WHEN GOD TAKES AWAY

LIVING WITH LOSS AND SURRENDER

Mark Steinberg, Ph.D.

ISBN: 153334907X
ISBN 13: 9781533349071

This book is dedicated to Neal Steinberg and all the people he left behind, including my readers.

VI AFTERWARD

PREFACE

Usually, I write about things I know. My previous books were how-to self-improvement guides—how to make your life, marriage, and so on better and how to conquer common obstacles within yourself and the world around you.

This book is different. Though I follow a similar theme of coping more effectively with a life and a universe that doesn't always give us what we want, now I explore territory less certain, less routine, and possibly just as confusing and overwhelming even as it grows more familiar. I am writing about *loss*, the phenomenon we all experience intermittently throughout life in varying degrees and with differing intensities and impacts specific to each of us at different times along our journey.

I lost my first-born son, Neal, to a drug overdose. This sudden tragedy impelled me to face issues and feelings I had put on the back burner, ambivalence and paradoxes I had only partially understood and that continued to obstruct my inner peace and the closeness I desire with God, the maker and taker of all. Death may be the ultimate loss, at least from our earthly perspective. The finality of death is unique, yet it joins other types of loss in the human experience of confronting deep emotional attachment and the puzzle of control and ownership with which every person contends.

The nature of survival is that we try to acquire skills, resources, and circumstances that protect, insulate, comfort, and embellish our lives; yet, it is ultimately a losing struggle. When death stakes a claim, it starkly reminds us of the limits of our control and brings the dilemma of ownership front and center. When an earthly life ends, unsettling questions arise for those left behind regarding the finality and meaning of that life (and our own) and regarding the ultimate scheme of things and our individual places and purposes. These questions are more painfully apparent when death strikes unexpectedly, perhaps to a young person or one who is perceived as innocent or undeserving of abrupt termination. The grief and pain of loss forces us to confront our most basic and tenacious intellectual, emotional, and spiritual understandings.

When God Takes Away is an exploration of the palpable hurt of loss, the mystery of proprietorship and control (even of our own bodies), and the possibilities and rewards of surrender to a mighty God and the destiny and knowledge he allows us to experience. As stated earlier, I am on new ground, uncertain that what I know (or thought I knew) is the full story. It's my hope that this writing will help me with the overwhelming challenge of losing my precious child—and that it will help you in accepting and adjusting to the losses you face.

There is a saying that I have found to be true in my practice and my life: "No one cares how much you know until he knows how much you care."

This book is an attempt to share with you how much I care—about people, about what God intends, about making sense of what seems like undue pain and injustice, and about coping with loss and suffering to experience and surrender to the will of a God I *do know* loves me beyond what my mind can even imagine.

I hold no easy or proven answers to the anguish of loss. It is my hope and intention that by sharing my thoughts, feelings, and experiences, I can help you be better able to grow and to face and surrender to the loving and omniscient plan God has for you—a plan by which he takes things away that are yours only for the time being anyway.

Loss and surrender are tender mercies through which God reminds us that he is in charge. He challenges us to accept life on his terms, to cherish and appreciate his gifts, and to yield to his timing and revelation of blessings to come.

May this book comfort you and help you weather painful losses. May you be encouraged to seek the treasures God has for you, even after he takes away.

I

WHEN GOD TAKES AWAY

CHAPTER 1
WHEN GOD TAKES AWAY

Living with Loss and Surrender

All of us experience loss. Things, people, and circumstances come and go, sometimes slipping away unnoticed or not missed in the course of busy and changing lives. Loss that we suffer, however, has a different character. This is the ripping away of what we protect, cherish, covet, need, and think we deserve. The real and meaningful losses we experience take a toll on our identity and challenge our beliefs about fairness and rightness. At its core, loss threatens our abilities and confidence in survival.

There are many losses throughout life, of course; it is the natural order of things. Losing a loved one is among the most difficult to bear—a family member, a friend, a pet, or someone you knew or identified with and who enriched you with meaning and humanity. One of the most difficult sufferings is the loss of a child.

On Memorial Day weekend in 2013, we lost our son, Neal. He was twenty-six years old. He died from an accidental drug overdose. The police came to our door in the middle of the night to respectfully deliver the tragic news, sentries of a nightmare for any parent. Instantaneously, we were transported into that unenviable group of parents who grieve and suffer and try to make sense of the unexpected and insensible.

How can I bear such a loss? How can I continue with my duties, swimming in a world of overwhelm, swallowing the salty tears, and flailing to connect reality with pretense? What shall I say to others? What will they say and think? Is it right for me to burden them with this grief, and is it deceptive or isolating to withhold it? What will happen with my heartache and sorrow, and how might God use it for good?

Why did this happen, God, since you love me and love my son? Why did you take Neal from us at this time? In your natural order, children outlive their parents, difficult as that painful finiteness is too. Why this exception? How shall I placate my analytical mind's unanswerable questions, and who will soothe my emotional angst?

In the midst of agonizing loss, vulnerability takes center stage, stark and unrehearsed. The carousel of emotions and coping skills spins aloof, and I'm incompetent at jumping on or off—hurt, despair, confusion, numbness, relief, misery, grief, love, self-pity, rationalization, anxiety, fear, and fatigue. Those common and reliable escapes—denial and anger—don't fit me well. I am loath to wear them, like some old fat clothes that no longer fit or the garish sports jacket that I wore in college when I was so full of myself.

I am plainly hurt, sensitive, and needy—exposed to the grim reality that what I hold most dear can be, has been, and, in varying measure and timing, will be taken away. This life that I cherish, act in and out, and pretend is my own exists in a context that has greater control than I can ever exert. The painful reality of loss asserts its sobering reminders that all I *own* is temporary. In the bigger picture, I am truly not even my own.

***

Loss is a natural, inevitable, and unpleasant aspect of life. It is far less predictable than we'd like and often strikes with sudden terror, leaving us exposed, shocked, and needy. Given the universality and intermittency of loss, we would think we could take it in stride, at least much of the time. But that is not the case, even with *minor* losses. Losing something meaningful feels deeply personal and threatening. When something is taken away, the experience cuts to the core of vulnerability, control, security, comfort, entitlement, and the organization of the world we take for granted.

There are no curricula for loss, no courses to teach how to give things up. Our culture exalts *getting* more and holding on to it. This market structure operates on an economy of material growth and confidence, catering to pragmatic needs but insensitive to emotions and the needs of the spirit. Even death has its proper associated industries.

Despite its unanimity, loss remains a private matter, leaving each of us to mourn, resent, pine, wish, regret, and adjust as best we can. When you experience a loss, you can find support groups, seek friends or family for comfort, and even find *replacements* for some losses. You can get a new car or bicycle, but you can't bring back the life of someone you cherished who has died. Whether the loss is minor or tragic, no replacement, substitution, distraction, or new opportunity provides the life lessons needed to *let go*—the practical and spiritual skills of *giving up* what you cherish, relinquishing your hold on the impermanent, and learning to adapt to what life deals you.

When God takes away something valued, giving up is a choice we can make in response to his sovereignty. When faced with loss, even a devastating, irreversible, irreplaceable loss, we can choose to respond in deference to God's will and with deference to the one who knows and can meet all of our needs. We may not understand what has happened, but we can learn to accept it, albeit with a broad spectrum of legitimate human emotions, including aversion, bewilderment, questioning, and pain. The process that can heal us leads to the ultimate acquiescence to God's inscrutable plan. This progression is called *surrender*.

Surrender is weakness and vulnerability leaving the soul and spirit. It is the renunciation of control and the capitulation to a force or will greater than one's own.

***

My wife grieves with me. She wails and laments that Neal will never have a wife or children, never know the challenges and rewards of a developing career, never experience the mixed blessings of aging. My heart echoes these laments, and my mind reflexively reviews the *coulda, shoulda, woulda, if only* thought loops that intrude in the aftermath of this tragedy. I know I did all I could for my son, yet the inexorable finality of losing him exacerbates my helplessness and the smallness of my power and competence in the universe. What is left for me when the emotional and spiritual maelstrom of figuring this out leaves only repeated fatigue and frustration?

I realize that I must yield to God's will and omniscience, for he is my strength and comfort. Accepting what happened and adjusting to life without my son and his future does not mean forcing away my pain and suffering. I know that God feels my feelings because he is the creator of those feelings. I trust God to comfort me and to bring about healing in his own time. My best efforts are put toward recognizing and yielding to his sovereign will.

It is difficult to think about what happens when you are gone; such thoughts don't compute with worldly reasoning, and it can be scary, especially without secure belief and reassurance about the hereafter. It is so overwhelming and confusing to experience and organize the thoughts and feelings of outliving a child. Yet life is a process of acquisition and loss, and the passion and security of attachment can only be ultimately disappointing. It is a great conundrum that fulfillment and peace appear through blessed involvement and, necessarily, through letting go.

Taking things for granted suits the natural mind, and this part-time illusion helps the nervous system relax and function. Eventually, everything in the material world goes away—but when loss strikes home, it is a traumatic challenge to the processes of attachment and surrender, these life experiences in the earthly and spiritual realms that God wants us to know and resolve through dependence upon him.

Oh, how hard it is to lose, to suffer, to accept and adjust, to yield and surrender to a world that doesn't follow one's plans and desires! For loss that comes unpredictably but inevitably with its trail of hurt and trauma, its specter of fear and vulnerability, it is the salve of surrender that gives the comfort, peace, and security that heals beyond expectation or understanding. And to whom is it safe to surrender? It is the one whose capacity and caring infinitely reaches beyond even the imagination and aspirations of his creations.

I suppose that in time the sharp pains of loss will abate and the open wounds will heal. Memories will soften and somehow fit with the passage of life. The agony will subside to a lessening and perhaps even occasional dull ache or pang, a reminder of injury that never quite disappears but that can become manageable. I hope...

I miss my son with a love beyond reason and words. I want him back—something I cannot have. Each day has multiple reminders of the stark change; I cannot call him or hear from him, give him advice, or respond to his frustrations and complaints. I cannot provide him food and comfort, watch him perform, share an Internet link, argue his ideas, or join him for a ride. The change is sudden and permanent. It is reality become chimera:

disappearance appearing as the new normal. It is shocking, disorienting, and pushing the limits of my reason and belief.

***

I have coped with loss many times in my fractured life and recovered well from the hurt, numbness, and sense of exposure and threat. I have many blessings, including a wholeness and stability that stand up well to challenge and trauma. From decades of personal and professional experience, I know that trauma is cumulative, so that those individuals most affected by life's multiple insults, injuries, and stresses will have the hardest challenge to accommodate the next tough surprise. Thus, I am charged with the responsibility of leadership, solace, and healing for my loved ones who also grieve and suffer greatly.

For this calling, I am ready. I know our God is a God who provides comfort and that his grace is sufficient for me. With the discipline of prayer, I defer my spotty understanding to the occasional glimpses of wisdom far too vast and magnificent for me to apprehend. Just as I accept the night as the earth turns even while I'm not making it do so or seeing the other side, I know by experience that the sun will shine on me again. Without a full grasp of this process, I stop to marvel and renew my faith that I will be blessed again.

Hope and faith may seem like clichés. But they are as real and necessary as oxygen. God gives and he takes away—the good and the bad, as perceived by man—but God works his own sovereign plan. And so, when struck with tragic loss, I suffer and mourn and work to heal, aided by faith and hope and dependence on a loving, omnipotent God who sees all that has been and will be and who knows everything. I choose the path of surrender, a lifelong practice of releasing my stubbornness and desires to God's will, letting him lead me to greater acquisition and grace. Hope and humility become the surrender that leads to clarity, perseverance, and peace.

When God takes away, he closes doors, often unexpectedly. In his providence, new doors open and opportunities unfold to discover and live out what God has in mind. Loss can be an opportunity to turn disappointment and longing regarding the past into hopeful longing and eagerness about the present and future. With God, the future is brighter. Surrender allows us to let go and move more fluidly toward what God has in store.

How does this manifest in practical ways? How do the daily hardships get handled, the overwhelm settled, the healing accelerated, the work done? How do I abide affliction, conquer fear, and carry on with triumph? And how can *you*?

Stay tuned.

NEAL RANDALL STEINBERG
1986–2013

Neal Randall Steinberg
1986-2013

A peaceful moment

CHAPTER 2
DEATH OF A LOVED ONE

Death is so inconvenient,
It happens into whatever you're doing.
Death is so persistent,
It won't go away.
Death is so personal,
It involves you.
Death is so present,
So distant from life long ago.

Mark Steinberg, Ph.D., 2002
(upon the death of my father)

Life comes and goes. God gives and rescinds. It is so plain, yet so hard to fathom. The constant cycle of nature continuously breeds life all around with so many species and forms. Cells and creatures come into being, grow, survive for a while, and eventually die. It is the template and pattern our great creator made, and it is a pinnacle of his creative essence.

We observe life and death, feel their intense joys and sorrows, and understand their biological parameters. We know intellectually that death will overtake each of us individually. Somehow, that knowledge doesn't quite connect as a concept with the ways we think about and manipulate other concepts. God has given humans the paradoxical ability to think about eternity, yet not to comprehend its full meaning (Ecclesiastes 3:11). Some mysteries remain unsolved. We can conceive mathematically that humans live approximately X number of years, and our minds can calculate that relativity compared with different animate and inanimate forms. We can adjudge perspective, compare and contrast, highlight and analogize. Our math tools work beautifully and reliably, but they don't solve the problem of how our short life span fits into the grand scheme comprising eons of life.

So much for intellect and concepts. What about feelings and spirit? Death is the ultimate vulnerability, the equalizer that humbles and reduces us all. It is one thing to think about death, to manipulate and revolve its aspects in the near and far places of our attentive mind. It is quite another matter when death strikes closely, taking with finality someone we love. The heartbreak of losing a loved one is like no other.

The death of a loved one confronts us with palpable sensations and desperations, tears, heart stirrings, love, fear, angst, and so many other feelings. It is overwhelming and sometimes insensible. We must deal with the onslaught of emotion and attempt to tailor with reason what doesn't fit well at all. We must pick up the pieces and move on, the shadow of our own mortality stalking us and lending a portentous glimpse in the wake of painful loss.

God takes away, and this is so hard to understand and accept. We argue with questions, pleadings, and contentions. *Why? Why now? It's so senseless. She was an innocent victim. He had everything to live for. What about the family left behind?*

These pleadings are natural. God understands. He welcomes the crying out and encourages the reaching out. He gives us the ability to be angry, and he gives us the grace, mercy, tools, and power of choice to put anger aside.

I don't presume to know why God does things his way, and I too suffer from loss and death. I do know what God says in his holy word, the Bible, and I apply these principles as best I can to live within God's will. Surrender is the process God uses to help us submit to his will and accept what he does, even though we don't understand much of it. God loves us dearly and wants us to love him and be in communion with him. But we are not God.

Ancestrally, we have been warned with prohibitions and forbidden to eat from the tree of knowledge. The cost of that ancient error is mortality and with it the awareness of our limited knowledge of the infinite.

It is difficult to swallow in the choked-up condition of losing a loved one.

Praise God for the provisions he has made for our loss and suffering! He has given us spiritual salvation, reliable promises, and practical tools for dealing with death and loss.

LIFE AND RELATIONSHIP

I love the statement made by Mitch Albom in his popular book, *Tuesdays with Morrie*: "Death ends a life, not a relationship." What a truly powerful idea! Its power encourages us to keep relating and valuing those loved even when they are physically gone. The idea that relationships continue after physical death gives credence to our efforts and meaning to lives that have material finality.

Each person born into the world carries a soul that is eternal. God, the maker and one who transcends all time, knew and knows each life before he makes it manifest. We are privileged to marvel at the appearance and passage of life and to wonder about its brevity and meaning. We also have opportunities to fulfill ourselves and participate in God's design through our relationships. Each soul born into this world makes imprints, both on earth and eternally. Relationships may be transformed or developed by circumstances, but they are not extinguished by biological limitations. A book written or a play performed does not cease to exist because it is no longer read or acted.

A person gone is a person still, one who made a difference, connected with others, fulfilled God's purpose—an individual soul whose eternal life can continue in the earthly memory of others. Even when God takes away materially, he supplies grace, spirit, and connection.

Relating to a person who has passed can be unsettling. Fond memories mix with sadness and longing and, for many, a helpless desperation that lingers. Remembrances are hauntingly private and bittersweet. Psychologically and spiritually, the death of a dear one reminds us on many levels that we too are finite and mortal. Paradoxically, significant loss makes us keenly value what we have taken for granted and yet become increasingly aware that we cannot take anything for granted. Death makes blunt the limits of our control, and this is painful to absorb.

The reality that death ends a life encapsulates the reality of that life, the person we knew, loved, interacted with, and cared for and about and who helped us and received our help—in short, the person who developed and enriched our own lives and growth. This is the part that continues in relationship, the wonderment that helps us surrender the departed one but keep and cherish that person's contribution to us and our respect and honor for the one who has passed.

God gave me one son for nearly twenty-seven years. I was very close to him, and for decades, I delighted in the intense joys and agonies of parenting. I couldn't forecast that God would take him away in this timing and manner, and I can't understand cognitively why what happened did happen. Emotionally, I am coming to accept this aspect of God's will and to spend more time spiritually and fervently treasuring the twenty-seven years that I was blessed with Neal.

My relationship with Neal will exist forever. Though he is gone from the material plane in which I still linger, he shaped me and affects me continually. Though Neal no longer argues with present human words and emotions, his character and nature live with me always. I know his preferences and can hear and predict his reactions to the experiences that season and punctuate my days. When I encounter a situation, a person, a song, an Internet site, or a cultural trait that Neal would have reacted to and shared with me, I feel the reward of his presence. I often want to share with him a thought or perspective that he would appreciate. Sometimes I want to ask him a question that he, with his advanced and inquisitive mind, could answer for me, saving me time and the embarrassment of seeming antiquated.

I miss the constant exercise of leadership and wisdom with which I supervised Neal. In the natural order of parent-child relations, I was gladly (and competently, I thought) fulfilling my duty. However, the natural order of things was upended with the passing of my child. I like to think that he is in a place of greater wisdom, propelled prematurely by his precocious nature, and that he is waiting for me to catch up to revelations he now knows.

These things are not for me to know at this time. The thoughts are far too lofty for me. I have faith that I will find out in God's time. Presently, I speculate and pine for a growing peace that still eludes me. No words can describe how much I miss Neal, how tenderly I long to touch and hear and smell him. Nothing can change his death, and nothing can change the life he lived and shared with me or the tremendous joy and growth he gave me as I developed the power and ability to love, sacrifice, and receive in our relationship!

I have surrendered my son, because I had to. I accept God's grace, and I dwell increasingly on my gratitude for the gift of Neal for twenty-seven years. I will always be in relationship with him, even as I relinquish his presence in this earthly life. I am so grateful that God gave him to me for a time.

LOSS, DEATH, AND A TRANSFORMED LIFE

I suppose that my experiences of losses, traumas, and deaths have not been excessive, according to what I have seen in the lives of others. Each person's pain, sensitivities, and limits are relative, of course. There is no value in comparing, analyzing, or competing in the realm of suffering.

On a spectrum of loss, surrender, and suffering, the death of a loved one must be at the far end. It is a dark and inevitable reality. I have learned through enlightenment, though, that reality is only a part of the truth. Praise be to God!

For death is not the end of the story. Thank God that death has been swallowed up in victory!

Listen, I tell you a mystery: We will not all sleep, but we will all be changed—in a flash, the twinkling of an eye, at the last trumpet. For the trumpet will sound, the dead will be raised imperishable, and we will be changed. For the perishable must clothe itself with the imperishable, and the mortal with immortality. When the perishable has been clothed with the imperishable, and the mortal with immortality, then the saying that is written will come true: "Death has been swallowed up in victory. Where, O death is your victory? Where, O death is your sting?"

"The sting of death is sin, and the power of sin is the law. But thanks be to God! He gives us victory through our Lord Jesus Christ." (1 Corinthians 15:51–56).

To those who are spiritually blinded, the hope and faith in life after death may seem a pipe dream, the belief in and reliance on God and scripture a fallacious crutch. I am sympathetic to that cynicism, for once I was blind too. But now I see what God has plainly revealed to those who would look, see, and believe.

Death is a very painful reality. But it is not the end. It is a continuation and a beginning of a new and different life. It can be the glory of eternal life with our creator. This is the pattern God has made from beginning to end, wherever the deceased may actually be, though unknown to us fully in our human form.

Physical life is limited. It is seeded by progenitors, often reproduces, and eventually dies. But the seeds proliferate and generate legacies. Jesus said,

> *"Very truly I tell you, unless a kernel of wheat falls to the ground and dies, it remains only a single seed. But if it dies, it produces many seeds."* (John 12:24).

Eternal life—spiritual life—is unlimited. From the perishable springs the imperishable.

> *But someone will ask, "How are the dead raised? With what kind of body will they come?" How foolish! What you sow does not come to life unless it dies. When you sow, you do not plant the body that will be, but just a seed, perhaps of wheat or something else. But God gives it a body as he has determined, and to each kind of seed he gives its own body. Not all flesh is the same: People have one kind of flesh, animals have another, birds another and fish another. There are heavenly bodies and there are earthly bodies; but the splendor of the heavenly bodies is one kind, and the splendor of the earthly bodies is another. The sun has one kind of splendor, the moon another and the stars another; and star differs from star in splendor.*

> *So it will be with the resurrection of the dead. The body that is sown is perishable, it is raised imperishable; it is sown in dishonor, it is raised in glory; it is sown in weakness, it is raised in power; it is sown a natural body, it is raised a spiritual body.* (1 Corinthians 15:35–44)

My wife believes that those who have passed are watching us, knowingly, lovingly. She describes Neal and our mothers as observing us with care and love and a knowledge that is supreme but inaccessible to those on earth. The Bible lends credence to this interpretation, as described in the story of Lazarus (Luke 16:19–31).

I can only surmise, hope, pray, and obey. I also know what I feel, and those feelings are grounded in material reality and in spiritual being.

Though Neal has perished, his being and our relationship remain imperishable. My seed gave birth to his physical being; his life sprouted the seeds of an imperishable relationship. I will be with him always.

Death ends a life, not a relationship.

God gives, and God takes away. In both of these ministrations, he reaches out to us, wanting us to draw closer to him and also to each other.

II

MY SON NEAL

CHAPTER 3
MY FIRST CHILD

It was a late August day when Neal was born. Barbara—Neal's mother and my first wife of decades—had an uncomplicated and fulfilling pregnancy. She was a woman who seemed at her best and most natural during pregnancy. As I look back, my simplified memory highlights the most significant prenatal challenge as selecting the right name. The potential Scotts and Terrys and Perrys and Ralphs receded in the race to become Steinbergs, along with all the other wannabe sperm that faded into nonexistence.

Neal Randall Steinberg was born into this world on August 28, 1986. Barbara was well-prepared and quite matter-of-fact about her first labor. Fortunately, she also had excellent medical care and support. In addition to their physician skills, obstetricians have to become adept at reassurance and at hiding their fatigue. As Neal prepared to enter the world, I gave thanks and prayer that he was blessedly received, cared for, and welcomed.

I remember the very small house we lived in then. I remember distinctly an eerie sensation from the nine months prior to Neal's arrival that some will find superstitious and meritless, but which I know to be true. I remember making love with Barbara on a November night and knowing—with absolute, doubtless conviction—that my first son was conceived right then and there. I am not given to otherworldly visions, nor to voices or mandates, but this experience was clear as a bell, and I knew the deal was sealed.

At the nursery, I remember looking at Neal in the bassinet just hours after his birth. This truly magical time is stamped indelibly in my heart and mind—the soft blueness of the swaddling blankets and the fuzzy cap and the gentle reassurance and cooing of the nurses fading in the background as I beheld my firstborn child.

He stared up at me, silent, steady, vulnerable. Time stood still. He looked at me with calm intensity. Quiet, content, anticipating. We had both been waiting to arrive at this moment. I became new and large and interesting in his fresh and marvelous world. I lifted him into my arms, trembling—the bond. *Welcome, my son. I love you already!*

His slightly protruding upper lip, the faintest overbite, shaping his image from earliest infancy caught my attention. We studied each other with rapt, devoted attention. It was the beginning of a new team—indeed, a father-son love affair.

My musings about what kind of father I would be were quelled by the bond I felt with Neal and the way he looked trustingly at me. Now that it was happening, fatherhood seemed more interesting and natural than I had imagined.

Neal Randall Steinberg, my son! I was a father!

Dad with baby Neal, circa 1987

CHAPTER 4
GROWING IN FATHERHOOD

Neal's early years were filled with love and nurturing and a comfortable, protecting environment. His mother and I were very attached to each other, and our love had brought us a wonderful baby son. For Barbara and me, it had been us against the world covertly, as we struggled to make our way through our thirties, establish ourselves economically, and cope with the pressures of the world and our own developmental challenges as new parents and partners. There were expectations to fulfill, as well as the nagging distraction of comparing our progress and fortune with those of others. Such is the ambivalent press of young adulthood, and we were glad to be in the fray, fortified by the blessing of a healthy baby boy.

Neal came home from the hospital to a modest San Jose home with a yellow room for him, filled with appropriate decals, toys, and mobiles. Adding stimulation to his development, there were our two dogs: Freedom, a golden retriever, and Diamond, a Doberman pinscher. The retriever (as is his temperament) vied for attention, exuding friendly camaraderie and lapping at the scent of fresh baby skin. I think that Freedom would have taken breast milk, if allowed. The Doberman, however, showed a jealous, protective demeanor. She was slow to accept Neal into her territory, but Neal didn't seem to mind.

We were poor. My practice was just beginning to take root, and money was always tight and in very short supply for many years. It was the norm to struggle and worry. We had the support of our parents. Despite economic struggles, life was good and looking to get better. I had transcended the tremulous first days of holding my new baby like a glass vase. I was easing into the challenges and joys of fatherhood, marveling at the delights and curiosity of a rapidly growing infant.

I admired how Barbara was blossoming as a mother. She was a natural. Diffident and cautious by nature, she flourished maternally, blending instinctive love with the resources from studying the *right* ways to care for a child. After all, she was a veteran nurse and professional librarian, well-equipped in the how-tos of care. Also, she was thirty-eight, old enough to subjugate self-indulgence to sacrifice and accede to most conventional middle-class values. We had grown past our days of hippie rebellion.

Fortunately, Neal developed as a normal child. He began talking late (just shy of three years old, as I remember), but once he started, you couldn't stop him. His curiosity and verbal skills portended the philosophical inquirer and "Philadelphia lawyer" personality, along with the cognitive style he would develop. He was easy to take care of, and he was a delight. This changed when his brother Jeremy arrived two years after Neal, but, from my perspective, they were boisterous, normal, active boys—bright, adventurous, curious, and increasingly overwhelming to their mother. (Barbara often would wonder out loud how anyone could handle more than two children, since a mother had only two hands!)

It is not easy to be a parent, but it can often be joyous. God does not bless everyone with children. Many who yearn for children and who are frustrated or thwarted in fulfilling this instinctual desire can suffer profound heartbreak. Yet, there are, of course, different lifestyles and different satisfactions. Many people deliberately choose not to have kids (and, in so doing, they save a lot of money!). Nonetheless, having a child changes one's attitude and lifestyle from that point forward. Becoming a parent admits you to a very large group of people who share a common and focal decline in specific memory functions: what life was like before children, when you could come and go as you pleased without having to constantly make "arrangements."

Regarding the blessings and challenges of children, I remember vividly a particular incident that occurred about two years before Neal's birth. I was preparing a lengthy and complicated document, and I was a novice at using computers. I sought the assistance of a consultant who lived in San Jose, and I visited him at home. He lived in a ramshackle house, overrun with toys and junk in the yard and, really, a disorganized and unsightly mess. He had four young children of assorted ages. As we talked, the kids were running around noisily, playing, yelling, clambering. Childless myself at the time, I silently wondered how the man could stand it. As if he could read my thoughts, he tilted his head up from the computer and said, almost reflectively, "Children are a chore. But I'll tell you, having kids is the best accomplishment I've ever experienced in my life."

Amen! I'll never forget the man's statement. How wise and true this became for me as my family grew and we developed individually and together.

Neal and Jeremy grew up in the Almaden Valley in San Jose. We eventually moved to a nicer house in a quiet bedroom community, close to creeks and trails. We regularly took walks with the kids and dogs along the wooded trails by the creek. There were signs posted along the creek that warned of "Contaminated Fish." Before Neal could talk, he would point at the signs very insistently and sound his preverbal incantation, *"Unh, unh, unh!"* What satisfied him would be when I pointed to the sign and read, "Contaminated Fish." When Neal could eventually talk, this ritual was replaced by his insistent reading of "Contaminated Fish." Weird but not bad for a toddler.

Neal progressed through his early years with the typical boy's interest in Legos and large machines. His early words and phrases were stippled with the excitement of noticing and exclaiming, "Bulldozer!" and "Front loader!" whenever we might pass one by or when he would see (and, of course, want) the Lego sets with which he could build these machines.

When Neal was a toddler, I would often carry him on my shoulders on a portion of our walks. Though physically stressful for me, it made me taller indeed (and, I do mean emotionally too)! Though the memory is clear, it's hard to reconcile this image with the man who grew to be about six feet tall and who played football and earned a black belt in martial arts.

When he was three years old, on nights when he couldn't sleep, I would hoist him on my shoulders and run up and down the street, yipping shrilly, "Super duper double dapper diaper dipper!" over and over again to his squeals of delight. I never much cared what the neighbors thought.

On many restless nights, I would put him in the car seat and drive aimlessly for several miles until he reliably fell asleep. Then I'd carry him from the car and tuck him into his bed. Thus, I discovered a practical, though unwieldy, method of getting a young child to sleep.

We enjoyed the many soft, sweet, cuddly bonding times of my reading to him in bed. Even after Neal could read (which he learned easily at a young age), he would ask me to "Read God," which meant to snuggle with him and read from books of children's Bible stories. This was precious, precious time for me! Neal would grab his sheepskin security blanket and snuggle up to me as we explored the comfort and mysteries of father-son bonding and God's Holy Spirit.

I remember bringing home this sheepskin blanket as a gift for Neal when he was about six. I had bought it in Puerto Rico while traveling on invitation to present a lecture to a medical group. He appropriated it immediately and possessively clung to it for many years, naming it "Geegul," which stuck through the many years of service and tattering. I can still picture Neal, curling within and grabbing his sheepskin Geegul, sucking his thumb, and enjoying the comfort and security, so desperately needed, that a cherished, tangible object can often bring to a young child's life. Even now, I can smell the sweet aroma of his young skin blended with the sheepskin—an olfactory burst of intense young human aliveness! I can still feel the tickle of the sheepskin as I bend to kiss Neal.

BONDING

When Neal and Jeremy were seven and five, respectively, we endeavored on a rite of passage: a camping trip. As I've never been the outdoorsy, survival type, this was a big deal for me. However, I felt it was important, and I was swayed by the invitation to join the church group of Treeclimbers, a father-and-son group I had been attending with my sons weekly for some months. This was to be a weekend of male bonding in the Sierras.

Following that adventure, I wrote a story about it in 1993.

A NOTABLE CAMPING TRIP WITH MY TWO YOUNG SONS

My back is killing me. I smell bad, and my beard is not pretty. Who knows what a shower will wash away, but I know that a hot shower will liberate me substantially from the misery of three days in the wilderness. I've just returned from camping with my two sons—seven thousand feet up in the Sierras, and I feel as though I've climbed every one of them.

Above my aching body, my mind is peaceful. My boys had a great time, and I have the secure feeling one gets from a sound investment. Through this camping experience, I paid another premium on family health insurance—the kind money really can't buy. I was counting on these experiences to insure my children against the ravages of drug addiction, the emotional injuries that are often part and parcel of growing up, the accidents of rebellion, and the pernicious malady of family and social alienation. There are no guarantees, of course, but I believed it was a wise investment. Dollar for dollar, I was certain that it would beat anything in the form of preventive family mental health care.

This primitive form of health care has reformed a number of ideas I've held about being a dad. Yes, there was a cost, a cost I was happy to pay: I lost several days of work. But there was a precious payoff. I spent time reacquainting myself with my children and with my own aging process. I discovered how arduous canoeing is when one is out of shape; memories of my agility in this pursuit have submerged beneath my own weight. I marveled at the value of a flashlight over a computer when one is in the forest. Some things remain unchanged: I still prefer beds to sleeping bags, and I still deplore guns. Some things have changed for the better: my ability to sleep well in unfamiliar places has improved, as has my prowess with a bow and arrow. Perhaps this is because I can concentrate more now and am better able to focus on the relevant. Thus, I paid more attention to my boys and noticed salient changes that clashed with images I retained about the younger children that they used to be. These differences manifested through their current fears. We spent a lot of time with fears; the boys and I, stereotypically following a traditional male prerogative, tried challenging nature to reflect both our strengths and weaknesses. I'm not sure we conquered anything, but we did experience and openly discuss our respective fears. Our fears were different, but the defenses were the same. The grip of apprehension was familiar, but how we shared our trepidations varied.

Five-year-old Jeremy surprised me with his anxiety in the water. He was frightened in the canoe and edgy and mortified at the prospect of a motorboat excursion. (This is the same child who, two summers ago, gleefully egged me to higher speeds riding on the Jet Ski.) In addition to his shaky water legs, Jeremy was also rattled by his fear of incompetence. Many of our activities were too demanding on his five-year-old strength and coordination—aiming a BB rifle, stretching a bow, paddling a canoe.

My poor Jeremy had succumbed to the grip of despair, which he expressed with sorrowful statements, such as, "I'm acting like a real wimp today," "I'm a loser at everything," and "Nobody cares about me. God doesn't care about me." It was clear that there was a crisis in the wilderness, and there was no hospital emergency room in sight. In this unsterile environment, I needed to bandage his self-esteem, which was ruptured and bleeding at the source. Of course, I reassured him and used this opportunity to explain how important and valuable he was to me and to God.

Seven-year-old Neal ambushed me with his question: "Dad, what are you afraid of?" I fielded his inquiry with a smug and clichéd paternal reflection of embarrassed wisdom, commonly experienced by adults when their children ask them where babies come from. In a quick moment, I returned from reverie to the wooded thicket where my son waited for an answer. This was a father-son heart-to-heart, one of many such communications that I hoped to encourage by dealing a straight answer.

"I'm afraid that you will grow up and no longer want to be with me, that we will lose the closeness we now enjoy," I responded. The gulp in my throat gradually transformed into an apprehensive abstraction. "On the other hand, I also worry that you *won't* grow up and that I will have to take care of you when you should be independent.

"I also fear—if you really want to know the truth—that I will somehow lose the love or presence of the people who really matter to me.

"I worry that I might get sick…"

"Dad," Neal replied with a mixture of sympathy and consternation, "what I mean is what *animals* are you afraid of?"

Caught by surprise, I sheepishly admitted that I was not particularly frightened by animals and that I worried more about other matters. Neal didn't miss a beat in pursuing his prey (me) who had just become ensnared in a classic parent trap. "Then I suppose it would be OK if we got a rattlesnake for a pet."

As I gazed at my son, pondering his unnerving fascination with reptiles and winning debates, he continued the spirit of the discussion with his seven-year-old concerns. "I'm afraid of the dark, like especially that someone is in my room at night. And also, I'm afraid of the black widow spider, not a *whole* lot, but just…"

I listened, absorbed in my son's trust and in the reality of this spinning web of bonding; it was the fabric of identity, confidence, and assurance as he was weaving strand by experiential strand. This was the stuff of protection and prevention, I believed, and the housing of health and emotional sustenance.

Over a parallel circuit, my mind processed the flow of anxieties unleashed by Neal's question. The concrete-associative fears of a child's thinking scurried through the foreground against a patina of adult memories and abstractions—my fears...yes, a thousand iterations of the apprehension that life will accidentally puncture my invincibility and, in so doing, irretrievably damage my ability to recover and repair.

The double whammy of aging and responsibility for the welfare of my family has increased the desire for security. I wanted a hedge, a safer risk than the unknown. My mind developed a multisensory fantasy. I pictured a wall of hedges, an impenetrable thorny thicket behind which I crouched, watching colorful balloons rise into the sky; they could not burst, even as they approached and cleared the sharp hedges. Simultaneously, I heard the inane jingle of an insurance commercial: "Insurance is lo-o-ove...(It's not insurance, it's love)...Insurance is ca-a-aring...(We'll bet you so many dollars a day until you die that you don't die.) Contact your Roulette Insurance agent today!"

In thinking about the future of my children's well-being, I wandered to images of the past. My father loomed large, like a giant poster in my chamber of relationships. He was my model, and he was brave. Oh, the man was riddled with fears, common and idiosyncratic. Yet he was brave by being himself, pressing through life with a hodgepodge of anxieties and quirks that rendered him more vulnerable to attack. I am not as brave as my father, but I may be smarter. Perhaps, in this hubris, I've simply had the benefits of his mistakes and learned through the innocence and faith of his generation. My father grew up through two world wars—but I had wars of a local kind through my growing up. The trauma of my adolescence is not forgotten. Like an incipient threat, I was vigilant for its contagion in the pattern of my sons' development and the denouement of our relationships.

I folded away the sleeping bags, contemplating the future and the prospect of health coverage. I've discovered anew that there are valuables that money itself cannot buy. I will spend, hope, complain, and follow the expected procedures of parental duty. Only a father, however, can provide a particular core of invaluable insurance benefits, particularly those involving mental, emotional, and spiritual health. It is a prescription plan to avoid pharmaceuticals. This kind of health care reform—where families have protection against the ravages of maturation—should indeed be universal.

Mark Steinberg, Ph.D.

(When I wrote this in 1993, it was originally entitled, "Health Care Reform: Benefits for Mental Health, Substance Abuse, and a Prescription Plan.")

PARENTING CHALLENGES

My children's early years reflect idyllic memories, but also harken back to the strenuous challenges of parenting. It's a wonder anyone does it, really—attending to a child's many needs, balancing discipline with affection and leadership, integrating a married life and work responsibilities with child-rearing, adapting to the bodily changes and consternation of getting older, and the ever-mounting financial expenses and demands.

My professional training and decades of clinical practice prepared me in many ways for the challenges and expectations that accompany raising children. Perhaps I was more prepared by proactive memories of my parents' overflowing (and often intrusive) love and my determination to omit from my own parenting the parts of my parents' I loathed.

I have a very strong memory of driving home from my office (many nights), exhausted and reflecting on the troubled children and families I'd seen that day—children very abnormal and hard to contend with; I remember thanking God that my children were *normal* and did not present such overwhelming obstacles. As I engaged in this thankful reverie, I drove into my driveway and pressed the garage door opener, only to find myself infuriated by bicycles and assorted toys blocking the driveway! Again! Aaargh! My gratitude would quickly give way to exasperation.

Entering the house like a trooper, I'd remonstrate and scold the boys, only to notice incidentally that Barbara was practically in pieces after a day of chasing them around and intervening in their scuffles. In so many ways, our family was typical—textbook, as they say. But no books (even my own) fulfill the preparation and implementation of what it takes to love, guide, cope with, and survive dear children.

SIBLING RIVALRY

Plan as you might, you take what you get in having children. We thought two was enough and that we were fortunate. Though Barbara had wanted a girl, we were content with our two sons, born two years apart. I thought, perhaps even rationalized, that the two-year difference was a good spread. However, Neal and Jeremy were fiercely competitive. I found it manageable, but the constant mediation was overwhelmingly wearing on Barbara.

It may be that the seeds of alienation that Neal experienced for much of his adolescence and adult life were planted in the conflict and competition between brothers. They were both excellent athletes, very smart, and had keen language and social skills. Yet they were different in ways that might seem endearing to onlookers but that kindled devastatingly manipulative behaviors as they each tried to gain the advantage.

Neal was a questioner and a person given to taunting. He liked to set people up and move in for the conquest. This often took the form of intellectual challenge and sophistry. Neal was also iconoclastic and perfectionistic. Though moderately aggressive and very determined, he was also concomitantly cautious and often took a long time to make routine decisions. He adored verbal enigmas, a precursor to his later fascination with esoteric problems of advanced mathematics and physics. He could drive you crazy with intellectual questions and puzzles. He liked to see people squirm and to challenge them intellectually. He was more interested in questions than answers and especially in the questions with no easy answers. As the years went by, it became apparent that his genius was marred by strains of impracticality and irresponsibility.

Jeremy was also aggressive, but he was a quick decision maker. He was adept at cutting to the chase. Though smart as a whip, Jeremy could be insensitive and blunt. Ironically, Jeremy was very sensitive to people's feelings, but his need to win trumped everything. The boys' common talents and individual differences comprised a formula for constant tension between them and instigated their battles.

Sadly, in later years, my sons were more distant than close. From childhood on, Neal developed habits of exasperating and alienating the very people he wanted to love and accept him. As his father, I could recognize and tolerate these quirks, using various opportunities to reflect and teach Neal about relationships and meeting the needs of others. But Jeremy and Neal developed habits of hurting and resenting each other. It was a wrenching thing for me to watch, being relatively helpless to repair the hearts of my offspring. Still, there remained decades of joys, frustrations, togetherness, and awe as my children made their way to adulthood and as I watched and helped them prepare for life.

CHAPTER 5
SURVIVING THE OLDERNESS

The following is a retrospective written long before my son Neal died of a drug overdose. It was written at a time when I was wrestling with family issues and crises that had an impact on their upbringing and helped to shape my views, expectations, and parenting behaviors.

***

Childhood is a magical time. It harbors the reach of imagination, the unfolding of novelty, the gradual revealing of the reasons for things; the inexplicable lapping playfully at the heels of what is explained. It is the period in which personalities are formed, outlooks on the world are chiseled, and far-reaching behavior patterns are assembled (at least, according to many experts).

It is during childhood that familial and social bonding is practiced and tested and the inner senses of competence and belonging are developed through experiences and self-evaluation. Children find out what kind of parents they have (or think they have), and parents find out who their children are. In this process, parents discover new dimensions of rewards and challenges and also become seasoned and wiser as the process of guiding their children fosters their own maturity.

For a child, the world is a mesmerizing and tempting place. Life is filled with the yummy and the yucky and turbocharged with rushes of desire and frustration. Children viscerally know that the world can hurt them.

They may often be sensitive and self-pitying, recovering from the latest impingement. Yet, despite the potential *owies*, children's natural curiosity and sense of adventure make the risks tolerable for the sake of pursuing the possible rewards, namely, the splendor and joy that are often the by-products of their innumerable acts of boldness, assertiveness, and success in obtaining what they want.

Children need guidance, protection, provision, nurturing, teaching, loving, and security. Fortunately, we are mostly hardwired to jump into this process (see the "Attachment" chapter). Children need adults, and adults learn to thrive in the sense of fulfillment derived from caring for children. It is an imperfect and often heart-wrenching system, but, somehow, that is the way we human beings survive and thrive.

The developmental years are a stage on which our children's processes of verifying security, developing skills and competence, mastering the rules and games embedded in the environment, and testing evolving independence are acted out. In their complex and confusing worlds, children must figure it all out. I call it *surviving the olderness*.

We all have traumas in life and throughout life. We may not think of them as traumas, partly because we have no early frame of reference for what a trauma is. As we grow and recognize the dangers and tragedies that beset people, we may minimize our difficulties in comparison with house fires, floods, shootings, lethal accidents, and so on. Yet, childhood is a period of intense sensory experience and of imprinting with impressions of what people, the world, and oneself are really like.

Growing up means surviving the *olderness*—that mysterious place and passage, both threatening and inviting, through which you pass and into which you blend as you become who you are destined to be. When we become parents, we remember patches of our childhood, including the traumas, through the filter of having made it to adulthood. We survived the swirl of confusion, hurts, and dependencies to the stage where we, in turn, are bringing children into and through the olderness.

Sometimes our traumas and memories of our own difficulties make us more compassionate and perhaps competent in dealing with our children. We would like to think so, and most of us work diligently toward that end. We often discover, in the ways we act, unsettling similarities to the habits and characteristic of our parents, whom we swore we would never copy or become. When we hear ourselves echoing our parents' words and tone, we are surprised (even shocked) by this recapitulation. As we age, our bodies change, and so do our opinions, tastes, and some of our values. It is a gradual and humbling transformation.

Like so many parents, I've wrestled with parenting styles, methods, and choices, as well as desires for my children's development and future and ultimately the control and influence I exert on the outcomes. I like to think I've provided well, especially with the nonmaterial stuff: love, emotional availability and security, good modeling, validation, acceptance, guidance, and leadership. As life relentlessly molds its products, I observe that I'm less sure than I used to be about the direct connections and cause-and-effect relationships between my parenting and the way my children turn out. How much of it is genetic determination, random events, cumulative and momentous choices, or the overriding hand of God?

From my own traumatic past, I am deeply aware of the impact of childhood experiences. As a psychologist, I know that children's impressions will affect their expectations and behaviors, as well as their formative images of their esteem and others' worth. Though not deterministic, early experiences can set the stage for decades of success or hardship. As a parent, I've tried to be respectful of these influences and maintain sensitivity to what my children have assimilated and accommodated, though I could only discern a portion of what they were really learning and becoming.

When Neal was six and Jeremy was four, their mother was diagnosed with breast cancer. She has survived, but at the time, we were traumatized and uncertain whether our children would lose their mother early in their lives. It was 1992. At that time, I wrote "Surviving the Olderness."

This story is a series of intermingled flashbacks, switching from my children's traumatic childhood experiences to my own, both in childhood and adulthood—me as a scared, oversensitive child and as a responsible and traumatized adult professional, husband, and father, facing the potential loss of my wife to cancer and the agonizing supervision of my children's traumas as I revisit my own. The story cries over the loss of innocence, something we all experience, even when things turn out well (and often they don't). It is a story full of truths—historically factual, but also spiritually recapitulative—about the yearning to belong, the fright of abandonment, and the terror and allure of the olderness into which we all must venture. The story flips among three generations of Steinberg experience, interspersed with staccato references to the biblical wisdom of Solomon. In recounting the facts, I have also taken posttraumatic poetic license. In so doing, I've interspersed different fonts, along with biblical quotes, to express shifting perspectives, time sequences, and my inner experiences across time.

SURVIVING THE OLDERNESS

Fugue in A Sharp Minor
What has been will be again, what has been done will be done again; there is nothing new under the sun.

ONTOGENY

My youngest son, Jeremy, is five. He returned from an afternoon at the park with yet more horror stories of being teased by the older kids. Jeremy persists in hanging around with older children, despite the obvious advantages they have by virtue of their advancement over his coordination, size, and (by implication) social standing.

As he says, "It's a jungle gym out there." Perils of the wilderness arise from nature. Perils of the olderness arise from the mature.

Cast your bread upon the waters, for after many days you will find it again.

This dichotomy of inclination and desire, poignantly expressed by Jeremy's angst, reflects a human irony: we cherish the stimulation and recognition attainable in the larger arena—the little fish in the big pond, so to speak. But we also need and depend upon the security and ego strength that come from familiarity, personal leadership, and the easy reward of exercising the skills we have mastered to the point of admiration.

This vacillation is played out on so many stages of development, the growth and excitement of challenge alternating with the familiar flexing of mastery and authority.

Through Jeremy's survival in the olderness, I experience life passionately and vicariously. My heart trills the octaves of emotion; the soprano of excitement and anticipation yields to the strident tenor of confidence—then, the sudden tumble through the bass depths of despair. The confusing facial foliage that hides Jeremy's humiliation glistens bittersweetly with remembrances of the olderness of my own yearnings.

I am determined to be wise, but this is beyond me. Whatever wisdom may be, it is far off and most profound—who can discover it? So I turned my mind to understand, to investigate and to search out the wisdom and scheme of things...

***

PHYLOGENY

Vivid memories of my own childhood experiences flood over me as I ponder my children's early development. My forays into the world beyond my parents led to unknown, varied, compelling, and often unpredictable responses. The maze of the olderness was complicated. Leaving behind my parental roots—sturdy trees I could climb for support and for a secure vantage from which to survey the environment—I repeatedly entered the labyrinthine temptations of the olderness, the world of those older, capable, confident, and secure. Everything was new and therefore surprising. The novelty alone was stimulating; excitement fed upon itself to entice me further. Fear hibernated beyond my senses, at least temporarily. People took me seriously, as if I could summon to the game board a new character who must be given his turn. Alas, the experiential dice inevitably sabotaged me. I became hurt, lonely, rejected, devastated. Characters in the olderness revealed themselves as predators, and the egoless, dangerous night would envelop me. My piece would be permanently (it turned out not forever but repeatedly) banished from the playing board.

...a time to embrace and a time to refrain...

Lost in the olderness, defenseless, without a retrievable foothold on worthiness, only the pain of my wounds sustained consciousness. I stumbled in retreat toward the sanctuary of my family, hopeful for succor, steeped in my humiliation, mindful that the nurturance I craved would not settle the score. *I must achieve victories in the olderness!*

As a father has compassion on his children...

The time machine is playing "Significance and Security" in the present. Jeremy is recovering from the latest bout of self-pity; I watch my solace drip automatically into his anguish. This parental potion heals, and injustice magically dissolves. Jeremy is fortified; he is ready once again to combat the mendacious ways of the olderness. He will prepare to engage by making up his own rules. This is indeed a wily strategy. He will ordain cause and effect so that he may win. Watch out, olderness! You are about to discover Jeremy's rules, a pervasive and persuasive armamentarium of illogic and need. You will defer, you must submit, you could at least accept...*please?* But the olderness is complex and unyielding...and its lure is irresistible.

Who is like the wise man? Who knows the explanation of things?

I couldn't understand the teasing. To this role of the stooge, I became accustomed. But the sense of isolation was onerous. Although the term *second-class citizen* was well beyond my ken, it was the embodiment of my role. I was tolerated according to conditions over which I felt no control and of which I had only partial understanding. I was often tricked, yet smart enough to see it coming. Like a prescient Huck Finn attending his envisioned funeral, this mental agility encouraged me to facilitate the games in which I was the inevitable victim. The olderness made room for me—as a cheerleader for my own demise.

At least I was involved in the fray and tumult where it really counted. I was surviving in the olderness! Soon, however, the other players tired. The game was dispelled, along with my connection to its players. I was not included in their other concerns—discarded, dejected, once again hung out to dry.

Tears streamed in a profusion of guileless sorrows. "Why won't they play with me? Nobody likes me-e-e-e-e...Gr-r-r-r!" An angry swipe of indignation.

I wince at Jeremy's ire as he girds in protection.

"I'll show them. It's all my lousy brother's fault. They like him instead of me. He makes fun of me. He copies me. I wanna be with them and do what they do, but they won't let me. Why not? It's not fair. I'm a person too. He plays with them, but they won't play with me. He plays with the bigger kids, and they won't play with me. This big kid took my ball and wouldn't let..."

...me have the ball, despite the double-teaming on him while I was free right under the basket. What's the matter with him? Doesn't he see me? Maybe he knows I'm here and thinks I can't score. Or maybe he's freezing me out on purpose, just like...

...when they ran me around, tossing my ball (shoes, jacket, book, toy...) among themselves, taunting, daring me to assert some dominant skill of interception. They paused, waited, hovered over my reactions as if fueled by my frustration. Let's play embryo—Steinberg's helpless in the middle. Watch him kick!

"Stop kicking the furniture, Son. That won't help you with the older kids. Let's talk about it."

"What's there to talk about?"

"The way it works is this: you play with the big boys; they make the rules. Usually, they take advantage. I know it's not fair. They won't listen to me either; they'll just pretend and be polite while I'm there (maybe). Why don't you play with the smaller kids, the ones around your age…"

"Less fun than being with the bigger kids. It's boring 'cause they can't do what I can do. Anyway, I like to do special stuff, and the big kids would appreciate it if only they'd let me and pay attention to me. Nobody has room for Jeremy! But they only want to tease me, and I…"

…don't think it's fun to tease the younger kids. The big kids tease me, and they seem to get a lot of fun that way. But I don't get fun from teasing kids like me or younger. Is there something wrong with me? I'm not interested in the kids who are interested in me. I am interested in the bigger kids and what they do—but they like to tease me, and I don't like that and don't want to do that to others. But I still want to be with the bigger kids; I hate it when they treat me mean! What's the matter with me? What do the older people know that I just don't get?

(Put on your big-kid stuff.)

Stomping clownishly in my f…
big I would be for my feet to fill …
the mechanical trenches of routine …
is the olderness then (toward u…
conquered? Where were his tears …

When I needed them, they were sometimes there for … security. Sometimes, I was left to fend for myself. I often wondered w… this was planned parenthood on the part of my mother and father or simply the result of their preoccupations or ignorance of my impending traumas. Increasingly, I sought to tread my trails in the olderness unchaperoned. I ruminated about whether this was the natural path or simply a reflection of my deviance. Over time, I grew warier, less sensitive to the thorns and thistles, quicker to swathe injuries, craftier in evading traps. I accumulated skills, defenses, and weapons. Self-preservation and exploration became more efficient. At times, I had fun in the olderness. Still I pondered, as I stalked solitarily, Was I becoming more civilized or more beastly?

***

(Put on your big-kid stuff.)

The commissioners glared at me during the oral examination for my license. Membership restricted—would they let me join the club? I glanced diffidently at the man questioning me. Irrelevant thoughts meandered into consciousness: *his tie is insignificant; it's not a sign. You can't tell from his expression what he's thinking.* Sure, I'm nervous, *but look at his feet...he's sitting in an open position. Those shoes remind me of...*

...My father, on his day off, would frequently visit libraries in Manhattan. These large, majestic structures held fascination for me; they contained innumerable books (which I enjoyed) and mysterious hallways and corridors (which I loved). I coveted any opportunity to visit these palaces, especially with my dad. Proudly accompanying my father (whose omnipotence included finding his way there by subway!), I alternated between the studious pretense of reading advanced tomes and the adventure of exploring the nooks, crannies, and connecting arteries in these intriguing buildings. Unaware that the stairwells of the Donnell Library above the ground floor were locked on the stairwell side (these were meant for emergency fire exit), I ventured into one and became immediately imprisoned behind the cavernous thud of the heavy door.

I tug, yank, and scream to no avail. This fire door has a foot-square window of wire-enmeshed safety glass located well above my head. In a state of panic, I launch running jumps to raise my eyes level with the window for fleeting seconds. Several glimpses of my unresponsive father make me feel like a drowning victim. Thrashing, flailing, pounding against the unrelenting door. If only somebody could catch the attention of...

"Dr. Steinberg," the commissioner began, as he fired another challenging question, "what would you do if a patient came to you with..."

Cancer! This nonkosher word does not belong in our vocabulary. It must be a myth, like Santa Claus. Unwelcome and nonexistent in my world, it nevertheless has stubbornly invaded my wife's body. This philandering disease intruded upon my safe and limitless world, an assailant who robbed me of illusions of competence, bullied me away from the embrace of oneness, and shackled me with alienation, hurt, and embarrassment.

...a time to be born and a time to die...

Gazing dreamily at my wife, I see the memory of our first child, Neal, in the hospital nursery. He gapes at me with that peaceful just-born stare that bonds us in future closeness. With the magnets of time, we will cling and repel. Time will propel him, too, into the olderness. Will his parents be there to guide him? Will his mother live to see him as a…

"Teenager, that's what I wanna be. 'Cause teenagers have fun, and they can do all sorts of brave and wild things," Neal drones on. "Like cool stuff and rock-and-roll and going places without their parents and not having parents always watching how…"

I am cast aside. It is Yom Kippur; after the synagogue service, there is little to do but wait for the sun to set on this surreal day of deprivation. On the tarred schoolyard ground, Alan is apparently unconscious but is softly whimpering. He fell from atop a schoolyard fence where he ventured between our stickball games. Alan is much older, a teenager; in fact, I look up to him with adulation and marvel as he embodies a picture of my potential. But now I am looking down on him, uneasy with this new development. Defensively, I decide momentarily that Alan is faking, that he will suddenly arise with color in his face and an animated grin that says, "Gotcha!" But he is pale and softly moaning, "Momma…" Abruptly pinched by reality, I realize that Alan is seriously hurt. I feel paralyzed but must act. Shaken, I must get help; it is time to venture into the olderness…

(Put on your big-kid stuff.)

…So I run, out of the schoolyard, accelerating into the world of the olderness. Breathless and scared, I flee, mindful of fear and adrenaline chasing me. I must get help. They must notice me in the olderness. I must alert them that youthful essence languishes in the schoolyard. My perception narrows in panic, and rules of the olderness recede. I sprint into the street amid unconcerned traffic. A random car bears down on my path, the inevitable terror escalates, and I jump…

…up and down to raise my eyes level with the window in the desperate hope that someone (my father?) will notice my helplessness and imprisonment in a library stairwell. Don't let this be a terrible metaphorical ending to a childhood of intellectual isolation. Someone must take action! I need help from…

…above…

…the car hood, which has screeched angrily to a resentful pause at least a foot beyond my intersecting leap. Heart pounding louder than the driver's horn, driven by the heel of his hand, I am driven by my heels and toes and the panic…

…And the next day is a swirl of timeless confusion, fear, and grief. The smears of dirt on Alan's cheek glare in my mind against the whiteness of the ambulance as they entomb him in its mystery and sirens. I cannot separate the tears and smears on Alan's face from my own when I find out he has died. Yet, I feel separated; all the while I, too, am moaning, Mom…

...and I want to retreat from the olderness, to locate and climb into the arboreal reaches of my family tree of security. That place of magic, where fascination parades unfettered with danger. A place of love and total acceptance where all things work out well. We are supposed to live happily ever after in this fusion of child and adult states, where I am a secure child.

(Put on your big-kid stuff.)

But now I have a wife who may die if the doctor...

"Steinberg, we'll let you know," the commissioner said in abject non-disclosure. *I stared vacantly at this grown-up whom I needed to satisfy and please, so much in the character of...*

...my father! He appears to notice...Yes, he's headed toward the locked library door! With curious and incredulous attention, he moves toward me, a flicker of rescue between my fatigued and frantic jumps. The door opens, and I can catch my breath. Time to gather myself. Composure is a new acquaintance, a foreigner with mysterious allure. Deliverance has strangely accelerated my descent into cool aplomb.

(Put on your big-kid stuff.)

I was just exploring. Nothing serious. I'm glad you came and opened the door, Dad, but you really didn't have to worry. I was just waiting for you to finish reading so we can...

"Sir! You can see your wife now." A call from the present pokes at my numbness. I have been sequestered in prayer, and the words pouring upon me about multiplying mutant cells clutter like so much dandruff outside a busy brain. In the doctor's presence, I studiously try to comprehend his scientific dribble about the nature of cancer. In my private Piagetian translation, I assimilate these technical words into the fabric of my existing thinking. *Repel the Philistines!* We are hostage negotiators (my mind tells me), and the terrorists hold my wife. (*Anything* to make this more human! But how can you combat *multiplying* terrorists?)

...be fruitful and increase in number...

It is *terrifying*!

(Put on your big-kid stuff.)

How can God let this happen? Surely he knows how much I need my wife, how much our children need their mother, how overwhelming is the olderness. *He made the olderness!* (Better yet, in cosmic appeal) God *knows* the difference between good and bad cells...

He causes his sun to rise on the evil and the good and sends rain on the righteous and the unrighteous.

The olderness engulfs me with its wicked ways. Heaven seems far away and inscrutable…

…because he is kind to the ungrateful and the wicked.

A tumor is eating my wife, and it's hard to make dinner conversation.

***

Jeremy has a problem he finds difficult to discuss. This is understandable, and, without many words, the message gets across. He feels left out because he has not yet learned to ride a bicycle unassisted. Afternoons at the park hold the specter of his barely contained chagrin over this puerile insufficiency. The olderness has many weeds, and this day at the park may overgrow Jeremy's developing and precarious balance.

Teaching a child to bicycle offers rending and poetic similarities to the push-and-pull process of parenting toward independence. The child, of course, must learn balance and must eventually embark on solo operation. The parent must also balance support with letting go. Too little success will injure the child, both physically and motivationally. Too much support breeds resentment, a stifling dependence, and a rebellious desire to break…

…away from the constraints and limits of riding within usual boundaries, I pedal ferociously down Sheridan Avenue, a familiar half-mile stretch of sidewalk whose every bump and crack I know as intimately as the contours of my own elementary body. This time, I would test the limits of kinesthetic knowledge and stretch physicality past its natural confines. Resisting the reflexive instinct to brake at the last building before the bottom of the hill on Sheridan, I choose instead to experience a climbing velocity. What a thrill it will be to whiz past the corner I have known only in the sobriety of cautious slow motion! Frozen by determination and the brisk fatalistic wind in my ears, I hunch over the handlebars, legs askew from the pedals, as I speed off the curb into the churning traffic. Fleeing the grasp of gravity and adult-imposed limits, I charge into the olderness, pursuing freedom and the Icarus of unencumbered flight.

He rebuked the Red Sea, and it dried up; he led them through the depths as through a desert.

The car screeches to an agonizing halt just inches from my involuntary swerve. Jerking the handlebars to the right at the last instant saves me from collision but catapults me to a lacerating impact with the street as my bicycle abandons me. I lie bruised and dazed in the gutter, thankful to be alive, but wondering if the army of motorists may still harm me. In the fog of disbelief and encroaching pain, I stagger among onlookers to the safety of the curb. Feeling sheepish and guilty over my Mister Magoo—like caper, I retreat under the castigating gazes of the olderness. With some concessions to reality, I have again miraculously survived.

Remember, Son, in traffic, if it's a tie, you lose.

He wavers precariously a few precious yards down the driveway; I hesitate for an eternal second before lunging from behind to grab Jeremy's bike, lest he tumble. I catch up with him, winded. Like some reverse rickshaw caricature, we plod forward: Jeremy oscillating the handlebars like a cornered sniper and I thumping my feet as brakes. I am his breathless father, acting as training wheels, and we both know this cannot continue.

"Gr-r-r-r! I can't do it! I'll never be able to do-o-o-o-o it, o-o-o-oh!"

I am moved and mortified by this unabashed blend of despondency and whining complaint. I provide consolation and encouragement. Hesitantly, I reflect that the honing of his skills will bring self-tests beyond my forbearance and awareness. There are stickers and thorns out there in the olderness. Tires deflate in the middle of nowhere, bicycles sometimes mysteriously steer their own courses, and no matter how hard the imagination may try (I learned), the bike can't fly.

Until he masters bicycling, Jeremy must find equilibrium with the crowd in some other manner. With his feelings as balance beams, he discovers the tilted scales taunting him in the olderness.

When the teasing gets out of hand and I am told about my children's merciless group escapades at the park, I question each of them about the heartless one-upmanship. I hold Neal to a higher standard of behavior because he is older. Hoping to spare Jeremy the ignominious spurning by a clan that includes his older brother, I emphasize for Neal the importance of setting a good example.

As we talk, Neal discloses his remorse over the teasing and his awareness of his role in rejecting others and perpetuating torment. I praise him for showing this side of himself and suggest that he might take the lead in sharing these feelings with the group of friends. He grimaces. "Nah, my friends would think I'm an imbecile if I talked about my feelings."

...a time to be silent and a time to speak...

I am shocked by this stark revelation. How I have underestimated the depth of my son's experience and his capacity to discern and tolerate the backlash of the olderness! He is struggling with the ageless dilemma of integrating the hunting instinct with emotional sentience. To cope, the tough veneer and cavalier put-down are unconsciously summoned to bind the affect and anxiety; by this common temptation, the olderness seduces wanderers to attack by machete. Then, the olderness redoubles its flora, enveloping its pilgrims in forests of emotional confusion. How can I lead him through this thicket, lest the fronds of the olderness camouflage traps and hinder his progress? My meditation deepens, and the response is occluded by a choking memory of...

...dust swirling up from my feet stamping the batter's box in mock determination. I am a ten-year-old summer-camp all-star. As a hedge against striking out, I crouch in protective anticipation, reducing the strike zone further. The umpire is college All-American athlete/camp counselor Stan; he is vending unwelcome field chatter. "Very little human being up at the plate. Tiny strike zone because he's so small. Hardly any batter." *I cringe crimson, wanting to swing at his head—"very little human being"—and I am weakened in the knees and about to cry. My hero has disparaged me. I am crushed and hopeless. My only recourse is to act tough and smash the ball way out into the olderness. But I am consumed with feeling! Where shall I cry out? My hero has forsaken me with his insolent banter. They would tease me and call me an imbecile if I expressed my distress. But I am human and have these strong feelings. Now, amid public disgrace, I am choking on this dust...*

...for he knows how we are formed, he remembers that we are dust.

(Put on your big-kid stuff.)

...and the dust returns to the ground it came from...

RECAPITULATION

As for a man, his days are like grass, he flourishes like a flower of the field; the wind blows over it and it is gone, and its place remembers it no more.

After forty-plus years surviving the olderness, I gaze longingly for a glimpse of milk and honey in the Promised Land. All I see, however, is milk and cereal, a messy breakfast before our sojourn to their promised land—a baseball field, site of my pledge to teach my boys, I hope, some skills for flourishing in the olderness.

They will need body skills and interpersonal skills, mastery of some craft or trade to ply, a measure of faith, dogged persistence, humor, and a respect for the unexplained convolutions and dangers in the olderness. In their feisty youth, they experiment and compete exuberantly (often with each other) as they cut their teeth in multilayered preparation.

Be happy, young man, while you are young, and let your heart give you joy in the days of your youth...So then, banish anxiety from your heart and cast off the troubles of your body, for youth and vigor are meaningless.

As it always has, the olderness lies in surreptitious control, and sometimes, to gain advantage, my sons join forces and conspire...

...to play a trick on Grandma (the world's most caring and gullible babysitter). I set the game plan with my brother. It goes like this: I'll perch on the windowsill, and you call Grandma in a panic. When she comes, tell her hysterically that I'm threatening to jump, but when she tries to come and grab me, hold her back. We'll both tell her that if she comes any closer, I'll jump. She'll be hysterical, but she won't dare to rescue me. It'll be fun to see how she reacts, and besides, when we tell her that the only way to get me down is to give us extra dessert, she'll give in...

...to gain footholds with the most accessible generation. The olderness is so challenging; we are kept so often under the ruling thumb of mere survival that we forget to be...

...grateful! They got the mutant terrorists (for now; there are always more in the olderness, you know). My wife has healed, the threat repealed. *Whew...*

...heals all your diseases, who redeems your life from the pit and crowns you with love and compassion, who satisfies your desires with good things so that your youth is renewed like the eagle's.

***

My children sit on the couch, and we slump toward the previews of the next episode in a popular television series. They are captivated by the commercial drama and allurement for next week's viewing. Rapt and spellbound, they naively echo the ritualistic refrain, "Dad, is it to be continued?"

"Yes, it's to be continued."

"For how long, Dad?"

"Until the end of the season."

"But why, Dad? Why, until the end of the season?"

"Because life goes on, children."

...from everlasting to everlasting...

Maybe, even past the end of the season.
There is a time for everything, and a season for every activity under heaven...

Mark Steinberg, Ph.D.

Ecclesiastes 1:9
"What has been will be again, what has been done will be done again; there is nothing new under the sun."

Ecclesiastes 3:1
"There is a time for everything, and a season for every activity under heaven..."

Ecclesiastes 3:2
"...a time to be born and a time to die..."

Ecclesiastes 7:23–25
"I am determined to be wise—but this is beyond me. Whatever wisdom may be, it is far off and most profound—who can discover it? So I turned my mind to understand, to investigate and to search out the wisdom and scheme of things..."

Ecclesiastes 8:1
"Who is like the wise man? Who knows the explanation of things?"

Ecclesiastes 11:9
"Be happy, young man, while you are young, and let your heart give you joy in the days of your youth."

Ecclesiastes 11:10
"So then, banish anxiety from your heart and cast off the troubles of your body, for youth and vigor are meaningless."

Ecclesiastes 11:1
"Cast your bread upon the waters, for after many days you will find it again."

Psalm 103:3–5
"...and heals all your diseases, who redeems your life from the pit and crowns you with love and compassion, who satisfies your desires with good things so that your youth is renewed like the eagle's."

Psalm 103:13
"As a father has compassion on his children..."

Psalm 103:14
"...for he knows how we are formed, he remembers that we are dust."

Psalm 103:15–16
"As for a man, his days are like grass, he flourishes like a flower of the field; the wind blows over it and it is gone, and its place remembers it no more."

Psalm 103:17
"...from everlasting to everlasting..."

Matthew 5:45
"He causes his sun to rise on the evil and the good, and sends rain on the righteous and the unrighteous."

Luke 6:35
"...because he is kind to the ungrateful and the wicked."

CHAPTER 6
CHILDHOOD AND ADOLESCENCE

As our two sons grew through the toddler years toward school age, we decided to homeschool them. Barbara had researched homeschooling and was convinced of its many benefits. It was also a way for her to maintain close involvement and control in important areas of their development.

I was also supportive and sought involvement. As a veteran professional in the field of education and child development, I had viewed for decades the insufficiencies and decline of educational systems, both public and private. Though I still believed in public education (I had taught and served as a psychologist in many public schools in New York and California and had taught education and psychology courses in graduate schools), I thought we, as parents, could do a better job than the schools. I also viewed homeschooling as an opportunity to instill Christian values in my children. In addition, I knew the many pitfalls that young children faced when they entered school without being developmentally ready for curricula that had become increasingly push-down, demanding skills development and achievement at younger ages and chronological grade levels. This was particularly difficult on boys, a high percentage of whom have visual-motor delays and are restless or have hyperactive natures when they are five or six years old. In this regard, I felt both Neal and Jeremy were at risk for being affected by the excessive developmental pressures and academic demands from schools during the early grades.

Barbara doubled as Mom and their core teacher. Though she did not adhere to any particular curriculum, she managed to provide what was needed in basic direction in an educational process that seemed, for the most part, to run smoothly. Neal and Jeremy were natural academic learners. They took to reading, math, and language expression quickly and easily. In many ways, they taught themselves.

We had behavior problems, of course, but obviously not because of class size. There were only two students. When trouble surfaced, it was always the other kid's fault. Barbara was a very competent and patient instructor, but she struggled with enforcing discipline and decorum. Often, she sent the boys to the principal's office—which, at our homeschool, was our bedroom. There, I would assume the authority role and adjudicate conflicts and administer consequences.

From my perspective, this arrangement went very well. The boys were bright, curious, active, and advanced academically. Despite the lack of structure, they easily mastered the fundamentals and absorbed with alacrity the intentional and incidental learning from adults, peers, and their environments. Their homeschooling years were filled with social opportunities (playdates and park days galore), cultural and academic events (museums and private classes) and many, many field trips.

Neal and Jeremy were active in sports too. Though not keen on baseball and basketball (the sports of my own youth), they loved roller hockey. They played in the street and schoolyard constantly. For years, they played in organized hockey leagues. I didn't know much about hockey, so I couldn't coach them, but I eagerly schlepped them to practice and games, where I sat on bleachers in a very smelly rink, cheering them on and developing my own increasing back pain. It was a lot of work—grueling, routine, often thankless. Every parent knows what this is like. Whether it's music or dance lessons, sports, tutoring, therapy, and so on, you put out for your kids. You make arrangements, pay for things, and walk the walk of parenthood. I'm glad I was given the opportunity and was able to follow through. Those were precious years!

As they approached and entered puberty, Neal and Jeremy segued into major changes in activities and lifestyle. We decided it was time to enroll them in public school. They both began their public education at our local middle school, Jeremy in the sixth grade and Neal in the eighth.

Conventional schools are strange environments for kids unaccustomed to them. Soon after Jeremy began school, he came home with a paper and asked me, "Dad, what's up with writing your name and date at the top of the page? Why is that necessary?" Jeremy smirked but accepted my explanation of this convention along with the many other routines and traditions in classes comprised of thirty students that served pragmatic organizational and record-keeping functions and helped make the teacher's life easier.

When the boys were young and homeschooled, I augmented their instruction by teaching them with methods adapted from my training with Ralph Reitan. Dr. Reitan is one of the world's most renowned neuropsychologists. He has authored over two hundred books and publications and developed the Halstead-Reitan Neuropsychological Battery. He also pioneered and developed REHABIT (Reitan Evaluation of Hemispheric Abilities and Brain Improvement Training), which is a comprehensive method for remediating cognitive deficits and generally improving brain functioning. Although originally designed for the rehabilitation of brain injury and developmental deficits, it can also be used to teach critical thinking skills and to sharpen and improve many areas of cognitive abilities. I asked Dr. Reitan if his system would be useful and appropriate in the homeschooling of *normal* children (i.e., those without brain injury or learning disabilities), and he replied, "That would be a useful and eminently appropriate application of REHABIT."

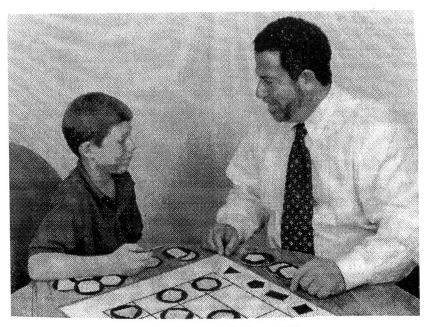

Dad teaching Neal, circa 1993

To an extent, all parenting involves experimenting with your children, and we do this in different ways. Perhaps those with professional training in psychology, child development, and education ("shrinks" such as myself) are more aware of this dynamic and therefore take precautions against being overly controlling. I believe that my influences on my children's education enhanced their abilities to reason, discern, and take better advantage of the abilities God gave them. It is a process that takes decades and becomes fruitful as children grow up, start to become increasingly independent, and begin to carve out their own identities.

Teaching my boys was fun but also a great deal of work. Through this process, our entire family became more keenly aware of our strengths and limitations, as we worked both individually and collectively toward growth, competence, tolerance, awareness, and insight.

SPORTS AND MARTIAL ARTS

Both my sons were very athletic, but my older son, Neal, persisted and excelled. Jeremy would argue that he was the better hockey player, but Neal was the skateboarder/risk-taker and he was the one who persisted in martial arts to the level of earning a black belt.

Vivid in my memory of the adolescent years are the smelly hockey rinks and the myriad trips to karate practice and events. Whereas Jeremy enjoyed martial arts for its social value (and quit after earning a few belt levels), Neal persisted for years. Fortunately, his mentor and the leader of the martial arts enterprise—Jim Buhisan—was a man of character and an outstanding role model and leader. Neal was disciplined, devoted, and appropriate in his martial arts development and was never a show-off or overly aggressive. I have always been *very* proud of him for those characteristics and his achievements in this arena.

Neal getting his black belt in Karate

THE TREE EMBARRASSES ITS FRUIT

As children develop, they imitate their parents consciously and subconsciously. Nonetheless, the genetic codes unravel through the years, assisted by teaching, circumstances, and the inevitable and instinctive similarities in appearance, gestures, expressions, and personality. There are natural tensions and conflicts in this process, as each child works out his or her own pattern of modeling and desatellization from the gravitational pull of parents. The adolescent years notoriously reflect these underlying conflicts in the behaviors of rebellion, rejection, and embarrassment acted out by teens toward their parents.

Adolescents commonly feel embarrassed (even mortified) by their parents. They mock, criticize, and flee from what they construe as their parents' bizarre mannerisms and habits. Psychologically, this is a way of processing feelings and taking proactive steps toward acquiring independence and identity, but it often brings conflict and wear and tear on the love and tolerance among family members.

In my family, I was the chief comedian. Though we were all very verbal, I often exerted leadership in sarcastic wit. Though I was typically good-natured and playful with others, Neal bristled at my exercise of comedy and wit, especially in public. For a number of years, he lived in the shadow of embarrassment, lurking at every turn of his father's interactions. Before rushing to judgment, please read the following.

These poignant episodes in Neal's struggles to adjust and accept moved me to chronicle in parody and satire some memorable moments. I wrote this story in 1995 when Neal was nine years old.

DR. CHUCKLE AND MYSTIFIED
PART ONE

A Cut-Up Develops a Split Personality

The inevitable has happened. My son has decided that I am embarrassing to him. Imagine! *Me?* The psychologist/father who has spent decades developing and refining tastes, eclecticism, humor, and a predilection for really cool things, as well as making it my business to understand what children detest about their parents...It's my *job* to be hip! (Is it OK to use that word?)

I figured this would happen, but I am surprised at the quick onset; my son Neal is only nine. Perhaps every victim bargains with similar plaintive innocence: "So soon? Why me? Is it my time yet?"

The symptoms are neither suspicious nor subtle, so I am spared the futility of pretending. In his anxious appeal, Neal blurts the directions that devastate my self-image. He tells me how to behave at the karate club party. "Don't talk to anyone, Dad. I don't want you to embarrass me. And, most of all, *please do not tell any jokes.*"

I am speechless and mystified, a sudden and depersonalized split from my identity as the infamous Dr. Chuckle, the veteran paternalistic, puckish prankster. I look in the mirror and greet the welcome hybrid of Santa Claus and Robin Williams. My son's vision does not reflect this jolly and benevolent appraisal.

Neal beseeches me with a contorted expression of filial respect and the pain of his wresting humiliation. It is agonizing for him to confront me. He is caught in that warp of development between the imminent polite skills of socially correct reproof and the raw certainty of his discomfort with my behavior. The pressure reminds me of stomach cramps.

"Da-aa-d!" he bellows. "I hate it when you joke around and talk to other people. It makes me embarrassed."

"What would you like me to do?" I reply indulgently, figuring that my calmness will both humor him and hide my growing mortification. After all, this is ridiculous; surely, my son does not expect me to be a mute chauffeur, detached in the formality of my role and bashfully deferent to the social cadence of children. In the face of my seeming consideration, Neal will realize his egocentric folly and will verbalize his appreciation for my wit and charm. "I should just stand there, smile, and not say anything?"

This logical invective seems to provoke him. "Dad..." he begins in tight-lipped disapproval, slightly shaking his head in a pretentious correction. "Don't say anything. Don't *smile*. Just *be* there, but don't talk to anybody. You embarrass me. Don't you get it?"

The knell has sounded, and I am nearly deafened by its impact. My son is placated only by my promise of restraint, and I grant him this as I withdraw into fantasy. With all the boldness and beauty of a turtle, I yank my ego inside and fold my personality into protection. I am Dr. Chuckle—benevolent, receptive, spontaneous, funny, understanding, and matured to immunity from my rebellious offspring. I worked terribly hard to develop this way, as can plainly be verified by comparing me with *my* parents. I could/would never be like them! They were not even my *real* parents—they *couldn't* be! (Remember that one?) Same deal here. My *real* children would appreciate me. They would recognize the vigilance with which I avoided becoming a jerk, committing myself to the sacrifices that would improve me to the status of a father worth taking pride in and having around. Part altruistically and part vengefully, I carved and molded my personality away from the queasy memories of my father's interactions. It sickened me to hear his repeated jokes and to watch his animated expectations of laughter and attention. It was all I could do to refrain from jumping at him and screaming, "You've told that one eight times before!" Instead, I sat there and tried to force the laughter at my father's entertainment, telling myself that diluting the audience's disdain was a suitable sublimation of my disgust.

Having this precedent, I grew with a fail-safe guidance toward becoming humorous. I would sidestep boorishness with the aplomb of a running back. Truly funny, yet taken seriously, that's what I would be—and so evolved Dr. Chuckle—intellect and respectability, with a punch line.

Now Dr. Chuckle is mystified. My personality is split by Neal's maturation through the evolving stages of his identity. During his earlier childhood, I was his security and strength, his bastion against a world that was too big, indecipherable, and threatening. The fountain of my knowledge cascaded into his bottomless admiration. In the middle years, his developmental tasks would revolve around mastery and the growing exploration of his independence and competence. It is coming time for Neal's personhood to assert itself; my role develops into part-time sparring partner for the training and tempering of his identity. Competition exists so Neal can defeat and reject me. The glimmers of pubertal chaos are too soon, too real. No applause for Dr. Chuckle. I know the process well, yet I am entrenched and mystified. It is high time for Neal to experiment with the varieties of pushing me away. The Jekyll-and-Hyde iterations of identity development pass through the generations. My son doesn't want me around for the world to see on the outside what he feels and fears lives within him. He is right, of course, though it is still training camp for the vigorous sport of adolescence. As the season unfolds, there will be cheers, adrenaline, and perhaps injury, as biology and environment vie for championship.

Exasperation and perspiration may later ensue. The games begin with a plea, a scoff, some put-downs, and the shielding psychology of one-upmanship and talking trash. I am thankful we are not yet at that stage. I have time to prepare for the incipient horror of Neal's rejection of my dress and appearance. No man's ties survive the cultural attack of his son's coming of age. In my closet, a neckwear collection hangs without defense against the passage of time. I peer into the future, skittishly sketching his mockery of my cravats.

For now, a proud developmental task is at hand. Neal's first necktie has been purchased, and he anxiously awaits my instruction, so he can present himself with fashion at the upcoming party. We have a minor skirmish over his insistence on practicing with a polo shirt.

"You can't wear a tie with that kind of collar!" My sense of taste is offended. Pompously, I fret that heritable dishevelment has skipped only my generation.

"Why not, Dad?" He pouts with surly insistence.

"Because it looks ridiculous!" Oh, boy. Dr. Chuckle is generously scattering the coffin nails now. In a few years, Bozo will look more fashionable than Dr. Chuckle.

"OK, OK." Neal capitulates, and we fumble and struggle to coordinate minds and hands in a knot over his new shirt. This act is symbolic, touching, and farcical—the father, the collar, the cloth, the laying on of hands, the confession of his immaturity. As if to etch our struggle of wills in dexterous contrast, we confront my right-handedness with his left-handedness. My automatic habits are a conundrum as I look at the world through Neal's eyes. I laugh once again through tears of mystification.

"What's so funny?" he snorts indignantly but with a contagious amusement.

"Never mind. You look great. You'll get the hang of it." I pat him approvingly and watch as he gingerly pulls at the tie and marvels as the knot rises to his neck.

With this temporary reprieve, I am valued again. His tie is loose, but I am choked up. I can tie knots in his tie, but he knots my stomach and throat. At the party, he will bear no sign proclaiming, "My dad helped me tie this tie (and taught me so many other things)!" What is available to see is that he is my son, a proud announcement he does not want me to make.

"Thanks, Dad," he utters as he scampers off.

I nod. "You're welcome," I say to the air.

***

As I arrive home from work one evening following such encounters, Neal greets me solicitously. He runs barefoot toward my car, eager in his purpose and oblivious to the cold driveway.

"Dad, there's something I've got to show you!" In the clamor of reentry to the family abode, he leads me to two long branches straddling each other amid fishing wire.

"I made fishing poles, and we went fishing for crawdads!" An impromptu display of his gear ensues, and I follow my practiced discipline of easing into the house and out of my business attire, while fielding the excitement of the day. Going to the bathroom could wait—my son, no longer estranged by embarrassment over me, shares his exuberance. We both enjoy this familiar transition into the roles that have often worked so well. Neal and I would share eagerly for a while in a barter where tacit territory is understood. He offers a recounting of the day's events and anxieties, while I, in turn, listen without judgment, censure, or invasive inquiry. I play my part and remind myself that these are the good old times I will remember.

"Really? How did you do that? I mean, where did you get the idea for fishing poles?"

"I just did…I found the branches and then we cut them down, and Mom gave me the fishing wire…Dad, you should've seen how the crawdads went after the bait. They really like hot dogs."

"How do you know they really like hot dogs? Did they hang around for mustard?" Dr. Chuckle is back.

Early the next morning, we review the crawdad fishing over dip'n egg (sunny-side egg with a bagel). The sunrise peers over the mountain through the window and falls across the table in slats of sharp effulgence alternating with shadows. The yolk of Neal's egg glows; fresh sunlight stripes his hair with early brilliance. Breakfast platitudes develop into deeper discussion.

"The fishing poles are OK…" he says, mouth full of bagel dryness. He takes some time to masticate the thoughts and bread. "But it didn't turn out the way I wanted."

"What do you mean?"

"I mean the fishing poles didn't come out the way I pictured; they're different. Lots of times things don't turn out the way I picture them in my brain—I mean, when I try to do them, they come out different. It's frustrating."

"You know, that's something I experience too. For many people, there is a *big* difference between what they think about, say, or want to do and what actually gets done. You're not the only one."

Neal looks at me quizzically, with genuine interest and reflection.

"Part of growing is learning to bridge the gap between what you have in mind, the way the world seems to you, and what you can get across to other people so that they see and experience the same things that you do. Part of living is also accepting that there *are* differences, sometimes major differences, between what you intend to happen and what actually occurs."

"Is it that way for you, Dad? Do you make stuff that turns out different from the way it's supposed to be?"

"Yeah, Neal...even my jokes." (Dr. Chuckle has to chuckle at this.) "I guess that many times I come across way different than what I mean to... and I know that I can embarrass you and make you feel funny and worked up and annoyed."

My son is studying me. This performance will be written into his philosophy, I sense jitteringly.

"Just like your fishing poles came out different than what you pictured when you started to make them, my humor and attitude and the things I say can have a different effect than what I mean or want. It makes me mystified."

"What's *mystified?*"

"It's like a part of Dad that's a different personality. One part of me is in charge, confident, knowing from practice and experience how things will turn out. That part of me jokes, plays with people, turns on the lovable charm, acts automatically. But there is another side of me that gets confused when the things I try to do turn out otherwise than what I had in mind—when people react against me or what I thought would happen doesn't—then I get puzzled, mystified."

"O-o-oh," Neal coos in that beguilingly precocious tone he has. "So, *mystified* is what you are when I don't like the way you act as a parent!"

Right.

"Or when I don't like the way you behave as a child. We've both got a lot of growing up to do. And it may not turn out the way we had in mind." I chuckle.

Mark Steinberg, Ph.D.

DR. CHUCKLE AND MYSTIFIED
PART TWO

Sown in Stitches, Grown to Ḥeal

"I don't deserve to live. I wanna die...I'm just gonna take a gun to my head!"

This plaintive bellow echoed from my son, sitting next to me in the car, across legions of advice I'd given to parents over the years when their children appeared suicidal. I knew it was a yelp of severe angst, the flair of a perturbed state, and not to be magnified beyond the expression of a person absorbed in making himself miserable.

I felt calm within myself, working moderately and successfully at not being provoked. But I was in the paradoxical pain of knowing my son's quandary and being rebuked and pummeled in the face with the obvious solutions I extended to him. Excited and out of control, he ascribed his dilemma in every conceivable manner to the conspiratorial events and people around him. I was the bad guy—me, Dr. Chuckle—the prankster sent to torment him. In his state, his soul was conned, so he would not be consoled!

***

Life teaches us to defend ourselves against the intermittent onslaught of insults, affronts, fears, and provocations that parade under the banner of anxiety. We develop coping skills, learn techniques, and assume veneers that become our roles, our personalities, and sometimes even our careers (Dr. Chuckle, for example).

The nature of upset is fiction. Its story line appears real, as if the environment unfolds events, feelings, and experience independent of the characters. The *response-ability* of being actor, observer, and author at once is usually beyond us. So our coping attempts often include subplots of victim, aggressor, and stage foil. Some of us abandon the production altogether—we put the book down, walk out of the play, withdraw from others, and leave the work incomplete.

Some folks blame the devil for these painful lies. Good fiction, after all, must be believable, and the devil is the master of deception. He makes us believe what is not true. He also uses humor with its many well-honed blunt and sharp-edged varieties. The devil has quite a repertoire of humor, as most will admit, though his humor consists of weapons rather than tools. Recoiling from the horror of being duped by sly infliction, we realize the value of beating the devil at his own game. So the jokes must be quick, witty, and carefully aimed and we must be vigilant to joust the devil where he lurks. Don the shield of funny self-protection and watch it work in mirthful ways. The devil hates to be exposed; he disappears from light. The light of humor brings Dr. Chuckle alive, and with him come the merry angels of raillery, parody, caricature, ridicule, banter, mimicry, impersonation, pretense, buffoonery, fantasy, and many puns. The humor must be funny without being hurtful, and there's the rub. For the devil's humor wounds, and in this hurtfulness, blinds us to the drama's falsity.

Accepting life on its own terms and responding with the lightness of jest empowers us to see truth, accept reality, and engage seriously with respect for life's rules. The devil hates to be topped, especially in good spirits. When the joke is on us, it is coming from "out there," outside of ourselves. We are mocked by life's penetrating intrusion. When we make the jokes, we make light (in the abstract literal sense) and we create a new perspective and see the reality more brightly. On this stage, Dr. Chuckle makes his entrance.

***

"Son," I began, "I have a story to tell you."

Neal rolled his eyes and inhaled slowly and purposefully, the breath of gathered tense resignation; it was his acknowledgment of my incipient lecture.

"I went out to get a haircut the other Saturday. When I arrived for my 5:30 appointment, the hairdresser was still working on someone. Though mildly disappointed at the delay, I sat down quietly and waited my turn, which surely would come in several minutes. I thought about the propane tank in my car, which I needed to fill to barbecue the dinner that you and the family were waiting for me to cook. I regretted not stopping at the gas station before arriving at the hairdresser and also for being rushed and not allowing a few extra minutes to fill the tank.

"As I sat waiting, I became impatient, and my thoughts turned from guilt about having to delay the family dinner to righteous indignation about being kept waiting. With my eyes aimed at a magazine, I could feel my anger directed at the hairdresser. I felt twisted by an embarrassed concern that she would somehow sense my ill will and rage. My concern was ironically misplaced because she seemed neither to notice my impatience, nor did she apologize for the delay. After twenty-two minutes, she glanced at me and said, 'Just a few more minutes, and I'll be with you. This lady has a lot of hair.'

"*And a lot of nerve, the both of you!* I was quietly fuming and incensed. I let out a sigh and cast a clearly aggravated glance at my watch. *Ten minutes later*, she beckoned me briskly into the chair. During this time, I was plotting how to vent my displeasure. Now, mind you, my motives were tempered by the fact that I respected and liked this hairdresser a lot and she had been cutting my hair for years. But I had these pent-up feelings, my family was waiting for dinner, and everything was late. I'd come for her to cut my hair, not my pride.

"I decided to tell her politely that the next time she would be running more than a few minutes late, I would really appreciate her letting me know that as soon as I walked in the door, so I could accomplish whatever errands were pressing on my very busy schedule. In the adult gamesmanship of etiquette, this would be enough to vent my upset assertively. I knew I had to do this, and I waited for an opportune moment. Her daughters were hanging around, so I couldn't risk embarrassing her. As I counted the minutes she did not apologize for the delay, I seethed. For twenty minutes, as she snipped and cut, she talked about her recent vacation (which I envied), and it was evident that the vacation had not been restful for her. She prattled on to people in the hair salon, kept a watchful eye on her daughters, and answered the phone. Her scissors dangled above my head for long pauses as my family withered with hunger at home. I noticed how tired she looked, how busy she was, and I remembered my appraisal of her tendency to stretch herself to accommodate many people's needs and demands. I also noted that she had accommodated my request for an appointment on the same day—as was our pattern over the years. These thoughts were inconsistent with my recent frustration; I began to feel sheepish. Yes, I *am* busy but also self-important and imposing.

"Into my reverie, the hairdresser shook her head and lamented, 'That lady had lots of hair. I been cutting her hair since a *quarter to five*, just cutting!' Seventy-five minutes of shearing, and I missed over half the show at the salon. And our weary hairdresser usually starts at 7:30 on Saturday mornings.

"'Her six-year-old son is so cute, but her ten-year-old is kind of retarded. You know, very slow.'"

"What? Who? Oh, the selfish, hairy customer preceding me. Who was slow? *I felt slow.* Snapping back to the present, I decided to forego my assertive communication and to concentrate on my haircut, which was turning out very nicely. The phone rang again, and the hairdresser turned her attention away from me. My mind wandered into an attractive place filled with thoughts of pride and fortune. I had accomplished much today—the shopping, the haircut, the exercise I did, the time I spent with my family. I would soon go home and cook a good meal. There was another weekend day ahead. The hairdresser turned back to me and continued snipping. I noticed the time she was spending with me, and I felt her care for me. She had been caring for me for years. How had this delay stressed her, and what kind of breach might she have surmised had occurred in our relationship? I decided to let go of my frustration and ill will. The happy thoughts returned with my complacency. Perhaps the loss of hair let fresh air into my head and evicted the pernicious thoughts. I walked out of the salon mystified at the change that had transpired in me over the past hour. It was not the first time."

***

Dr. Chuckle emerged from recounting this anecdote into the pondering quiet of Neal's gaze.

CHARACTER AND CARELESSNESS

Neal was a very smart and caring person. He was also very sensitive, and he eventually learned to hide his sensitivity and anxiety behind defensiveness, intellectualization, and derisiveness of others.

Try as I did to encourage his becoming acquainted with his feelings in more psychologically and socially adaptive ways, Neal persisted in being his own person with his particular manner of managing his emotions and manifesting his feelings and behavior with others. In retrospect, I suppose that his own feelings of entitlement led him to defend, lash out, and to protect himself by cloistering his anxiety in an effort to fit in and become socially accepted.

Neal had flaws that I noticed over time, especially as he became more autonomous during adolescence; he was careless with possessions, and he seemed to accept his carelessness with a sense of entitlement. Neal would easily lose things—a hockey glove left at the rink, a sweatshirt left at the park, a helmet in the schoolyard. Though he was contrite and apologetic, his remorse seemed somewhat shallow, and it did not modify this behavior of carelessness about possessions.

Even more disturbing was Neal's tendency to "borrow" my possessions without permission. On one occasion, he loaned his friend my expensive video camera, which the friend then lost. I was furious and exasperated. Neal did not do this regularly, but such incidents were notable etchings into his character, and they were, I now realize, portents of his subsequent escapades as a drug addict.

It is difficult for me to think and write about these aspects of my beloved son's character and his misdeeds. Yet, they are a part of who he was, my memories of him, and our lives together, the imbroglio in which I try to reconstruct and make sense of the course of his life. There are so many qualities I cherish about Neal, so much of his charm and character I remember and relive. Alas, there were also the careless, selfish, mischievous, and irresponsible parts of him that made him, in many ways, so alienated and hard to live with. I am ambivalent and haunted by these thoughts and memories. At the end of many redundant paragraphs, thought patterns, and circles of emotions, I am left with the humbling evidence that I can be so in love with a deeply flawed human being.

DRIVING IN STEALTH

During his high school years, Neal had become more distant from and rebellious toward his mother. Our marriage had deteriorated progressively and significantly over the years, spiraling its way toward the denouement of divorce shortly after Neal left for college—but I didn't anticipate this while he was still at home and in high school.

One day, Barbara came to me and confided that she believed that Neal had been sneaking out at night and taking her car. I thought this was preposterous and chalked it up to her resentment against Neal and her suspicious nature. Over a period of weeks, she reiterated her suspicions to me, citing the evidence that she had been tracking and recording her odometer. Barbara was, above all, meticulous and detail-oriented. Finally, at her urging, we confronted him. To my utter amazement, he readily confessed! My son was a car thief!

Unfortunately, this was not the end of it. Some months later, I returned home in the middle of the day at an atypical time. No one was home, yet I sensed something was amiss. Suddenly, I realized that my van (a second vehicle) was missing from the driveway! In a rare episode of doubting my own perceptions, I hunted in my mind for what I could have overlooked. Did Barbara take the van? No, she never drove it, and, besides, her car wasn't in the garage. Did I bring the van to the mechanic? No—now I was either sustaining memory loss or becoming senile! Suddenly, aha, that's it! Though I shuddered to admit it, someone had stolen my van! I was just about to call the police when I had a thought, prompted perhaps by the recollection of Neal's recent subterfuge with Barbara's car. I called Neal's cell phone and left a message, asking him if he had taken the van. Minutes later, he called back, sheepishly confessing and apologizing.

Neal was routinely honest—after the fact. Perhaps that was why I gave him second chances. I valued his candor and seeming accountability. Many years later, I realized that this was a shield for his wiliness and sense of entitlement. His modus operandi when caught red-handed was to give up and apologize with transparency. Trouble was, even routine and austere consequences didn't rehabilitate the character fault that would manifest itself in repeated manipulative and boundary-breaking behaviors.

That escapade cost Neal a two-year delay in obtaining the first car I would give him, a vehicle he was expecting because of my previous promise. Neal was remorseful, and he followed the rules for a long time. Eventually, I gave him my 1997 Lexus. It was this car—his only vehicle—in which he made many trips between his college life (in Riverside and later San Diego) and the Bay Area and that would ultimately carry him in his forays to his destruction. It was this car that he slept in when he had no place to go. It was this car—the one I had used for years to drive him to school, to sports, to dinners, and for deep conversations, father to son—that eventually I was to tow from the garage in the San Francisco house after his death.

HIGH SCHOOL CHALLENGES AND ACHIEVEMENTS

Neal attended and graduated Leland High School in the Almaden Valley in San Jose. He was not quite used to public school when he entered as a freshman, since he had only spent one year (eighth grade) at Bret Harte Middle School subsequent to homeschooling. Neal did well in school, and he made an adequate adjustment, earning a freshman position on the varsity football team and eventually excelling on the speech and debate team.

However, he experienced an inner turmoil that festered and grew—about which we didn't know until years later. Though Neal had many friends, he felt isolated. He brooded about being a misfit. As parents, we heard his occasional complaints, but we attributed these to typical adolescent angst and a search for identity. After all, Neal had friends; we saw him interacting regularly and being part of groups; he was doing well in school, staying out of trouble, and participating successfully in extracurricular activities. What could be wrong?

In retrospect, I don't know that anything was wrong—at least in high school—except that Neal was growing ever more self-conscious about his self-perceived inadequacies. He claimed that he never did drugs in high school (which I believe) but that he felt very naïve, a sensitivity that he claimed his peers exploited. He often talked during his college years about how he felt that he was completely lacking in social skills. I was flabbergasted at his confessions and attributions, since there was abundant evidence of his multifaceted charm and successful social interactions. Listening to him complain about his social ineptness felt as bizarre to me as standing outside on a blazing sunny day and hearing the person next to me complaining about the rain. I couldn't make sense of it. For years, Neal blamed the roots of this perceived inadequacy on his homeschooling.

It is easy to surmise roots and causes to explain outcomes. We invent or rewrite history to supply our needed sense of continuity and rationale. The actual merit or accuracy of such explanations is hard to prove. Neal had his explanations and justifications for his struggles. I had different views of him. We often argued about our disparate perceptions and feelings about this complicated person, Neal Steinberg.

DEBATING

After a freshman stint as a benchwarming running back on the Leland High School football team, Neal abandoned varsity football in favor of his dedication to karate, which would eventually earn him a black belt. He also found a home on the venerable Leland speech and debate team. His forte was speech, and he became successful in competition.

Both Jeremy and Neal engaged this discipline, and they were both rising stars. Their school consistently ranked high nationally in competitions. It was a discipline we encouraged, along with contributing the necessary parental efforts—months and years of driving and playing audience to (and sometimes judging) competitions. There were many Saturday evenings that stretched into Sunday mornings at Santa Clara University, where local competitions were frequently held. I stayed awake as long as I could at these events, eventually succumbing to adventurous dreams of my children's future accomplishments.

My sons were quite talented in this realm. Jeremy was actually brilliant, but he was, at the time, callow and cocky. He thought his first draft should suffice, and he was rarely willing to put in the work necessary to refine his presentations. He wanted to coast on brains and quickness. Neal was wonderfully eloquent. He had a rare gift of glibness saturated with ease and authenticity. He could have sold snow to Eskimos were it not for his need to provoke adrenalin and conflict in argument and everyday life.

Nonetheless, under the superb guidance of the team staff and devoted teachers, Neal thrived and achieved. His speech team competitions and victories gave him a deserved bedrock of confidence.

High school varsity football

SCIENCE GUY

It became evident that Neal was a very bright student, although he shirked homework and had erratic and sloppy work habits. As he progressed through high school, he became more enamored of the physical sciences. He was also gifted in mathematics. He forged good relationships with his science and math teachers and became increasingly interested in scientific methods and intrigues. His attraction and abilities foreshadowed his collegiate studies and achievements in these areas.

PREPARING FOR COLLEGE

In 2004, Neal graduated Leland High School with a 3.2 GPA—nothing shabby, but neither was it outstanding in the mix of the exacerbating competition that was escalating in our world. He was accepted at the University of California at Riverside. And so, we prepared to send our firstborn son away to college, off into the world to find his way.

I was ready. Neal was ready. There are always worries, but we felt prepared, adequate to the challenges of Neal making it successfully on his own.

There are no guarantees. In retrospect, I have searched for clues and signals about Neal's deconstruction and tragedy. Repeatedly, I come up empty, if not blinded. For every harbinger I imagine, there are many more signs of his fortitude, resiliency, and positive outlook and expectations, which depicted his development and maturation. In retrospect, it is humbling to know so little, even with the benefit of so much history and information.

Months before Neal's departure for freshman year at university, I wrote a poem expressing my memories and feelings about my son growing up in our family. This poem portrays my attraction and deep love for Neal. It floods me with tears each time I read it.

I WILL MISS YOU

I will miss you when you leave and go to college.
Listening for the rumble of your skating, echoing in my ears.
I'll remember when I worried with the knowledge
That you'd fall—and stumble into tears.

Now I'm the one who fears this fall
From childhood when you amble away
To independent living in peer-filled fray,
And I shall grace the sidelines, scraping memories that stray.

Oh, the glare of what I tried to reinforce
When you were young and I could press my way
To stay upon intended course,
But nature had to have her say.

So, son, you grew and drew the source
From which you sprang into your independence.
I behold you with no remorse,
Just vivid pride and piquant loss at your descendance.

The dearth of MTV will give my eardrums rest.
Downstairs the kitchen reeks, a food-stained mess;
And still I rant my vain prerogatives for what is best,
I know that when you're gone…I'll have so much less.

Your music fills my head with rhythms loud
Enough to burst the membranes' generation gap.
Your artful skew of limits makes me very proud
Of how you vest your energy into maturity to tap.

When you depart from home, this womb of habits that we've spun,
You might review our parenting and counsel with disdain.
You may not see the chrysalis transforming and begun
To morph your freedom from the sinews of our heritage and pain.

I celebrate your youthfulness and dreams and straining toward the world.
I wait with diffidence and confidence for accidents to counter what you know.
You have a history and destiny about to be unfurled.
The stark reality is that when you go, my son, I'll miss you so.

CHAPTER 7
COLLEGE TEARS AWAY

We had attended freshman orientation, parents' day, and numerous meetings in preparation for Neal's beginning his freshman year at UC Riverside in 2004. It was a heady time. Neal decided to take advantage of an opportunity to attend summer school at Riverside preceding his official freshman entry in the fall semester. He would live in a dorm and assimilate with other students while earning credits and taking a study skills and an orientation course.

From my own youth, I remember summers away (even summers at a university while I was still in high school). Though I returned home periodically (and spent one semester attending City College of New York while living at home), once I left for college as a true freshman, I knew that I would never be the same or return home as the same "child." Thus, I looked wistfully upon Neal's new beginning with a mixture of excitement and conflicted feelings. Setting my ambivalence, trepidations, and personal reminiscences aside, I was very supportive of this critically important transitional process of Neal leaving the nest and striking out on his own.

As a gift and to ease the transition for this rite of passage, I took Neal for a getaway weekend at a beach resort in Southern California for a few days before heading east to the Riverside campus. Neal, an endowed athlete, was an amateur surfer. I sat on the sand and reveled in his adventurous spirit as he played in the ocean. My fears waned as I fully appreciated his obvious skills and watched him exult in the joy and physical challenges he eagerly pursued. Though I too had been an excellent athlete in my youth, Neal's breadth of physical abilities, his willingness to take calculated risks, and his persistent practice clearly eclipsed my own athletic prowess. He was a spectacle to observe as he cavorted on his surfboard, and I was as proud as any father could be of his demonstrable talents!

INLAND EMPIRE

Riverside, California, is about a hundred miles east of Los Angeles in a dry, smoggy valley known as the Inland Empire. Compared to Los Angeles, both its cost of living and its amenities are modest. But it is very much typical of California—dry, agricultural, and spread out geographically, with a very prevalent Mexican culture. And it is *hot*!

Whereas the city itself seemed to be impoverished and slum-like, the campus of UC Riverside struck me as jewel in a parched, desolate desert. It is a large university, well-endowed with important research that had begun to cast powerful beams into the future. At the same time, I had the impression as we walked around the campus that it was also infested with many dysfunctional students who were acting out their independence in destructive and immature ways. Unfolding events would subsequently reinforce these observations, and my disquieting and inchoate parental premonitions of danger would ultimately prove justified.

This was to be Neal's home, his school and stomping grounds, and he would have to navigate the temptations and pitfalls as best he could. As a freshman, he lived in a modern dorm that housed "pods" of students—six or so freshman in minicottages, sharing facilities in a high-rise on campus. Neal seemed to adjust reasonably well, given the required adaptation to living with peers having varying levels of cleanliness and territorial dispositions.

Toward the end of his freshman year, he became affiliated with a fraternity. Neal was passionate about his newfound brotherhood. Unfortunately, the fraternity was a noose in quicksand that would lead him to his undoing. That would be years in the making. At the beginning, the fraternity offered Neal conditional acceptance, peer support, and validation, and it was a place to hang out and try to fit in.

I was skeptical about his fraternity. The more I learned, the more I prevailed upon him to cut his ties with what I knew to be some mightily sinister and destructive influences. But, for Neal, it was his clan, and he did not heed my admonitions. In retrospect, I could have insisted. But then, how much of his life would I be increasingly trying to micromanage? It is a proverbial parent's dilemma. Given my son's ability, autonomy, and the nature of our relationship, I mostly played the role of listening and pointing out sternly the cautions and consequences of his more significant mistakes. I couldn't be there to supervise his every move, nor could I motivate his heart in the ways of the Lord. Despite my frustration and disappointment, I know that I tried.

PROGRESSING THROUGH YEARS AND HABITS

Neal made it through his freshmen year with the routine, but not overwhelming, conflicts and difficulties—roommate disputes, financial aid hassles, and academic progress and credits. He seemed to be doing OK. He returned home to San Jose to visit at regular intervals. I enjoyed listening to his exploits and the incessant ruminations of his busy and opinionated mind. Though I cringed at some of his confessions and bravado, I bit my tongue in deference to the knowledge that he had to find his own way. I wanted him to trust me and to know that he could confide in me. I tried to keep criticism and censure to a minimum in the hope that, eventually, wisdom would emerge and prevail.

SEPARATION AND ALIENATION

By Neal's sophomore year in college in 2005, I was in the throes of a prolonged and difficult divorce. I had moved out of the house that the boys had grown up in since 1992. Jeremy had chosen to live with me for his senior year of high school. Barbara and I put our house on the market and sold it just ahead of the housing crash and recession. We contested bitterly over money for the next two years, a familiar shadow that often follows the dimming light of a failing marriage. (Auspiciously, my attorney said, "As go people's marriages, so go usually their divorces.")

Through adolescence, Neal had been rebellious and cantankerous toward his mother. Our separation and divorce seemed to reinforce and accelerate his feelings of antipathy toward Barbara. Despite my problematic feelings about her, I was consistently careful—and, I believe, honorable—about not denigrating Barbara. I let my kids ask questions, and I answered them without sarcasm or vituperation. I let them express their confusion and ambivalence. I tried to be honest. I admitted my frustration and subjectivity, hoping to facilitate their individual working out of a wrenching family division. *At least they were older and more independent*, I told myself. Divorce is always ugly, but ours could have been worse—no custody battles, just quiet resentments, magnified by the haggling over money.

Unmistakably, however, there was a psychological rupture in Neal's identification and relationship with his mother. They were alienated from each other, carrying prolonged grudges and feuds until the end of Neal's life. Neal was often hostile toward his mother. This was such a torture for me. Barbara, my erstwhile and resentful partner, mother of our children, believed that I had turned Neal against her and that I had purchased his allegiance with material offerings. Neal, my defensive and contentious firstborn, was acting out some grievances against his mother that none of us (even I with all of my psychological acumen, insight, and clinical experience) could understand. I was in the middle, trying to mediate. It was a situation that, for years, I could only witness and lament, but could not repair—and it resulted in a profound sense of spiritual helplessness and despair.

A NEW LIFE FOR DAD

In 2006, I met and married Giulia. After twenty-eight years with Barbara, I knew I was a long-term relationship man and that I didn't want to grow old alone. I was fortunate. Giulia, eleven years my junior, had a fourteen-year-old daughter. She was Russian and Jewish, and we hit it off immediately. On the surface, our children accepted, blended, and adapted. Nadia, Giulia's daughter by a previous marriage, was a beautiful girl, gifted socially and athletically. Much of our early marriage revolved around Nadia's competitive swimming, a life full of eight-hour practice days, independent study, homeschooling, and worldwide travels for competition. It was grueling.

There were many adjustments, but I was happy. Weeks after our marriage, Jeremy moved to Southern California to attend UC Irvine. Giulia's mother occupied Jeremy's room, and Nadia moved into Neal's seldom-used room in my postdivorce house. I suppose my sons must have felt displaced, but they showed no overt resentment.

Neal and Giulia took each other very seriously. They often went head-to-head. Giulia is verbal, outspoken, artistic, passionate, aggressive, and *very maternal*. She immediately accepted Neal and adopted him in his need for mothering (with which he would ambivalently grapple). Neal had a hard time accepting and expressing affection. Though he acknowledged this struggle, he seemed to make no appreciable progress in overcoming it. I cannot blame this on Barbara. Though quiet and reserved by nature, she was an excellent mother to the children for many years. She was loving, affectionate, and nurturing to both of them. Unfortunately, Barbara's conflict aversion and inflexibility became real liabilities in overcoming differences between her and Neal. He too was rigid and uncompromising in his views about his mother and the ways of the world.

Neal transferred his woman/mom issues to my new wife, who had a different personality. They often clashed. As much as I love my children, I maintained an inviolable stand regarding the sanctity and leadership of the husband-wife relationship. My offspring would simply have to defer and adjust. I left their resentments and entitlements in God's hands. In my view, I was not abandoning my children; I was welcoming them into a new and healthier family milieu.

Still, Neal continued to test limits with Giulia. Some of his provocations were nastily hostile, and some were twisted pleadings for love. Giulia learned quickly and gave love profusely. Having never raised sons, she adjusted magnificently. Since I've known her, she continues to astonish me with the power and pervasiveness of female and maternal love. Slowly, Neal accepted her love—but always with a measure of caution and defensiveness. We loved Neal jointly, and we held him to reasonable standards of accountability.

Giulia, Mark, and Neal at a favorite restaurant, circa 2007

THE RUSSIANS ARE HERE

Like me, Neal embraced things Russian. He learned Russian words (especially idioms and profanity), practiced and performed Russian rap songs, attracted Russian friends, and gobbled delicious Russian foods. Over the years, it was a delight for me to take him on food shopping expeditions (one of my favorite hobbies). The Giulia era included stories about Europe, a history of the world from someone who grew up under Communism and whose mother survived a concentration camp, comparisons with San Jose suburbia, and a salting with my South Bronx origin and legends. We added to this mixture the flavors of ethnic markets, eateries, and recipes. With this stimulation and love, Neal crept readily into the fold. Russia, after all, is red. Neal, the redhead, was able to summon his Eastern European genetic fervor in embracing my new wife and her culture.

As her older stepbrother, Neal was protective of Nadia. But he also needled her and took advantage of her sensitivities and insecurities. Like many people, Neal developed the habit of building himself up by finding fault with others. He was often sneaky in his teasing, digging the verbal knife in just enough to exert dominance and extort passive resentment. Whereas he really needed love and respect, he often earned himself disdain and distance.

He was kind to Giulia's mother; he often listened patiently to her stories. He was very much the beloved grandson to three grandmothers (the other two being my mother and Barbara's mother). Sadly, it was some years later that, in the throes of his addiction, he would steal pain medication from Giulia's mother.

Neal, stepsister Nadia, and puppy Coco, 2007

Neal doing a Russian dance

Christmas 2007—Mark, Giulia (holding Kira, the Shar-pei), Jeremy (holding Kirby, the wire-haired Dachshund), Nadia, Tatiana (Giulia's mother), Neal, and Coco, the Golden Doodle

SOCAL AND NORCAL

During the course of his undergraduate years at Riverside, Neal progressed and achieved academically. He earned his bachelor of science degree in physics at UC, which is no small accomplishment. He became an acolyte of physical sciences, and he developed a "personality" minor in philosophy and skepticism. He went through a long phase of infatuation with *consciousness* in philosophy and metaphysics. He loved to engage anyone who would listen (few could tolerate his discourses, so mostly it was me he would talk with) in long discussions about metaphysics and the nature of consciousness. Given to intellectualism myself, I tried to be tolerant and accepting of Neal's cerebral meanderings, but I grew weary of these pointless mental gyrations and I would insert in our discussions my emphasis on the need to be practical. Sometimes Neal would fight me, and sometimes he would accept my advice. He clearly had a hard time making it his own and putting it into practice.

Throughout his undergraduate years, Neal visited us at home in San Jose regularly. I always looked forward to seeing him—a parent knows viscerally this mixture of attraction to, worry about, and excitement at seeing one's child again. Occasionally, I would visit Neal at Riverside. His appearance, his attitude, the content of his conversation and preoccupations, and his affect and connectedness combined to tell me how he was doing.

I knew that he was using drugs. During his freshman year, it was mostly marijuana and drinking. This was to be expected, though I strongly disapproved, remonstrated him, and I cringed. Gradually, he progressed into using opiates, mostly OxyContin and the like. He spent most of his time at the fraternity house (though he lived in various apartments with roommates in Riverside). This environment reinforced and justified his drug use and increasingly irresponsible lifestyle.

Neal was never careful with money. He spent whatever he had, even before he descended into full-blown addiction. I tried many tactics to get him to be financially accountable. Nothing succeeded in this regard. I continued to support him, as I believed I should and must during his undergraduate years. I also continued to hold him accountable about spending, hoping that some stability and responsibility would eventually take root. Neal had matured in many ways; he was increasingly adept at managing difficult academics on his own and was able to live independently and negotiate the ambiguities of getting along with peers, dealing with conflicts, and accommodating certain quirks.

However, in the realm of managing money, he failed to mature. This was noteworthy and frustrating, since we as parents had set good examples in this regard. His mother especially was very frugal and cautious about money. Nonetheless, Neal was a spendthrift, and his drug descent inevitably decimated his preexisting tenuous self-discipline with money.

When I got to see Neal, it was joyous and relieving, even amid his instability and irresponsibility. The natural protectiveness and desire of a parent for his child trumps disapproval and disappointment. I was not blind, just hopeful that my son would overcome his mistakes, learn from them, and grow out of his irresponsibility and hedonism.

We made trips to Tahoe, sometimes as a family and sometimes just Neal and me. Since I am not a skier, I amused myself with watching snow and fireplaces and hosting the environment in which my more daring family members could cavort and play. Neal was a pretty good snowboarder. I reveled in his taking on such challenges.

In the summer of 2007, we went as a family to Hawaii. Nadia's international swim competition served as the rationale for this excursion. We met her in Hawaii, watched her compete, and continued on to have a fabulous but brief vacation. Those were great times as a family. Despite his typical moodiness, Neal participated in our family communication and activities. It was a lush and memorable time. I am grateful for those experiences. The pictures in my mind are comforting, more so than the tears that flow when I look at photographs.

Hawaii, 2007—Nadia, Jeremy, Neal, and Dad

Neal surfing in the Pacific

Neal loved the ocean

Neal had a succession of brief jobs in Riverside. He worked at a hot dog restaurant near campus, and he found contract tutoring jobs. He was a good writer, proficient at understanding and teaching literature, and he was a whiz at math. He enjoyed tutoring, and he was especially taken with mentoring some of his inner-city students. Neal would have made an excellent teacher, had he chosen that career path. His brief stints in tutoring (and later teaching as a graduate student in the physics department at San Diego State University) gave him satisfaction, earned him some income, and provided him with the real-life experience and evidence that he had much value to give.

In 2008, Neal graduated UC Riverside with a bachelor of science degree in physics, a proud achievement. He moved back to San Jose to begin the next phase of his too-short life.

Graduation from UC Riverside, 2008

Neal with Mom Barbara at graduation, 2008

Neal reading on a plane on one of our many trips

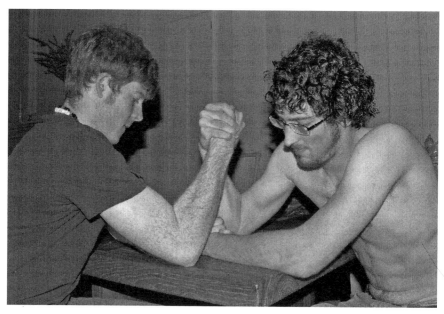

Neal and Jeremy arm wrestling

*Neal, Dad, and Jeremy at Grammy's eightieth birthday party, 2005
(Mark's mother, Pearl)*

Neal dancing with Grammy Pearl at her eightieth birthday party, 2005

Jeremy (holding Kira, the Shar-pei) and Neal (holding Kirby, the wire-haired Dachshund)

Neal about to eat a one-pound cheeseburger

A moment of repose

CHAPTER 8
A SEMIPRO YEAR

After graduating UC Riverside with a bachelor of science degree in physics, Neal moved back to San Jose. Like so many other college graduates, he didn't have a specific plan for what to do. He reassured us that he would look for a job, so I took a wait-and-see attitude, hoping that he would follow through and that he and opportunity would find each other.

For a few months, Neal lived with us—Giulia, Giulia's mother, Nadia, me, and our two dogs, Coco and Kira—in our San Jose home. Neal was charming and social, but the arrangement soon became uncomfortable. He did not have his own room, since all the bedrooms were occupied. He slept on the living room couch (which he said he did not mind), though we all knew the arrangement had to be temporary. Still, Neal was an inveterate night owl. He stayed up late and slept in late. His habits quickly got in our way. Also, he was untidy, routinely leaving the remains of his food around the living room with crumbs and food wrappers embedded in the furniture.

Despite our pleadings and his promises, Neal barely complied with the house rules about cleanliness. He almost never challenged the standards; he simply was lackadaisical about meeting them. Giulia worked hard to combine a need for his accountability with her profuse love for him. Ours was a fairly new marriage, and the blending of families and children brings adjustment and ambivalence. Neal's poor compliance and his reactivity created stress.

I frequently felt stuck in the middle, mediating my sons' needs for autonomy and respect with my wife's needs for consideration and respect. Despite the difficulty, I took a firm stand that Neal and Jeremy had to respect Giulia and comply with the house rules, parental quirks notwithstanding. Giulia could be domineering, and there were many times when she and the children went head-to-head. I was fortunate to be adept at navigating their personality differences and clashes, but it was stressful. I expressed and re-inforced through daily experience the sanctity of the husband-wife bond, as well as a delicate mixture of validating and supporting my children while instituting requirements for accountability and performance. It's not easy, as any parent can attest.

There were two aspects of family life that brought us all closer together: our dogs and Giulia's mother, Tata (Tatiana). Because of these lovable and dependent beings, arguments and conflicts receded in the presence of their needs and unending, simple love and affection.

Taking care of the dogs—walking and running with them, playing and fussing over them—was a constant source of entertainment and together-ness. Kira, the matriarchal top-dog shar-pei, was a regal and often aloof dog whom Neal adored. He would play with her, tease her, and practice his Russian language on her. It was a strange and adorable spectacle. As was often the case with Neal, he went overboard with playfulness and teasing to the point of annoyance. Though many times we had to intervene, the natu-ral communication and self-protection of animals enabled Neal to calm and temper his intrusiveness. Dogs are wonderful in that way.

When I married Giulia, I signed on to live with her mother as well. It has been a delight. Though there are tremendous responsibilities and limitations living with an elderly parent, the rewards, for me, have been a consistent blessing. In many cultures, living with and caring for aged parents is taken for granted. Say what you will about the apron strings of parent-child dysfunction and mitigated psychological independence (most of it true, I tell you as a veteran psychologist), caring for parents is one of the tenderest and most spiritually awakening experiences in this life. It is a duty that honors the humans who gave us life and the God who gives all life. It is humbling, and it teaches respect and models love, responsibility, and fidelity for multiple generations. It can be inconvenient and expensive, but this responsibility carries with it the deepening of human intimacy, a rich fabric of family life, and the confidence that commitment brings.

I feel fortunate to have this experience in my adult years. My own par-ents lived in another city across the United States until they passed away.

Though I visited them several times a year, the onus of care fell upon my brother, who carried this responsibility devotedly for many years. After the many freedoms and adventures of my young-adult and middle-age years, I've become content with the family God gave me—including a mother-in-law who was easy to get along with and who loved and favored me.

Tata spoke enough English to get by, and she communicated her needs and emotions very well. (I remember my glee at the time she wanted some pickles but couldn't find the English word. So she took out a cucumber and began salting it in front of me! I got it!) She would often talk to me about her youth in Russia and about raising Giulia (along with side comments about Giulia's stubbornness, which I loved to hear, as it gave us a tacit collusion in living with Giulia's idiosyncrasies). Though she rarely talked about her teenage years spent in a concentration camp, I felt a connection with her suffering, her bravery, and the simple pride she brought to this new world that somehow fused us as family.

Neal loved Tata and engaged with her joyfully and respectfully. There is often a certain magic in grandparent-grandchild relations that circumvents the trauma and conflicts that often pervade parent-child relationships.

YOU HAVE TO WORK

After several months of his hanging around the house and being unproductive, I put increasing pressure on Neal to find work. He was not yet ready to attend graduate school, and, in fact, had proclaimed his plan of taking a year away from academics even before he graduated. However, his postundergraduate torpor was grating on everyone, and I believed that his idleness and lack of direction must have some concrete resolution.

Though he reacted anxiously to reminders about finding a job, Neal made efforts to find employment. He had an interview here and there, but nothing materialized. What concerned me more than his lack of work was that he had no plan. Physics majors were not in high demand, and Neal had maintained a common juvenile fantasy that upon his graduation, one or more top companies would offer him a good-paying professional job. Within months of his graduation, this bubble had burst, and the terrible recession was growing and reaching destructively into the lives of millions.

Frustration abounded. Neal was sleeping late in the day, provoking intellectual arguments with people (including family members), and becoming an economic parasite. To turn this tide, I decided to take a big chance: I would hire Neal as a neurofeedback technician to work in my practice.

Aside from the potential conflicts from employing family, I had one overshadowing concern about Neal working in my practice: he didn't believe that neurofeedback was worth much. For years, Neal had loved to mock the "soft" social sciences. He believed in hard science, data, and the stuff of labs and lasers. (Ironically, he was just as devoted to cosmology and philosophy, intellectual enterprises with less empiricism than what he loved to criticize.) My skin is thick, and I could chalk up much of Neal's skepticism about my work to his developmental struggle for independence. After all, many children rebel against their parents' way of life. What better way to dig in the knife of criticism and dismissal than to skewer a parent's work? However, I worried about Neal's scoffing at social sciences and human-caring professions. Couldn't he see how important and legitimate these many avenues of healing were? It was like my son to be contentious, adversarial, challenging of the status quo. It was not like him to be insensitive and narrow.

So, I offered Neal a job at my office as a neurofeedback technician. I would send him for professional training, and he would be under strict supervision at my office. I had full confidence in Neal's competence, quickness, and ability to learn quickly and perform. He had demonstrated these attributes consistently across many activities and fields of endeavor throughout his life. My concern was about his attitude. Could he be effective in treating patients with a technology he didn't fully believe in? Would he convey his skeptical and dismissive attitude to patients and bother them or subvert the treatment? Was this even ethical?

After mulling this over for months, I decided to give Neal a chance. I reassured myself that practically everybody was skeptical about neurofeedback. It just came with the territory. We (professionals in the field of neurofeedback) have never had the luxury of acceptance. Laypersons and professionals alike demand that we justify and prove the validity of the treatment we offer. Despite decades of research and millions of treatment sessions, we are regarded with suspicion and marginalized. The employees I've hired and trained over decades have all come to neurofeedback either with tentative belief (and mostly because they needed jobs) or with some direct personal experience that greatly benefited them or a loved one. So, Neal was not unique, except for his filial relationship with me. In fact, both my sons had benefited from neurotherapy that I administered to them when they were young and I'd first started this practice (though it would be decades and more neurofeedback before they realized their benefit).

Neal needed gainful employment. I could offer opportunity and close supervision. I decided to make him earn his keep. Neal was a brilliant young man with few practical skills—an atavism akin to a proverbial chip off the old genetic block. As a friend proverbially and insightfully quipped to me decades ago, "Unemployable Jewish comedians make great salesmen, teachers, and psychologists." Perhaps the same can be said for neurotherapists.

WORK WORKS OUT

Much to my surprise and delight, Neal was a winner as a neurotherapist from the very beginning. With his background in physical science and his love for computers and technology, he learned and acclimated as efficiently as I had hoped. He picked up the technical skills quickly and naturally, like a sponge absorbing water. Fortunately, Neal's interest in physics and his years of knowing my friend and colleague Dr. Siegfried Othmer spurred his interest in the field and the validity of neurofeedback. Dr. Othmer first introduced me to neurofeedback. Eventually, we coauthored *ADD: The 20-Hour Solution*. Siegfried was a reliable resource and a good and credible mentor to Neal as well. Maybe Neal couldn't believe his dad, but Dr. Othmer had substantive credibility in Neal's eyes because he also had a Ph.D. in physics and had worked for decades in the aerospace industry.

The big surprise was how effective Neal was with patients. People *loved* him. He exuded a natural charm and affinity for almost everyone. Neal had a wide range of interests, a far-reaching mind, and decades of exploration in the esoteric to indulge his unending curiosity. These attributes, along with his charming personality, made a positive impression on an array of patients. Older patients felt comfortable with him because he projected competence and was nonthreatening. Younger patients related to him and felt his nonjudgmental acceptance.

When he was not under the influence, Neal was charming, hardworking, and delightful.

LIVING INDEPENDENTLY

After several months of living with us at home and clashing with family members, it was time for Neal to move out and live independently. He found residence in San Jose as a roommate to a thirty-something man who owned a condo in a decent area downtown. This fellow was employed in technical industry marketing. He worked a lot, had an active social life, and wasn't home much—which suited Neal fine. It seemed a good situation for Neal.

He lived with this fellow for the better part of a year until he left for graduate school in San Diego. They seemed to get along. I was hoping that the roommate would be a good role model for Neal, demonstrating financial and emotional independence from his parents, working productively, and establishing viable contemporary social connections. However, his life was busy, and Neal wanted more friendship and personal contact than the roommate had time for or was inclined to give. Still, they got along.

Neal continued to do a good job at work, developing his skills as a neurotherapist and also beginning to awaken some interest in the benefits of the treatment we offered to patients. Though he was skeptical, entrenched in his commitment to the hard sciences and prone to scoff and be dismissive, Neal did eventually become impressed by the consistent and irrefutable evidence that neurofeedback was helping lots of people—and that he was an important agent of these positive changes. The experience planted seeds that began to take root within the next year and allowed Neal to also experience the palliative and balancing effects of neurofeedback for his own difficulties, most notably his anxiety and compulsive tendencies to ruminate.

AN UPSIDE

One of my most memorable moments was the time that Neal appeared with me on TV, doing a segment demonstrating the use of EEG neurofeedback. We drove to the KRON TV studio in San Francisco for a segment during the morning news in which I talked about the benefits of neurofeedback treatment and Neal helped by facilitating and demonstrating the neurofeedback electrical hookup. This was a very proud moment for me; the event stands out in my memory of Neal as a professional, as a son, dearly loved, and as a sidekick who accompanied me on many trips around the Bay Area for shopping, errands, and this time—in his own right—a professional TV appearance.

Neal with Dad and news anchor on the KRON4 morning news,
San Francisco, 2009

Neal with Dad discussing EEG neurofeedback on the KRON4 morning news,
San Francisco, 2009

A DOWNSIDE

I know that Neal was smoking a lot of pot that year. He was also using opiates (especially OxyContin) and had been indulging in this practice on and off since his undergraduate days in Riverside. I did what I knew to discourage his drug use. I didn't take it lightly. I was stern, but did not push him away. I maintained standards, gave him data, literature, and fatherly advice. I encouraged him to seek therapy. He was superficially appreciative of my concern but remained characteristically dismissive of the idea that he had a significant problem. Neal tended to defend himself by intellectual forays and by rationalization. He seemed the poster boy for "Philadelphia lawyering." (Indeed, he was so good at arguing, so verbally skilled, that I had often encouraged him to attend law school. Neal engaged in persistent soliloquys about consciousness, the nature of the universe, and unanswerable philosophical arguments. This habit turned others (family and friends) off so much that few could stand to listen to him. I too had my limits. I tried to explain to him that his style of argument and intellectual superiority was a control mechanism that interfered with the intimate friendship he so desperately wanted, but he would have none of it. I realized that he was conflicted and stubbornly immature. He wanted attention and craved adulation, but he insisted on having it his way, despite the evidence for lack of takers. He still insisted on selling Neal, as he was. Life teaches lessons, as always, in the consequences of choices.

GRADUATE SCHOOL PLANS AND TRANSITION

In the spring of his transitional year working for me, Neal asserted his interest in graduate school. He wanted to earn an advanced degree in physics, a subject of his longstanding interest. To his credit, he researched graduate programs and applied to several schools. He decided to attend San Diego State University.

Neal was attracted to SDSU's graduate program by its reputation for research in the field of ecological ("green") technology and by the facility of the department chairman for attracting multiple grants in areas that interested him. Perhaps Neal thought he could ride on the coattails of this professor—a not unusual modus operandi for graduate students trying to find their way and procure their degree. I believe that Neal was sincere in his intentions.

I was glad about his decision on several levels; most important, he seemed to be motivated and moving on with his life in a positive, productive direction. San Diego is a lovely place, full of recreational and social opportunities, and a highly desirable place in which to live. And Neal would be within reasonable driving distance of home.

Giulia and Neal at the Empire State Building, NYC

Neal recording New York at the Empire State Building, NYC

Neal on the subway, NYC

CHAPTER 9
GRADUATE SCHOOL

The summer of 2009 was a bright and busy time. Neal was headed to San Diego in August to start graduate school, and there were preparations to be made. Chief among these was finding him a place to live.

I was happy about his motivation and determination. Though I had my reservations about his sobriety and stability, I thought that graduate school would help him mature, develop improved self-management skills, acquire increased responsibility, and enhance his capacity for independent living. I was confident about Neal's academic ability, and I believed he had the capability to land on his feet.

We made the road trip through Los Angeles and south to San Diego. It was fun to travel with Neal. His mind was always full of stories, challenges, riddles, and scientific trivia. He could be lively and engaging, and he maintained a constant interest in my view of things, as well as my legends, stories, and jokes. As far as I knew, I could tolerate Neal more than most. As well, his respect for and interest in me sufficed to make us look forward to and enjoy spending time together. I regarded him as my protégé.

HOUSE HUNTING

In the early summer of 2009, we spent a few days in San Diego, finding housing for Neal and going through the paces of enrolling in his graduate program. I met a few of his professors and, with Neal in the lead, roamed the sparsely inhabited halls and offices of the university physics department.

It harkened me back to my graduate school days a generation ago and, more recently, to my experiences teaching graduate school at California State Northridge University in the very early 1980s. I remembered the poverty and drudgery of grad school and my own relentless ambition and yearning to move beyond academia into the "real" world. I could not foresee what my son's future would hold, but I wanted him to seize his opportunities. So I kept my thoughts to myself about grad school.

We traipsed around San Diego, enjoying pizza at the Bronx Pizza place, an establishment founded by relocated New Yorkers. Neal asked if the pizza was truly representative of New York pizza, and I admitted that it was. Truth be told, back in the Bronx in my day, we did not have pizza with ricotta and white sauce or barbecued Asian chicken pizza with arugula. I remember from my youth that there were "pizza wars" along the Grand Concourse, where an upstart pizza joint threatened an established eatery by opening for business three doors away. Their competition lowered prices to *ten cents* per slice, so we, as consumers (and kids without much money), benefited from the commercial competition.

Eventually, Neal found housing with a professor who taught at the university and rented out rooms to students. Subsequently, during his first year, he moved again into a different house with a mélange of graduate students. I forked over rent money and felt satisfied that he was living with students who seemed goal-oriented and serious about their work and budding careers.

GRADUATE SCHOOL LIFE

It was important to Neal to develop friendships with his housemates. He craved fellowship and believed that those he lived with should be his friends. I couldn't fault him for that; however, people do have different interests and boundaries. Often, people end up sharing what is proscribed by communal interests. In Neal's situation, that involved a kitchen and living room. His housemates were cordial but aloof and preoccupied. Neal took this to heart, and he internalized their disinterest as further confirmation of his self-perceived social ineptness.

Ironically, Neal was very social and very affable, and he craved companionship. Watching him try to make his way during those college years, I saw similarities to my own angst as a collegian, yearning desperately for acceptance and intimacy, wanting to be popular enough but secretly on a mission to find a soul mate.

In retrospect, I wonder if I should have—even *could* have—seen signs that Neal was being driven by frustration and misinterpretation to root deeper into himself, developing wounds that festered in his soul and eviscerated his fragile sense of worth. *What else could I have done?* I was his bastion of support, providing encouragement, answering his questions about my own grad school experiences and struggles, and reassuring him of the bright light and profitable future that lay ahead. I provided direction but also related to him increasingly as an adult; still his father and providing support and sanction, I gave him the space and freedom to learn what he needed to survive and thrive. I had confidence in him, trusted him more than I should have, and believed in his ability to subdue his doubts and demons and to find workable, sustainable answers to his diffidence and confusion.

Neal had to find his own way. Though the rigors and milestones of development remained similar to those I'd experienced, he was living and emerging into a different world than I had experienced, one of frantic globalization and technology. I too had been an eager and energetic young grad student. But psychology is not physics. Bright as he was, Neal's challenges were extensive and overwhelming. And whereas I had put drug use behind me by the time I reached graduate school, Neal was becoming more entangled and suffocated—more rapidly and deeper than I knew.

MORE DRUDGERY

Through the semesters of his first year, Neal trudged, worked, and plodded through very difficult courses. He did reasonably well but became increasingly burdened by both the work and by his increasing and nagging sense that his peers were much smarter than he was.

Until graduate school, Neal took his gifted intelligence for granted, never boasting or overly comparing himself intellectually but rather delving into his interests and letting his curiosity and achievements speak for themselves. The graduate physics environment seemed to beset him with self-doubt. I tried to be supportive and to offer perspective. However, Neal was competing with and comparing himself to peers with much scientific engineering experience, some with advanced degrees. I could advise him about the nitty-gritty and street savvy of how to get through grad school, but I could not mediate the reality of his facing the scientific academic challenges and pursuits that were beyond my ken.

GRANDMA'S DEATH

In May 2010, my mother, Pearl, passed away. Neal was visiting in San Jose when we got the news. She was eighty-five and had been suffering and declining for years. We flew to Florida for the funeral with Neal in tow. Of course, it was a difficult time. My dad had died in 2002. Now, the finality of generational separation and mortality was upon us. In addition to the mourning and the missing of a beloved parent, an undercurrent of psychological aloneness crept upon me. The reality of losing my parents brought with it the undeniable awareness that I, the parent of my children, would also die. Little did I know that Neal would pass before I would leave this world. During that period, I could not help but wonder what Neal felt and what he really thought—about aging, parents, relationships, and the finality of earthly life.

Neal had sustained a kind of love-hate relationship with my mother. As he was her first grandchild, my mother held Neal in a special esteem and regard. She lavished attention upon him during her frequent visits in his childhood. She tried relentlessly to impress Judaism upon him. Not surprisingly, Neal rebelled, and much yelling, taunting, and disrespect characterized Grandma's visits. I had tried to mediate and maintain decorum, but my Christianity was too much for both of them.

Neal mourned with us. He was appropriate and respectful. I was so glad to have him around. I needed the family's support. Saying good-bye is terribly difficult and so important. To whatever extent Neal was using drugs at the time, he kept it under wraps.

RESEARCH, LONELINESS, AND TRAUMA

Neal spent only part of the summer with us. Soon he returned to San Diego. For many young adults, leaving home for college demarcates an unofficial emancipation from their parents' home and often from the city of their upbringing. They return to visit, to be nurtured, perhaps to regress, and sometimes with flu symptoms or baskets of laundry. Yes, home is always home—but for many, the homing instinct becomes transplanted to their new life, usually where they attended or are attending college. This was the case with Neal. San Diego was his new home base.

He immersed himself in difficult and technical courses, fulfilling the remainder of his required curriculum. He spoke of continuing beyond a master's degree and pursuing a doctorate. I was gratified and proud of him.

Continuing trouble was on the horizon. The ensuing two years in San Diego gripped Neal with despair, anxiety, loneliness, and increasing drug abuse. Though he and I had a pattern of regular communication by phone (ranging from several to many times per week), there were periods when Neal withdrew and became incommunicado. He was becoming more isolated and behaving immaturely and irresponsibly.

One of his more egregious acts was using his self-initiated student loan money to purchase a motorcycle. Neal had always been a spendthrift, but this took irresponsibility and impulsivity to a new, disheartening level. Some months after the acquisition of his new toy, Neal crashed his bike on a freeway outside of San Diego. He was airlifted by medical helicopter to a local hospital. He had dislocated and broken his shoulder but was otherwise spared of potential and life-threatening disaster. Soon afterward, he flew home to San Jose, where I arranged a necessary surgery to repair the shoulder. As the orthopedic surgeon wryly quipped about Neal's life lesson in the physics of centrifugal force, I fretted over the issue of pain medication—a routine adjunct to surgical recovery, but also a danger to Neal, who had been abusing prescription pain medicines. I shared this confidence with the surgeon, who took it under advisement. Still, protocol and procedures made these powerful painkillers a continuing part of his consumption.

SLEEP PROBLEMS AND IRRITABILITY

Neal had always been a lousy patient (surely, a chip off the old block)—fearful, irritable, defensive, and fantasizing doom and demise. His mounting and debilitating problems with sleep over the past years became exacerbated with the pain and recovery from surgery. Undoubtedly, his frequent use of drugs had an adverse impact upon his tenuous self-regulation. In short, he was a mess—a tangle of frayed nerves, irritability, moodiness, and bouts of aggressive tantrums. It was hard to take care of a child who, as an adult, was immaturely pissing in other people's faces.

After some recuperation, Neal returned to San Diego. The motorcycle was wrecked, and the medical bills had piled up. Though insured under my health insurance as well as his student health plan, Neal neglected to file paperwork to cover his bills. I exhorted and reminded him repeatedly but to no avail. He was apparently too distracted, stoned, and irresponsible to follow through.

DRUDGERY, DRUGS, AND THE ADDICTED LIFE

The period of Neal's life between 2010 and 2012 (when he left school and returned to San Jose) remains a difficult blur for me. My typically acute and detailed memory is smudged with glaring bits of memory that emerge in random order. When I try to sequence the details and make sense of the chronology, I become helplessly blank. If I did not know better, I could attribute this to emotional repression, the cognitive decline of my own aging, or the general pain of obsessing about the past. But I do know better. None of these hypotheses makes as much sense as the conclusion that I was wrapped up in my own life, before and after Neal's tumultuous escapades, and in the aftermath, I remember notable events, episodes, and feelings in a nonsequential and narratively desultory manner.

I remember being regularly frustrated by Neal's lack of follow-through on many things. A notable irritant for me was his lack of following up on a salient job lead I secured for him in San Diego along the lines of his expressed career interest. A former patient whom I had treated (actually, Neal had assisted in this person's treatment when he worked for me as a neurotherapist) supplied a lead (and a personal phone call) to a CEO of a company in San Diego who was waiting for Neal's call to give him an interview and possibly a job.

There were other opportunities for Neal, but all went by the wayside. I beseeched him many times to seek therapeutic help. I even placed a call to a very competent therapist in San Diego I knew through collegial association. I offered to pay for any reputable therapist Neal chose. He never initiated a step in that direction.

What I see in retrospect—and making devastating sense—is that Neal was in the throes of drug addiction, that his focus was constrained to relieving anxiety and withdrawal, that his capacity for reasoning and maintaining composure was relentlessly diminishing, and that his brain (that wonderful, brilliant, striking mind) was invidiously coming apart under the influence of drugs.

He was making stealthy and frequent trips from San Diego to Riverside to hang out with his "buddies" and to score drugs. Under the auspices of maintaining old friendships from his undergraduate days, Neal was sinking further into the prison of hard drug addiction.

I remonstrated him, scolded him, limited his funding, and set and reset conditions for my financial support. *Was I blind?* No, I knew what was happening. *Why didn't I take more drastic and controlling measures?* This is a difficult question, one I've reviewed many times in my journey through sorrow, guilt, and confusion. The best I can reconstruct leads to a combination of conclusions. Neal was an excellent manipulator; like many addicts, he was talented and experienced at concealing, resurging, wheedling, evoking sympathy, and making feints at turning over a new leaf. Not only did I want to believe him, but I didn't see other options. In San Diego, he was living independently, attending school, and teaching graduate courses as a paid teaching assistant. I knew he was using drugs; we talked about it, and I emphasized the destructive consequences and reinforced my disapproval. I straddled the fence between directing and alienating him—a very rough ride that the family members of addicts know intimately. He did not seem in the helpless crisis that propels many people into rehab centers (and which would characterize our taking charge and placing him in such a hospital in late 2012). Critical to his stealthy decline, he was living remotely, hiding his behavior to a large degree, and refusing any kind of professional assistance or treatment.

Would I do things differently, knowing what I know now? That is a painful question, one I have revisited repeatedly. There is no answer that makes sense to me. To have my son back alive, I would do anything. In that regard, any answer or scenario I provide could not fare worse than what happened. The problem with this hindsight is twofold. Firstly, the mere mention or allocation of alternate reactions or possible interventions convicts me of negligence or irresponsibility. Secondly, in conceiving an alternate potential for Neal, I cannot help but imagine his young adult life of continued irresponsibility and drug dependence and a potentially marginal adult life and middle age. This is depressing, but it seems likely given what I know about the trajectory for many involved in drug addiction. Some are successful and turn their lives around (I did); many have multiple relapses and live tethered or imprisoned by their demons.

I was passionate about Neal, and I was generous, supportive, and careful. After many cycles of evaluating the situation from different angles, of hosting self-doubt and the possibility of my own denial, and of wondering if I needed or constructed defenses against culpability, I am at peace with my proactive and helpful activity as well as my helplessness in what happened to Neal.

The doubts and remorse are subdued by fond and passionate memories, by treasuring Neal's legacy and the fulfillment and maturity he gave to me during his all-too-brief life. In telling his story, I must consider the questions and divulge my hauntings, wonderings, and closure. If I follow any paths of regret, they ultimately lead backward across every milestone and conflict in his childhood and upbringing, through the thickets of marital strife, conflict, struggles in my own maturity, and the decision to have children. Having been there and done the examining, the torturing, the suffering, and the healing, I choose to let it be and to move forward.

DENOUEMENT TO GRADUATE SCHOOL

In the spring semester of 2012, Neal was not faring well. In his third year of graduate school and finished with his courses, his challenge was to complete his thesis. This was no small project; it involved original research, including many hours in the lab (where lab resources and time were competitively sought by other students).

He was having overwhelming difficulty getting organized, staying motivated, and getting things done. Obviously, the drugs were defeating him; they were addling his thinking and making academic progress all but impossible.

During this period, Neal had begun a relationship with a woman graduate student in an allied department at San Diego State University. She was working on her Ph.D. I was delighted that he had a girlfriend. However, soon I found out that she was also a drug user and had not entirely disentangled herself from a marriage. This was much to my dismay, but I was in no position to dissuade him from connecting with another human being and from developing intimacy in a relationship—something he needed (we all need) and which I hoped would give him support and bearing to extricate himself from his morass.

During the late winter and spring months of 2012, Neal went through periods of deep depression, debilitating anxiety, and insomnia. He would often call me at night, confiding his immobilizing despair, asking to be heard, to be reassured, and to vent his frustration and complaints. He would often rant (as was typical of him, especially when he was in the throes of irritation and withdrawal), but almost as often, he would ask me to treat him with Voice Technology to banish his misery.

He also had periods of withdrawal from communication. For weeks, he would not contact me or other members of the family. I just let him be. In March of 2012, I underwent two heart surgery procedures. Though Giulia, Jeremy, and Nadia informed him, he didn't reach out to me. It was only months later that he sheepishly acknowledged the event with barely an apology (more of an excuse) for not contacting me.

It was easy for me to forgive him but not so easy to recognize his absence as a hallmark of self-absorption and irresponsibility. Neal was a very caring person. The ravages of his drug addiction emaciated his ability and motivation to consider the needs of others. It was indeed a downward spiral.

A PLEA TO COME HOME

By late spring, it was plain that Neal was simply not functioning. My advice, support, and exhortations about finishing up his work fell on deaf ears. He was hurting badly and sinking into more depression and despair. I had talked with him about taking a leave of absence and had coached him on how to talk with his professors to depart with either an agreement to finish his work independently (and possibly at San Francisco State University) or to leave a door open to return to San Diego State at a later time. He was just unable to gather himself to face his department.

It was during a tearful phone call that I realized that Neal needed to come home. Perhaps he had been subtly requesting permission or acceptance of his need for return and protection for a while. I knew it clearly from our communication late that spring and heard him tearfully ask me if it was OK to come home.

"Of course, Son," I said. "Come home. We'll work it out. I love you."

Contemplating in the kitchen

Neal mixing music as a disc jockey—
one of his favorite activities

Neal with Kirby, the wire-haired Dachshund

Neal and Dad shopping—one of our favorite activities

CHAPTER 10
DECONSTRUCTION

Neal moved back home in the early summer of 2012. He was in sorry shape—depressed, lonely, homesick, emotionally fragile, and mentally disorganized. He was reeling from rejection by his former girlfriend and from his inability to gather himself to any purpose, much less the completion of his thesis and master's degree at San Diego State University.

During his last weeks in San Diego, he had been calling me frequently, seeking solace, advice, reassurance, and connection. All of these I was glad to provide. He had not spoken to me very much during the winter and early spring months, a sure sign that he was immersed in his world of torpor and confusion. In those months, he returned my calls with an undercurrent of reluctant impatience, as if he knew that the conversations might turn into minilectures, highlighting his omissions and irresponsible actions.

It was not in my heart to castigate him. I felt sincere and tender love for him but also a growing helplessness and frustration. Also in my heart were literal blockages that had to be repaired surgically in the early spring, and I underwent two heart surgeries. As mentioned earlier, though Neal was aware of my medical situation (through family), he barely commented or offered solicitations. Although this hurt me, I took it as a sign that his mind was absorbed in drugs and his sensibilities, judgment, and behavior were continually impaired in a condition that was becoming routine for him. I never doubted his love for me, nor that he would have expressed more outward concern if he were not so blunted and preoccupied.

His calls from San Diego as summer approached became more childlike and desperate. He was lonely and wanted to come home. I welcomed him, tenderly reassuring him that leaving San Diego at this time was the right decision and that he would continue his scientific career pursuits or start anew in other circumstances when he was ready.

ON THE PSYCHOLOGIST'S COUCH

Neal's arrival home brought a few days of quiet joy and relief. My son had returned to safety and protection, or so I temporarily believed. Quickly, however, it became clear that he was in a drug-ravaged funk, a compulsive condition that made him vacillate between sleeping on the couch over twelve hours a day (usually into late afternoon) and displaying a short temper and frequent frustration and deliberation over minor and mundane matters. I wavered between letting him rest and recover and calmly but persistently reminding him that he had to do something besides lie around the house. His interactions with Giulia were growing more combative. This was not new, but its heightened intensity raised the level of tension and made me feel more helpless and lonely. These conflicts reinforced my awareness that Neal had to find his own way. Though we could support him, it was necessary for him to live separately from the family.

A crisis arrived on our doorstep just days before Giulia and I were to decamp on a planned weeklong vacation. We were notified by the property manager that the owner of the house we had been renting for years needed to sell it. We would have to vacate in thirty days!

We returned from vacation and somehow managed to find a new home to rent in Palo Alto. The move would be gargantuan and stressful. This was also the springboard to insist that Neal go somewhere else. He was soporific, cranky, disorganized, and mostly stoned. In fact, he had taken to stealing Giulia's mother's pain medications! I've learned that, with addicts, what you think is the last straw turns into one of many manipulative straws that undercut and suck out your resources and patience. Neal's descent was gaining momentum.

I thought I could respond to these emergencies by orchestrating our move and using the circumstance to ensconce Neal in a new situation in San Francisco. I had just recently rented a beautiful house in a great neighborhood in San Francisco. This house was to serve multiple purposes. It was a part-time getaway for Giulia and me. It was a waystation for me during and between my many trips to the city on business and for my own recreation and networking. Eventually, it would become home for Giulia and me, as well as a convenient residence near my San Francisco professional office. In 2012, it seemed a fitting place to let Neal live and reorganize his life. So, in the summer, he moved into our San Francisco house.

AN OPIUM DEN

As the summer months progressed and the fog dutifully rolled in off the ocean, reaching toward the seething inland, Neal became progressively more isolated and paralyzed in the grip of drug addiction. I was stepping up my pressure for him to find employment. I kept holding out the carrot (and my own hope) that when he cleaned up his act, he could return to work for me as a neurotherapist, as well as continue and complete his graduate studies. In the meantime, he would have to get a regular job of some sort and reestablish his stability and responsibility. This also meant getting clean.

Neal kept promising me he would get on it. He eventually found work with a San Francisco company that dispatched workers to run errands and serve as office temps for businesses in the city. I was quite skeptical because I knew that without a regular schedule and enough hours, this contract employment would not sustain and regulate him. But at least it was a start.

There were days when Neal seemed more like his old self. He could be chipper and full of humor, receptive to conversation, and willing to offer his own questions, answers, and opinions on contemporary events and philosophical matters debated since antiquity. These periods of alertness became sparser, and I would soon realize that his moments of seeming lucidity were crests on the roiling inner waves of his drug highs and withdrawals.

Several times a week, I would drive to San Francisco and find Neal in varying states of idleness and torpor. Often he was sleeping, and sometimes he would lie in his bed on the floor, covered up and moaning, obviously in the agonizing state of withdrawal. I didn't know what to do. I felt torn between wanting to kick him and wanting to hug him. I chose the path of affection and support. I bought him food, which he was usually too sick to eat. I rubbed his back and tousled his hair, hugging him when he would let me.

IRRESPONSIBLE DECLINE

With his brain addled and his mind and behavior in addictive throes, Neal became increasingly desperate and enslaved to feeding his cravings. One day, I entered the house to find that my large-screen TV was gone. It was shocking! My immediate rage was quickly aborted by the sight of Neal cringing, crying, pleading, "I'm sorry, Dad...I'm sorry."

It is so painful for me to write these words. This image of Neal, helpless, defenseless, deteriorating in front of me, along with similar images, haunts me continually. When you love someone intensely and that person misbehaves into defiance and danger, you become wracked with ambivalence. The mixed impulses to protect, scold, rescue, vilify, interrogate, hug, blame, and forgive descend in crushing confusion, and a whirl of cascading blurry emotions quickly overwhelm you.

As I censured Neal, I observed the interactions as if I were removed from the situation. It felt eerie and a bit dissociative. *Was this really my life and my child?* I saw myself—terse, intense, not given to yelling, but clearly angry, hurt, and shocked, realizing suddenly that I was witnessing and participating in the dramatic stereotypic scenario of an addict who would do anything and betray anyone for another fix. My son, the true victim, had sunk pathetically to this nadir!

I knew something had to be done. It would be a short matter of time before we removed Neal from the house and placed him in rehab. In the weeks between this shocking discovery and his entry into rehab, there would be other incidents of drug-fueled desperation and irresponsibility.

Letters from the DMV and the city were piling up with demands for payment and notifications that his driver's license had been suspended. The old Lexus I had given him now had a bounty on its rusted being for many unpaid citations. Neal had finally parked it in the back of the garage, not daring to venture out where he might be arrested for driving without a valid license. Before rehab, the car would be his homeless shelter, a respite from the street. This would happen right after he sold my second bigscreen TV for drugs!

After the first incident, I installed a lock on my bedroom door and forbade Neal to enter that room. Soon, thereafter, however, I entered the house to discover that the lock on my bedroom door had been broken and the door damaged and the TV was gone. I felt as if I were living in some sordid, low-budget crime movie.

A MOVE TO REHAB AND HOPE

Things were spiraling out of control, and I knew something drastic had to be done. Neal was leaving drug paraphernalia around the house and engaging in desperate and frightening behavior. One day, he drove to San Jose and invited an old friend of his into the Lexus where Neal displayed his "works" and invited the friend to shoot up with him in the car. I found out about this from Jeremy, who was horrified by Neal's bizarre and pleading behavior.

Neal had no money. When he became hungry—famished and undernourished from his binges and withdrawals—he would call Jeremy and beg him to order and pay for takeout pizzas that Neal could pick up near the San Francisco house. What an agonizing bind for Jeremy!

I had stopped putting money into Neal's account. Much as I wanted him to eat, he could not be trusted with any money. Incredibly, it took me *months* to finally close the joint account I had set up for him (the bank claimed it couldn't close the account with overdrafts, and Neal kept overdrawing faster than I could pay the account into the positive). I drove to San Francisco several times a week to check on Neal and buy and deliver food to him. It was a desperate and dysfunctional treadmill.

As quickly as I could, I shifted gears and researched chemical dependency in-patient programs in the Bay Area. Rehab had become an ever more urgent priority. Neal had resisted before, but now he would have no choice. As my wife had plainly (and prophetically) said, "From this activity, it is either jail or the grave." I knew that we were fighting against both.

In December 2012, we placed Neal in a thirty-day chemical dependency treatment program at Alta Bates Hospital in Oakland. He went willingly. It seemed like a great relief for him. This program was housed in an unlocked facility with a typical set of rules and daily procedures—medical care (especially helpful for detox), regular meals, group meetings galore (AA, twelve-step type), and occasional individual counseling. Neal readily adapted to the routine, and he expressed an unexpected affinity for and appreciation of the meetings and group support. He attached much value to learning how (typically) his escalating drug dependency steeped him in isolation, quickly extending a vicious cycle of increased drug use and further isolation.

Neal was among the few young adult resident patients. Most were middle-aged and older patients who had tread this path in rehab and relapsed several times previously. Not surprisingly, Neal was popular among the patient population as well as the staff.

The rehab program invited and expected family participation. I visited Neal weekly, attended group meetings with him at the hospital, and joined him in two conjoint therapy sessions with a marriage-family therapist on staff. In these private conjoint meetings, I felt good about expressing to Neal that I wanted more than promises from him. I expected follow-through. As a concrete example, I wanted him to find work and gradually repay me for the two TV screens he had sold from the house. He agreed. The therapist told me privately that when young adults remained clean and sober for a time, they often matured at an accelerated pace, making up for stagnant time during the arrested development phase of their addiction. I was hopeful.

As the end of his thirty-day stint in rehab approached, we looked for a sober living house into which he could transition. This was the recommended next step in recovery.

SOBER LIVING

Neal was accepted into a sober-living house in the Excelsior District in San Francisco, not far from San Francisco State University. He shared a room with two other men in a home that housed about fifteen recovering residents. For this privilege, I paid $1,200 per month. There is a burgeoning market in sober living environments for recovering alcoholics and addicts—a need that spawned an industry subculture.

There are strict rules for residents in sober-living houses, including mandatory daily house meetings, absolutely no drugs or alcohol, mandatory attendance at AA meetings (one mantra for recovery is "ninety meetings in ninety days"), and keeping your room and the common living areas clean. Neal accepted these rules and obeyed them, at first. Gradually, however, he strayed and got into conflict with the house manager, a strict but caring woman named Dede. She held him accountable with a maternal sternness and objectivity I truly appreciated. She called Neal out on his sloppiness, his attitude, and his slipping follow-through on attending AA meetings.

When he first entered sober living, Neal was gung-ho on AA meetings. He enthusiastically traveled around San Francisco by public transportation, going to different meetings, forming loose friendships, enjoying the camaraderie, and learning within the structure how others struggled and followed steps to recover. Given Neal's history and personality, which predisposed him to fault-finding, independence, and sovereign independence, I was surprised and delighted that he seemed to fall into line and under the leadership of sober and accountable influences.

I drove to the city frequently to visit Neal, check on him, and bring him food. I still could not trust him with a bank account, so I would give him small amounts of cash for transportation and incidentals, and I would purchase his basic needs for him. As we drove around the city together, I delighted in being with him and supporting his recovery. Occasionally, he'd confide in me that he still had constant cravings. When we traveled through the Tenderloin or certain South or Market neighborhoods (notorious for drug dealing), Neal would confide that if he were there by himself, temptation might overcome him. He had a keen eye for itinerant dealers, and he spotted needles in corners I did not notice.

Just before Neal left in-patient rehab, he was given a $600 injection of long-acting Naltrexone, a medication that acts as an opiate blocker. This is an increasingly recommended proactive head start for recovering addicts to help them avoid relapse. The chemical action of this drug is such that if a person uses opiates, he cannot experience the high. It can be a useful deterrent to falling off the wagon, and it also diminishes cravings in some individuals.

Neal was instructed during rehab to find a physician to continue his Naltrexone prescription by pills. He procrastinated this task to a point beyond the effects of the long-acting injection. I found myself constantly reminding him to find a doctor. At one point, I offered to drive him to our family physician in the South Bay. He rebuffed my many overtures to help him obtain prescription medication for his recovery.

I remember one particularly irritating event related to the Naltrexone in early spring 2013. We had arranged for the physician at Alta Bates Hospital to phone in one last Naltrexone prescription to the Walgreen's near my home at the time in Palo Alto. It turned out to be a huge hassle, since I was to pay for and pick up the meds, but Neal was required to be present—which, of course, he was not. The pharmacist was trying to be helpful, and eventually (with much fuss and complication), I had to pick up the medication in person and deliver it to Neal in San Francisco. By this time, I was beyond my irritation threshold, exasperated with Neal's irresponsibility and questioning whether I was being helpful or simply enabling his dysfunction.

I railed at him, "Why must you make everything so *damned difficult?*"

Neal apologized on the surface, but I could feel his resentment and lack of enrollment in his own recovery. My familiar helpless feelings about him rebounded.

It was his last capitulation to Naltrexone. Soon after, I realized the truth: Neal didn't want to block getting high. He wanted his opiate escape—hewn under its spell, trapped, hooked, desperate. I was losing my son to the sea of addictive destruction, the tide relentlessly dragging him out beyond reach.

RELAPSE AND EMERGENCY

One day in March, I got a call from the landlord of my San Francisco house. He was in the garage of the house, entering to do repairs I had requested. He told me calmly that as he drove up to the house, an ambulance was pulling away from the garage with lights and siren blaring and that he saw several young men running away. Upon entering the garage, he had discovered "works"—drug paraphernalia, including needles and rubber tubing.

I was horrified and almost in panic. The landlord was diplomatic and indirect, but I knew it was Neal and I knew that the landlord also knew. I had evicted Neal from this house months previously, and I'd replaced and redoubled the locks. However, he had broken into the garage and shot up heroin with some of his cronies. As I later reconstructed the story, Neal had overdosed and they had called an ambulance and had subsequently fled, leaving my son at the mercy of paramedics or else at death's door.

Nearly out of my mind, I began calling every hospital and emergency room in San Francisco. Eventually, I found out that he had been taken to St. Mary's Hospital, near to the house. Although the emergency room physician told me they had admitted a Neal Steinberg, she could not give me any information without his written permission. By this time awake (and, I was thankful, alive!), Neal was ashamed and refused permission. Oh, how livid I was! I told the emergency room physician to tell my son that unless he immediately gave consent to communicate, I would call the police and have him arrested for breaking and entering and illegal drug use. At that point, he consented. At least my deranged son was safe and alive.

After his relapse, we had a very tense meeting at the sober-living home—Neal, house manager Dede, and I. Neal was typically defenseless and contrite, and I was enraged and exasperated. At that point, I seriously considered leaving him to his own resources—that is, refusing to continue to pay for his sober-living residence. Out of duty, fear, and love for my son and remembering God's forgiveness, I relented and gave him another chance. We embraced, and I had a hard time coping with and expressing my emotions.

Neal had strict marching orders, and we would be monitoring him carefully. His mandate was to find a job.

PERKING UP WITH A JOB

Soon after the emergency room debacle, Neal found a job at Peet's Coffee in the SOMA district near downtown San Francisco. I was relieved and grateful for this positive step. I wanted to see it as a harbinger of his turning the corner in recovery. I praised him repeatedly and stopped by several times to order coffee from him and leave him a tip. Despite his personal struggles, which brewed continuously after his hours percolating in the work environment ended, Neal seemed content. He was jovial as he bantered with coworkers and went through the routine chores of his stint as a barista. He spoke positively of his peers at Peet's, and he seemed to fit in and was consistently eager to go to work and thankful to have a job. I was encouraged.

SOMA is an acronym for South of Market—an area near downtown San Francisco, known for its blend of artsy residents and businesses, light industry, and emerging upscale renovation with tech giants, such as Twitter, Salesforce, Google, Dropbox, and others. The Peet's location where Neal worked allowed him to interact with a wide variety of people, including shakers and movers, misfits, buttoned-down executives, and transients. It was minutes away from his sober-living home via a MUNI public transit line. Even better, he had a work schedule that required him to get up early in the morning.

I was hopeful about his adaptation and confident that a steady, "normal" job would help anchor him in self-regulation and rebuilding. Watching him behind the coffee bar in his brown Peet's smock, I took pride in his achievements and capitulation to the humbling processes of recovery. Here was a brilliant young man, working to overcome his demons. He was a scholar, willing to pour coffee and mop up spills as he wrestled with anxiety, addiction, pain, confusion, and lack of confidence.

In those days, which were to be the twilight of his life, Neal spoke hopefully of enrolling at San Francisco State to get his teaching credential. He looked forward to getting a place to live in San Francisco's Mission District, where he felt he might blend in and establish a new life for himself. He had dreams, desires, fears, and considerations, and I felt blessed that he shared them with me. I listened and encouraged him. I loved being his father, though I never expected to be tasked and burdened in the ways that he and I were. I was getting used to accepting my son in the reality of his fragility and foibles, rather than the superstar I'd once thought he would be.

My son was special to me, though to the legions of customers he served, he was just another barely visible moving gateway to their caffeine fix and to getting on with their day. How many thousands of cups of coffee have I taken from servants across the counter who had private lives, loves, aspirations, and conflicts as had Neal?

How could I know that looking across the counter at that Peet's store, loving and approving my son, it would be the last time and place I would see him alive on this earth?

Neal working at Peet's Coffee in San Francisco—
about two weeks before his passing

THE STRANGLEHOLD CONTINUES

Sadly, the positive period between his relapses did not last long. Neal wavered in his sobriety. He lapsed in going to twelve-step meetings, and quickly his connections with support groups and peers dwindled.

As do many recovering addicts, Neal understood that isolation is one of the devastating and pernicious characteristics of addiction. Isolation plays a major role as both cause and effect. Knowing about this cycle is a step forward, but awareness is not enough to overcome its stranglehold.

The secrecy and shame that pervaded his addiction led Neal to shy away from contacting me as regularly as he would during more sober periods. Whereas normally I would speak with him almost daily, there were stretches of days with no contact. I didn't want to hover over him, to reinforce his dependency on me, yet I worried about him with good reason. The dysfunction in his life resulted in his coming to me frequently with either a desperate need (no money for food) or a report of or excuse for his latest mishap. Between Neal and me, communication and expectations could be double-edged swords.

Sometimes Neal would just call me and confess his latest relapse. He'd blather quickly, as if to expel the confession from his system, saying, "It sucks, Dad. I just make mistakes. That's the way it is. I'm not perfect." This had the effect of stifling me. What does one do in this situation? Scold? Remind? Offer consolation and advice? Pretend to be positive? No doubt, I tried a combination of these approaches. Surely, Neal could sense my disappointment and frustration. How could I hide this from him? Somehow, somewhere in the interstices between accountability and support and validation, I had to give him encouragement, acceptance, and hope.

During the last months of his life, Neal would frequently call me and complain about his loneliness. He was continually anxious. He parried my suggestions that he see doctors or therapists and consider appropriate medication to help him through his withdrawal and angst. He just wasn't willing.

Neal relied upon me, and I was there for him. He wanted solace, connection, and relief. Many nights, he was so desperate that he would call me and beg for Voice Technology assistance to relieve his depression and anxiety. I was glad to help him, and we routinely eliminated his desperate symptoms when they were present. Sadly, Neal did not follow through in dealing with the psychological reversal that threw him repeatedly into relapse.

I did my best, though my answers were no match for his pain, my resources insufficient for his wounds, my love not enough to carry him through.

EVICTION AND REDIRECTION

Toward the end of April, Neal's relapses and rule violations exceeded the tolerance of the sober-living home. He was asked to leave. With an admirable combination of sternness and maternal oversight, Dede evicted him. There was an open door, however, a path to returning and resuming his recovery stint in a sober-living residence. The minimum requirement was proof of enrollment in an intensive rehab program.

Neal had nowhere to go. He had worn out his welcome with almost everyone. He couldn't live with me and Giulia and her sick (and medication-dependent) mother. Neal's own mother wouldn't take him in. He had no money and no real friends. This was torture for me, but I had to stand firm.

He was able to find temporary housing and respite in the garage of one of his buddies—Corey—who lived in Concord, a city in the East Bay, about thirty miles from San Francisco. Corey was an intermittent friend with whom Neal shared a hobby of pyrotechnics. Neal loved to dance and whirl and do routines with lights, glowsticks, and fire. Apparently, there is a growing subculture inspired by this creative pastime.

Though I didn't know Corey, I later learned that he was a solid guy who didn't use drugs and who cared a great deal for Neal. He set strict rules for allowing Neal to stay at his house for a very temporary period. There was to be absolutely no drinking or drugs.

Neal was relieved to have a place to stay. He also complained about the inconvenience of commuting into San Francisco to work. The BART (Bay Area Rapid Transit) train took him almost door-to-door, but it took time and cost money. He did make it to work most of the time, excusing himself when he had no money for train fare and appealing to me to help him out.

Again, I was put in the untenable position of wanting to stipend Neal's basic needs (like transportation fare) but having no practical way to get the money to him. We had already exhausted the bank account transfer routine. Neal could not be trusted. Such is the immaturity and irresponsibility that pervades serious addiction.

I kept nagging Neal about entering a rehab program. To my dismay, he was reluctant. He dragged his feet about looking into programs, so it was left to me. Eventually, he agreed to enter a reputable program I found in San Francisco. He went for his intake interview and evaluation on Thursday, May 23, 2013. He was supposed to move in the following day.

FATEFUL PASSING

I didn't hear from Neal in the days following his report about his interview at the Ohlhoff Center in San Francisco. I should have known something was amiss, as these short fugues were indicators of relapse. I didn't want to push him further, and something in me needed to avoid the suspicion that he was again using. I fought my internal worries, kept busy with my usual routines and responsibilities, prayed, and reminded myself that I would need to follow up and get Neal situated at Ohlhoff Center. Certainly, their requirement for payment would get the ball rolling and reinitiate communication.

Our doorbell rang in the early hours of the morning on Sunday, May 26, 2013. There were two policemen and a man who identified himself as the pastor of a local church. The brief interval between letting them in the house and hearing that Neal had passed seemed timeless. Giulia and I wailed and wailed, the ushering in of the grief and sorrow that would mark this new phase of our lives.

Those moments were eerie then, and they are eerie still when I call them to mind. My son was not there for all the attention given to him, all the attention he needed and deserved. I remember listening to myself sob and talk and hold hands with the pastor as a policeman touched my shoulder. I wanted to run away but also felt the pull toward sheltering Giulia. I am a very emotional person, but truly, no one sees that. Perhaps it's because I've long since mastered the submersion and taming of hysteria. I am not ashamed of feelings, and I welcome them as a natural and enhancing part of life. But I am perceived as analytical and stoic by those I wish would register the deep feelings I regularly experience and express.

The policemen explained that Corey had found Neal cold and unresponsive on his bed in the makeshift garage bedroom. The Contra Costa coroner had been notified.

The shock led me to clutch my bathrobe and talk about Neal's life and drug problem in a desultory manner. I clung to the hugs offered by the people in the room. I found the wherewithal to thank them repeatedly for being there and to speculate how difficult such duty must be for them.

I felt far away. I hoped that my relative calm would not seem like an act to them. I remember the thought that had repeatedly intruded on me for years. *Neal will not live past thirty years of age.* I'd felt spooked by this thought; I don't believe I ever shared it with anyone. I believe in premonitions yet am not superstitious that entertaining them makes them happen. But Neal was only twenty-six! It was all too early—and too final.

My son was gone, and I was helpless. There was no fight in me. It was time to surrender.

REFLECTIONS

I think about Neal continually. I have adjusted since his passing, though life is not the same without him here. There are periods when the grieving comes in waves, unexpected despite the regular recurrences—a tsunami of overwhelm and sorrow. I weep and wail, and then it passes, leaving me rent and almost normal again. Often, he is in the background of my brain, a watchful presence amid the rumblings and turmoil of mixed attention. Neal was never quiet, even when he wasn't talking. He was intense in his exuberance and frustration—real, needy, charming, demanding. In my mind these days, his spiritual visitation and memory are more subdued, as if he's come to terms with the narrow dimension of his physical life, a stretch of history I've not quite processed and accommodated.

I have quasi-conversations with him—pleadings, praises, remonstrations. I don't expect him to answer, but I want him to know I am still with him, as he is with me. There is no rational sense in this, and yet it is perfectly natural and important to me, even though he is not physically present. Somehow, letting him go is still compatible with holding him dear.

The late comedian Joan Rivers told the story about breaking the ice in talking about her husband's suicide. She reported, "He wanted me to be with him always and made me promise to visit him regularly after he was gone—so I had him cremated and I sprinkled some of the ashes around Neiman Marcus."

Shocking or incongruous as this morbid humor may appear, I get the point that we all have habits and that carrying our loved ones into our habits and daily thoughts and experiences is a natural way of including them and continuing the relationship. It is also a way of easing into the acceptance that once a loved one has passed, the sharing and remembrance is up to us who remain.

I never had the opportunity to admire Neal as a husband or father, never got to appreciate his maturation and fulfillment of a career. It wouldn't develop that he would bring me a grandchild or that he might care for me as I grew infirm and dependent. How devoted might he have been? This remains fantasy, a make-believe that, I am thankful, doesn't much entice me. Alternatively, I do speculate upon the possibilities for Neal's development, had he lived—specters of unpleasant scenarios that make me shudder and even wonder if his death was a blessed curtailment of potential suffering for both of us and the other lives he touched.

This is a painful and difficult thing to discuss: spreading his ashes as I shop at Neiman Marcus, so to speak. But I must be honest, because God sees all things, all my feelings, reservations, desperate resentments and confusion, and the reality that manifests his will. Speculations about the future or its alternate scenarios (the what-might-have-beens) are proscribed by the limits of human control. When I think about Neal in the context of what if or what might have been, I can't help but wonder if he would have maintained his addictive patterns and matured into a marginal and stunted lifestyle as an older man.

Would he have gone to jail? Would he have been victimized by violence? Would a dysfunctional marriage, damaged children, or other severely broken relationships have ensued? Surely, his lifelong pattern of spending and financial irresponsibility would have likely continued. Would this have fractured our bond into resentment, rejection, or hostility?

I cannot help but wonder about these potentials. Sometimes, I stray from the path of these thoughts into the tangled thicket of ruminations about whether God did a good thing and blessed me by taking Neal away before his life and its effects on others could become even uglier and more destructive. These are not pleasant thoughts—my mind and heart seem to override with cautions about such speculations. But deep inside me, in a place I cannot define nor have consistent access to, I know that God is guiding me and that he allows such questions. I am too humble to expect answers.

Entertaining the idea that Neal got what he deserved—the natural consequences of years of poor choices and destructive behaviors—seems at once like a raw desecration of him. How could I be so cold and dismissive? Yet, this is not my position or attitude, merely a perspective included among the swatches of reality I work to stitch together as I go about my business. Neal is always with me—*me*, the father who loved him, who taught him right from wrong, who helped him pay for his mistakes over and over again, who rescued him repeatedly, who suffered with him in agonies and also took pride and joy in his accomplishments and victories. I am the father who righteously intones, "I told you so," and who shrieks in the next moment, "My beloved son, I miss you so!"

I toss and revolve in my mind and heart Neal as an innocent victim of an accident and Neal as a perpetrator of his own demise. Heroin is a vicious killer, a merciless satanic python. The wicked cycle of withdrawal, abstinence, and relapse carries with it the uncertainty and poor regulation of street drugs; overdose is common and probable. Was Neal's fatality a miscalculation? A dire misfortune of pure drug? A mercurial last-fling indulgence before again submitting to rehab? Was it a suicide? And how do we determine the parameters of intentionality in such a circumstance? Did I contribute unknowingly, yet stupidly, by giving him money for food and transit fare?

I'm not tortured by these questions, but I do need to revisit them periodically. I don't think it is disgraceful or taboo—or disrespectful to Neal. I love you, Son, from the depths of my being, so let's try to be honest in love. I would like to make sense of what you and God did. Sometimes, I feel left out of it. Mostly, I'm immersed in this tragedy.

I am a psychologist who helps others with personal problems, including addictions. Yet, I couldn't save my own son. Where is the logic in this, and is the irony even relevant? I feel responsible to my beliefs and faithful to my values. For me, the "ashes in Neiman Marcus" means that my son's memory and failures parade with me in the course of my normal activities. I preach and practice self-regulation and self-control, abstinence from drugs and alcohol, and a striving to follow God's ways and depend on him for the strength and direction to do so.

My son had trouble following a good path. I mourn this tragedy. I mourn for him. To tell the truth, I don't even know whether to blame him (or how much)—that's how perplexing, humbling, and overwhelming is this whole business of losing him.

Life goes on, as it must for the living. I traipse through the Neiman Marcus aisles of my activities, looking for purpose and good bargains, looking for value and sometimes returns. Neal is with me, as he must be, as I want him to be. He is silent and invisible to those around me. But inside my heart and mind, he dreams, listens, expresses, and loves me beyond any reward I ever imagined possible.

There are many devastating losses. So vulnerable are we, such lumps of clay with temporary breath and heartbeats, so desperate that we cling to all we need and want and covet and love and think we cannot do without. Perhaps the ultimate and most insatiable loss is the failed claim to what we never get but think we are *entitled*: the loss of privilege to rule absolutely over our own lives and the outcomes in the world around us. God never gave us that, nor is that among his bountiful and certain promises. The greatest loss is the surrender of what we think rightfully belongs to us, whether we have gained and lost it or never attained what we thought we should have, our contrived rightful due. To give up what we think is owed us is the grandest, most virtuous loss and surrender. In its place, God gives us more than we can ever imagine.

THINGS NEAL LIKED

Seeking attention and knowing what's true
Debating, arguing, and conquering you
Questioning God and being a Jew
These are the things Neal liked to do.

Coffee at Starbucks and coffee at Peet's
Pizza with pesto and sugary treats
Chinese and pasta and burgers with cheese
These are some things Neal liked to eat.

Physics, philosophy, math, and science
Cosmology, autonomy, and lack of compliance
Challenging authority and passive defiance
Neal would admire intellectual giants.

Skateboards and sports and athletic pursuit
Snowboarding, glowsticks, Asian girls he found cute
YouTube, Reddit, and Internet memes
Neal's curiosity flourished, it seems.

Mountain moguls to snowboard, hockey goal shots to slap
Hip-hop and trance music mixing to rap
Running and biking and taking a nap
Neal liked neurofeedback and learned how to tap.

Playing with pets and playing guitar.
Neal's moods could swing wildly, his mind would range far.
The thrill of speed, martial arts to spar.
Neal knew so much about all kinds of cars.

Calculus, string theory, nuclear fission.
Solving equations he did with a mission.
Neal was a talented academician.
But he could take days to make simple decisions.

Neal loved to read; he craved movement and speed.
Japanese racing bikes followed his lead.
His keen smell collected arrays of colognes.
He preferred socializing over being alone.

Neal enjoyed life; he valued his many friends.
He practiced good fashion, was conscious of trends.
He shared thoughts and feelings, could talk to no end.
About certain topics, your ear he would bend.

He liked his neck rubbed, his back massaged, too.
He loved watching movies and giving his view.
His charm and his brilliance could make people swoon.
Neal, we miss you! You left us far too soon.

III

SURRENDER

CHAPTER 11
THE PARADOX OF SURRENDER

Living with loss is ongoing and reminds me just how much living means losing. They are intertwined.

—Laura C.

We learn throughout life to stockpile the goods and skills that make for well-being and security. Our elders train us in the rudiments and finer points of self-care and self-management skills, as well as the paths toward marketable competence and the fundamentals of attracting and getting along with people.

Ours is a dog-eat-dog world in which the strongest survive and profit while those less fortunate or capable serve those more powerful. Striving for power, material wealth, achievement, and recognition occupy most of our time and energies. We worship the almighty dollar and often base our self-worth and satisfaction on material acquisition. For some, identity, emotional survival, and purpose center around the connection with, achievements of, or protection and approval by others.

The sayings "Possession is nine-tenths of the law" and "He who dies with the most toys wins" may well describe many people's actual behavior, if not their expressed creed. This is not cynical but rather realistic. Of

course, I'm not exempt, and I cite this ethos to frame a fundamental problem for all of us: *How can we cultivate and exercise determination and perseverance
while maintaining an identity and security that neither resides in nor depends upon
the gifts and possessions that are, in reality, temporary?*

If labor is begrudgingly learned and executed, then certainly we deserve to enjoy the fruits of our labor—isn't that just and right? The problem is that work and rewards and duration are disproportional. Life is not
fair, even by any stretch of the most creative reason or imagination. And if
justice is hard to figure out in terms of earnings or luck, it is even harder to
abide in terms of keepings.

One of my father's oft-repeated sayings was, "Now that I can finally
afford steak, I can't chew it properly." (And my father was a dentist!) In
this world of cruel ironies, where acquisitions and glory are ephemeral,
where thieves break in and steal, and where moths destroy and rust cor-
rodes, there are constant streams of grace and mercy. God gives, and God
takes away. In his inscrutable pattern of doing so, he gives us a method of
accepting what we cannot control and of experiencing a peace that passes
understanding.

This method, a path that can become a fruitful way of life, is the blessing of *surrender*. It is the capitulation to God's will because he is greater
than we are and he made it so, along with everything he allows to happen—
even when it is so painful and devastating to us.

Each of us struggles not only with loss—things wrested from us against
our will—but with the senselessness and injustice of oppression, devastation, and cruelty. When someone else's house is destroyed by fire or when
innocent children are killed, we shrink back in helplessness and horror. We
get scared of disease, incensed over crime and discrimination, and angry
about injustice. We are often compassionate and also secretly relieved that
it didn't happen to us—this time. But there lingers the knowledge of inevitability—we cannot escape hardship and loss.

How are we to live with this dilemma of impending certainty and
timeless uncertainty? We are bound to lose things and people of great importance to us. How can we recover when calamity descends and our taken-
for-granted stability is disrupted, our security ravaged, and our sustenance
robbed?

It is the act of surrender that provides liberation. Surrender is antitheti-
cal to resistance. It is the willing and deliberate choice to submit to that

which is not under our control or will. However, in the context of lifelong training to take charge of one's direction, to plan, work, and strive to determine the outcome in one's favor—essentially to win and prevail—giving up and giving in doesn't make sense. Surrender can seem like weakness, a desertion of determination and duty. In the world of acquisition, you win the game by holding on at all costs.

But the game rules change when God takes over and confiscates your markers. Loss decimates your resources and strategy. It is a checkmate of your wiles and your will. When loss strikes at the heart of your being, it is time to concede.

The paradox of surrender is that you gain by giving up. Surrender is weakness and vulnerability leaving the soul and spirit. It is the renunciation of control and the capitulation to a force or will greater than one's own. *Surrender enacts the yielding of the object of attachment, not the ability to attach and to value and love.* When you surrender, you relinquish claim. Therein lies the peace that brings wholeness, regardless of possession or presence.

How is it possible to give up claim? To abandon what you've worked for, to accept the theft of what belongs to you? A dogged redoubling of tenacity and proprietorship seems consistent with all the effort that goes into acquisition—except that when God whisks it away, your demands for ownership and restitution come to no avail.

Indeed, the options in the face of loss are limited. You cannot manufacture or reconstitute on demand what has been destroyed. When it comes to a life lost, there are no substitutes or surrogates.

What do you gain by surrendering to loss? One gain is a resolve to adapt to new circumstances and not depend on what is no longer available. It is not easy to do without. Certainly, there is no replacement, nor is there adequate salve for the pain of losing a loved one. Surrender allows the process of carrying on to resume and to strengthen. Another gain is the comfort and peace that eventually accrues through acceptance. To live with what has occurred, to find new joys in the exercise of sacrifice and other attachments, is to resume a life of connectedness and renewed resilience and hope.

Surrender creates a focus on the present and the future. It is a catalyst for healing. Surrender is the exercise of flexibility and deference, the acknowledgment of vulnerability, and the yielding to forces greater than one's own. It is not weakness or destitution; rather, it is the participation in a universe of natural cycles of exposure and erosion, nurture and protection, hurt and healing.

Most important, surrender is the process by which God can manifest his rightful place as creator and owner of the universe and let us experience his vast love, comfort, presence, grace, mercy, and protection.

When you surrender, you give up ownership and entitlement. There is no reason to fight for what is no longer yours. You relinquish encumbrance, and you trade continued responsibility for freedom and lightness.

Surrendering to your loss does not mean that you give up your feelings. Instead, you become better able to feel your feelings purely. You experience them as triggered by and related to events but not mandated or continued by circumstances. You practice the artful grace of detachment. You exert this ability by virtue of a joint power of your self-control and the owner of all life who invites you by difficult circumstances to become humbler. Paradoxically, you learn to become less dependent on particular things and people and more dependent on the enduring promises of the one who gives all things.

God took my son, and I have surrendered his passing. I mourn for him, and every day I miss him. I look forward to the days when my thoughts of him may be unobstructed by clouds of pain and memories of him will surround me with welcome warmth as rays of sunlight touching my skin and soaking into my heart. More and more, I am able to blend my sorrow with the joys of fatherhood that, for Neal, lasted for less time than I would have wanted. The Holy Spirit who dwells within me nurtures my hope and shows me, paradoxically, that when I lose a part of me so intrinsic to my identity, I find a strength I did not know was possible.

When God takes away, he closes doors, often unexpectedly. In his providence, new doors open and opportunities unfold to discover and live out what God has in mind. Loss can be an opportunity to turn disappointment and longing regarding the past into hopeful longing and eagerness about the present and future. With God, the future is brighter. Surrender allows us to let go and move more fluidly toward what God has in store.

CHAPTER 12
ATTACHMENT

We are designed to want things. From earliest infancy, we seek what we instinctively realize will help us survive. Starting with the most basic needs of food, protection, and comfort, we learn to attach ourselves to those who provide the materials, nurturing, support, and love we must have to sustain us. Attachment is a biological imperative, for without it, none would survive and flourish.

In the human species, as in many other species, during the vital primary months of development, babies attach themselves to their mothers physically, neurologically, and emotionally. Thus, a powerful bond is created, beginning in utero. Infants are genetically programmed to depend on this core relationship and to anticipate that their needs will be understood and met. It is from this repeated expectation of needs fulfillment that their sense of trust evolves, security becomes predictable, and confidence builds. This process of reliance, of course, continues throughout early childhood, middle childhood, adolescence, and beyond in stages and phases that are biologically and culturally mapped.

This biological and social bond is a foundation of evolution and nature. It is what makes parents fiercely protective and possessive and what enables children to thrive and learn about the world and people. From earliest experiences, children form notions of what to expect and how their overtures will be received. They accumulate experiences that tell them about themselves and where they fit in (or do not belong). They learn what behaviors will get attention and gratification and how likely they are to be successful and satisfied. In other words, the child-as-forecaster acquires predictive skills about the probability of success in gaining what's needed and wanted.

Attachment is a vital though imperfect process. Its trajectory facilitates emotional connection, empathy and compassion, social adhesion, and the abilities necessary for social relationships. When attachment goes well, it empowers the child to differentiate him- or herself from the mother figure and progressively move toward independence and relative self-sufficiency. The child's brain and nervous system become adept at self-soothing and self-regulation. He or she is increasingly able to withstand adversity, absence, deprivation, uncertainty, ambiguity, and eventual sacrifice. Self-control, reasonable risk-taking, and tolerance develop from trial-and-error experiences built upon expecting and attaining success, gratification, protection, and security.

CONSEQUENCES OF POOR ATTACHMENT

When attachment is ruptured or impeded, the consequences can be devastating. Early deprivation often results in a nervous system that cannot effectively quiet itself. This leads to heightened arousal—a fight-or-flight response—as the default state of the brain, causing the individual to be overly vigilant, restless, defensive, and lacking in the capacity to trust and form attachments. An absent, detached, or preoccupied mother leaves a child with primal experiences of neglect, abandonment, and loss. The child learns to expect hardship and perceive the environment and its people as threatening and unsatisfying. It becomes enduringly difficult and burdensome to draw close to people, and the skills of satisfying behavior exchange are ineffectively practiced and refined.

Though classic examples of the roots of attachment disorder abound (such as with scandalous Eastern-European orphanages or drug-addicted, prostituting mothers), it would be simplistic to reduce attachment problems to early childhood harsh or adverse conditions. The larger problem is that children can *perceive* neglect and deprivation, even when their needs would seem to be met routinely and material and emotional resources are abundantly provided. Jealousy of attention given to a sibling, victimization by bullying or ridicule, busy schedules or travel by parents, or the inherent alienation that can develop when a child feels he or she doesn't measure up can progressively harden his or her heart and stultify his or her ability to form healthy attachments. It is also the nature of human sinfulness that contributes to character flaws, which might include a sense of entitlement—beliefs and feelings that all that we desire is rightfully ours. Thus, when these desires are not granted or are taken away, the resulting frustration becomes overwhelming and morphs into reality distortion, resentment, and behaviors that are disproportionate to the situation. This sets the stage for a self-aggrandizing sense of entitlement to develop and potentially for narcissism to ensue.

In some cases, children who are very emotionally needy become *too* attached. These youngsters become overly anxious and have trouble separating from their parents because of excessive fearfulness and dependence. Given the multitude and probability of factors that can sabotage attachment, it is astounding that the necessary process ever happens. However, attachment flourishes regularly, for it is the norm. As such, it is resistant to most intrusions once it has had a chance to take root. The ability to form attachments is robust and rewarding; yet it is delicate and intimate, requiring nourishment, practice, and reinforcement.

ATTACHMENT AND LOSS

Attachment can be damaged by loss. Withdrawal or disappearance of a dearly loved family member, cherished friend, or valued love object (such as a house lost in a flood or a book of cherished photos lost in a fire) can have a profound negative impact on one's sense of security and wholeness. The more you have developed and established satisfying and healthy attachments, the less likely you are to disintegrate in the face of loss. Nonetheless, the effects of loss are influenced by degree, perception, and timing. Neediness and vulnerability cannot be calibrated by circumstances, achievements, or the perceptions of others. Onlookers don't walk in your shoes. Children born of the same genes and raised in the same environments can turn out very differently. One child may grow up to be a self-indulgent criminal, while a sibling becomes a self-made leader and philanthropist. In my family, Neal succumbed to drug addiction, but his brother (same genetic and environmental conditions) has grown and developed with a different set of values and self-discipline. It happens all the time.

Loss is both actual and subjective. It may occur in reality, or it may be perceived to have occurred. It may perseverate (continue and be expanded upon) beyond and sometimes in the absence of a specific event. If I think or feel I am damaged by a loss or cannot go on without something or someone, this outlook will profoundly affect my attitude, coping mechanisms, adaptation responses, and even my physical health.

It is my ability to *attach* that materializes the experience of loss. The precious qualities of loving, needing, connecting with, depending upon, providing for, and experiencing joy and sorrow with another living being carry inherently with them the vulnerability and potential for grief, hurt, loneliness, anguish, and suffering. The very essence of what enables me to find self-actualization and fulfillment by relating to others leaves me exposed and susceptible when what I love is taken away.

In what manner is it possible to navigate and manage this delicate balance? The duality of attachment and surrender defies logic and is often imbued with confusion, tension, and even desperation. Life is a struggle between attaching, yearning, acquiring, protecting, and developing and detaching, surrendering, yielding, letting go, and giving up.

Loss appears to be a sharp instrument that God uses to separate us from the ownership that is truly and only his. God gives many gifts and is able to supply all needs. In addition to the many things and people that comprise his blessings, he gives us the priceless gift of the ability to grow fond of them.

The ability to claim God's blessings and enjoy his provisions must often be tempered by the humbling sacrifice of relinquishing what is taken away. To accept such sacrifices, we must understand and even embrace the paradox of surrender.

CHAPTER 13
STORING UP TREASURE

CONSECRATED CONFISCATION

I love the God who gives me things and reasons,
Who gives me things without reasons,
Who gives me songs and seasons.

I hate the nature forcing me to give up things I want—still *want*—
When I'm not ready.
Willing or steady in resolve to be OK,
Complete in confiscation.

Take away, take me away,
Don't punish me with absence.
Lift my burdens, hear me say
That emptiness is nascent.

Consecrate this forfeiture instead of wresting trauma,
Give up the entitlements without the trenchant drama.
Oh, God, I'm awed with fortune, how you populate my life
With work and foods, conflicting moods,
With children and a wife.

Yet in the end, around the bend, it all becomes rescinded.
I run the race and find my place, the trek has left me winded.
Remaining breaths appreciate the time and matter left to stay,
For soon enough, it is enough,
And then God takes away.

Out of the ashes of defeat and misery comes glory.

The experience of awesome splendor, the witness of astounding beauty, the satisfaction of achievement, and the magnificence of peace are a sweet, sweet contrast to the ache of pain and loss, the grueling familiar toil, and the dejection that fill so many days of life.

REFLECTIONS ON MEANING AND MATTER

Where is glory in this mess of a world we live in? Why is pleasure so elusive, so fleeting, so costly? In the end (and along the way), what is worth achieving, and what efforts are worth sustaining? What about *holding on?* Is it merely a survival instinct embellished by character strength? Or is holding on a selfish illusion that stubbornly conflicts with the reality that everything is temporary?

Sometimes, my obligations are overwhelming. There is so much work to do, and it usually involves more effort and obstacles than I anticipate, even after years of experience with this phenomenon. Each bit of progress I make seems to bring with it the awareness of more tasks, complicated next steps, and the realization that I will never be finished with the stream of endless requirements. The satisfaction of paying bills is quickly replaced by the requirement to pay more of them, and the needs of people are pressing and ongoing.

I am used to this cycle of events, the mundane repetition of human activities and natural phenomena that King Solomon described in the biblical book of Ecclesiastes as "Meaningless. Everything is meaningless!" Fortunately, I have learned to be productive and to cope with frustration. Maturity has given me some useful perspective, and I have experienced enough success and achievement to know that these come in waves and require patience, hard work, and perseverance. I enjoy material things, and I strive in this dog-eat-dog world to acquire them. Every so often, I am stopped in my tracks by an experience that makes it all seem so pointless.

Something is taken away! I am surprised, angry, confused, dejected, and even traumatized. A valued possession disappears or breaks. Worse yet, a relationship devolves or someone dies. Also, there is the maddening irony that I often get what I want, only to find that it's not that great or satisfying after all. When this occurs, it typically happens gradually. The relentless loss of pleasure and interest in what I formerly coveted and aspired to attain leaves me disappointed in life's rewards and shaky in my confidence and expectation that I can appreciate and sustain them. In other words, life can become bleak and insipid, interrupted by moments of unsettling stimulation.

When this condition persists, it is labeled *anhedonia*, a Greek and psychiatric word denoting the loss of or inability to experience pleasure. I don't know whether King Solomon suffered from this condition and he tried to cope by amassing incomparable wealth and accomplishing unparalleled projects. I do know that his conclusions and frustration resonate with my experiences in the twenty-first century. I work and work and look forward to the fruits of my labor. The sparkle of the prize lures me. But much of the time, whether I get it/there or not, things fall apart. This, I've learned, is the norm. I have heard this common experience called *destination sickness* or *destination disappointment*. There are exceptions, of course, moments or months of elation, pride, recognition, or coasting in the zone of delightful fulfillment or effort that regenerates itself. Then, there are periods of abyss—the shock of loss and trauma and the long, steep road to recovery. This may sound like bipolar disorder, but it is rather the more common, natural cycle that most people experience to a greater or lesser degree.

Encountering a profound loss—as I have with the death of my son—catapults these realities beyond philosophical inquiries into a daily and palpable struggle. The questions that keep emerging, louder than the rollercoaster cacophony of feelings, are: *What is worth working for and toward? Since everything gets taken away eventually, what is worth achieving? Can I gain or do anything that will last? What are the real treasures? How can I find and enjoy them? Are there any treasures I can keep?*

In seeking and wanting, there is insight and reward intermingled with the pain. For God promises:

Ask and it will be given to you; seek and you will find; knock and the door will be opened to you. For everyone who asks receives; the one who seeks finds; and to the one who knocks, the door will be opened". (Matthew 7:7–8)

GOD SPEAKS THROUGH CIRCUMSTANCES

Let me share with you an example of how God works in me and with me.

On a Sunday morning several months after Neal had died, I hurried to get to church, as is my ritual. I was late, arriving after the sermon had started. I slid unobtrusively into a pew in the back of the sanctuary. As I tried to focus on the sermon, I noticed a young man sitting in the row in front of me, and my jaw dropped. This person was the spitting image of Neal—same red-orange hair with the same texture, the freckles on the back of the neck, the manicured beard tracing the contour of his jaw, the olive-green shirt contrasting nicely with his hair and complexion, and blue jeans. As the congregation stood for a song, I noticed his athletic build. He seemed to be my son, reincarnated. I remembered so tenderly how Neal would often request that I rub his neck and back and how he would sigh in relief when I did so. *That feels so good, Dad, thanks.* I kept staring at this young man in church, not wanting to make him uncomfortable but knowing that he couldn't see me. It was uncanny and surreal. I wanted to touch him or at least make contact with him. He was sitting and exchanging occasional words with an older man.

When the service ended, I introduced myself. To my surprise, this fellow didn't want to talk to me. He wouldn't shake my hand or look directly at me. It was awkward, and I sensed his discomfort. I told him he looked amazingly like my son, but I didn't push the conversation. Instead, I talked with the older man, whom I assumed to be his father or relative. Neither of us could engage the young redhead, and I thought to myself, *Is this guy angry? Is he here under protest? Is he so self-conscious or mortified that he won't make small talk? Is he left-handed and troubled like my son Neal was? Is he struggling in life, feeling overwhelmed and unsuccessful?*

I talked with the older man and showed him pictures of Neal on my phone. The man was solicitous and welcoming. He agreed that Neal looked remarkably like his young fellow, who also happened to be twenty-seven—Neal's age. I found validation and comfort in reaching out and making new acquaintances at church. I don't know if I will interact with these people again. I hope I didn't stress the young man in my eagerness to engage and compliment him. Perhaps he thought I was just some weird guy with an offensive agenda, a blip on his cynical radar screen of life's intrusions and unfairness. Maybe the older man was struggling—as I had with Neal—

to awaken the young man's spiritual yearnings, to discourage unhealthy habits, and to teach and encourage him in winning ways. These were my speculations, the imaginary correlates of a brief social encounter, emanating from my wistful memory of Neal and my reading into circumstances certain physical and emotional similarities. I needed to insert myself into the lives of others, to discover and accept what fits and does not, to carry on and carry with me the history, personality, and sensory vividness of Neal and the twenty-seven years I spent with him. I felt gratified by this encounter, glad I had taken the chance, pleased with my motives. I fantasized that maybe in the future, I would be given opportunities to recognize and aggrandize parental love and perhaps to facilitate more powerfully the rescue of young people who had lost their way. In those moments in church, Neal was with me blessedly, even as I missed his physical presence.

Out of the ashes of defeat and misery comes glory.

LOSS AND TREASURE

We lose things—material things, people, relationships, ideals, hopes, and trust. We age and lose physical capacity. Eventually, we lose the breath that sustains us. Each day that you live, your life becomes shorter (using the logic that you are closer to your death than you were the day before). Is anything truly lasting? What is worth acquiring, developing, and adhering to? Are there things that cannot be taken away or undone?

The answers emphatically are yes! There are efforts and achievements that are truly lasting. Buildings crumble, records are broken, and living creatures die. But the way we live, how we react and develop character, what we do with the opportunities and circumstances given us—these are the determinants of the treasures that each of us acquires and retains. Consider Psalm 103:

As a father has compassion on his children, so the Lord has compassion on those who fear him; for he knows how we are formed, he remembers that we are dust. The life of mortals is like a flower of the field; the wind blows over it and it is gone, and its place remembers it no more. But from everlasting to everlasting the Lord's love is with those who fear him, and his righteousness with their children's children—with those who keep his covenant and remember to obey his precepts. (Psalm 103:13–18)

If we are to store up treasure, to acquire and develop material and spiritual possessions, capacities, achievements, and qualities that endure, we must embrace what God values and what he wants for us. It must not be a contest with God, for he sees everything and knows everything. He created everything, even the desires of our hearts and our ambitions. (And God even created and allows free will and the desires of our hearts, which sometimes stray from him.) God is eternal, but our earthly wants are finite, as are our breath and time on earth. God created us this way, and *he knows how we are formed, he remembers that we are dust. The life of mortals is like a flower of the field; the wind blows over it and it is gone, and its place remembers it no more.* While in this mortal body, however, we can develop and store up treasure that rewards in this life and whose value lasts infinitely. God made it so, and he encourages us to follow his path to lasting treasures. A peaceful and rewarding life cannot be a contest with God to claim dominion or cling to or hide things so that he cannot take them away. Such a contest is futile, for everything belongs to God. Yet God, in his mercy, grace, and lovingkindness, wants us to have things that endure. He encourages us to store up treasure that lasts.

What endures beyond our temporary life spans, achievements, and pleasures? Here are some lasting treasures.

SALVATION

God gives us, freely, the greatest reward possible: eternal life. It is up to each of us to claim it. We all lead double lives, the material and the spiritual. This is the nature God gave us. In the material or fleshly realm, it is darn difficult to grasp or relate to something nonconforming to sense or reason. We have palpable needs and pressures—bills to pay, many other pressing obligations, limited resources, pain, and conflict. The story of Jesus sacrificing so that we could have eternal life seems hard to reconcile with earthly reason and experience, despite its clear factual, historical basis. That is the whole point! To accept this history, this sacrifice, this future, we must rely upon faith to bridge the gap between material and spiritual realities. Faith necessitates believing in what our senses cannot ascertain. It is an act of trust and a commitment based on belief and conviction.

Salvation that brings eternal life is the quintessence of storing up treasure. It is neither a delusion nor a postponement of dealing with daily realities. It happens in the future and in the present. It has also occurred in the past. It is the basis for security in a world of transient matter and events— people, possessions, and circumstances. The very idea of salvation—the acceptance that Jesus sacrificed and died for our sins so that we can live forever—lifts the heart and mind beyond carnal limitations and bestows a security and mind-set that transcends circumstances, painful and consequential as they may immediately be. When you know the ultimate outcome, playing the game with endurance and confidence becomes a whole lot easier and sure.

God has the power and prerogative to take away anything and everything. But he promises that he will not take away our eternal life, our lasting presence with him, if we commit our belief and faith in him. It is truly the most powerful choice each of us has to make. What greater treasure can there be, both in the future and in the present?

Salvation, the reality and gift that depends on faith, colors how we regard possessions, loss, ownership, and permanence. Belief is the bridge that makes the intangible knowable and accessible. God takes away things, people, and opportunities that are important to us in the moments of our carnal human nature (a nature he gives us). None of us can ascertain why he does what he does when he does it. We hurt and want to possess and feel pride and entitlement; because of these sensations, we feel deprived, resentful, confused, and even angry when something or someone we think belongs to us is confiscated. It is not entirely knowable in this life why God takes away what and when he does. However, God clearly gives us consolation, kindness, and a mandate for belief and trust in his love, protection, security, and supremacy. It is his way of directing us to what is truly and supremely important, even in the midst of our pain, despair, self-absorption, and limited reasoning. He gives us a *lasting treasure*, a delight and security that he will never take away

Never will I leave you; never will I forsake you. (Hebrews 13:5)

SPIRITUAL TRANSCENDENCE

In this ephemeral world, full of pain, disappointment, and struggle, God gives us the challenge, ability, and support to surpass immediate circumstances and our self-serving reactions to them. The spiritual world is beyond, different, yet interactive with the material world that we operate in on a daily basis. The laws of science and logic that bind us to daily existence, the non sequiturs that perplex, the extraordinary phenomena that captivate us and inspire marvel and humility—God created all of it! He invites and encourages us to partake in his larger reality, the true reality in which material events and knowledge are only partial.

The ability, desire, and habit of accessing and participating in this nonmaterial world may be called *spiritual transcendence*. It is the act of acknowledging and surrendering to the God-supervised reality of spirit. In the spiritual reality, events and relations are not limited by human ideals and values or by physical limitations. For example, faith is the belief in what is not seen. The assumption of faith is that reality exists beyond our senses, reason, or tools of measurement.

Spiritual transcendence requires a commitment to believe in God's abilities and works beyond our own knowledge and capacity to fully interpret, track, and predict them. We get glimpses that astound and convict us. These experiences, in turn, build faith, security, and confidence in a lasting presence and protection. Along the way, we have pain, frustration, and challenges that test and delude our pride and self-sufficiency. The ability to weather disappointments, setbacks, and even devastating loss is buttressed by the knowledge that God *is* in charge. To live in the spirit is to *go beyond* rationalization and self-serving logic. This practice breaks the limitations of time and physical circumstances. It allows us to play by God's rules, even when we think we are not winning. Because God is faithful, our acknowledging the spiritual aspects of experiences gives us access to treasures otherwise not found.

We cannot fully know why God takes away that which is of great value to us. Sometimes, we find out later that a loss was a good thing—for instance, a better job or more suitable partner comes along. Much of the time, though, there is mystery and disappointment, even lasting heartache, when loss befalls us. What good can come from my son's death? What better child can appear?

When loss strikes—surprising, devastating, incomprehensible—it is by the practice of spiritual transcendence that healing, trust, and even some knowledge comforts and blesses us. This is the language that God speaks, and he wants us in communication with him. The mechanics of this language are prayer, trust, humility, faith, and surrender.

GOOD WORKS

Most people want to do good things. Many people strive successfully to enact constructive, compassionate efforts, born of the desire to help others, express love, and give back. Others intend to be helpful, generous, loving, supportive, and so on but often fall short of these intentions. And, yes, there are also those who, for reasons hard for most of us to fathom or accept, act with bitterness, inconsideration, hate, violence, self-justification, and a startling lack of remorse.

When good things happen, we are quick to take pride and claim credit and virtue. When bad things happen, we are inclined to blame, criticize, excuse, or recoil at the *unfairness* and injustice. We want to believe that what goes around comes around and that eventually equitability will prevail and people will get their just desserts.

Yet injustice abounds, and we are left to cope with horrible things that God allows; we are compelled to deal with gross inequities by dint of limited human reasoning and the conflicts and complications of sin and desire. In the face of inequity, one choice is to carry on by doing good works, becoming a *good person* who acts benevolently toward others and the planet in general.

Surely, these attitudes and habits cannot be impugned—except on one basis: they do not overcome sin, and they do not earn admission to heaven. This is the whole point of salvation, that which is both the supreme gift and stumbling block. God has declared that none of humanity's works are good enough and that the only path to him and his kingdom of heaven is through his son, Jesus Christ (John 14:6).

Humans can wrestle admirably with the thorny dilemma of what good is *good enough* and by what standard. However, the most logical minds and eloquent debaters cannot provide conclusive answers to the quandary of what qualifies as good enough or best. And this is because it is impossible to qualify a human standard to that which is superhuman.

What, then, of good works? What good are they, and why should we do them? If our efforts and material achievements do not last—in fact, do not earn entrance to heaven—what is their point? Can good works store up treasure?

Yes, good works do store up treasure! They do not earn salvation, but they *matter* (James 2:14–26). They are meaningful and righteous to God and to our fellow creatures, whom God created and loves. The reasons for and effects of doing good unfold on both secular and spiritual levels. Here on earth, we generally reap what we sow. Though it's not a perfect mathematical model, it's reassuringly predictable that being productive yields better results than dissipation, that bad guys usually get caught and punished, and that sincere compassion and sacrifice are eventually recognized and appreciated (though not necessarily recompensed).

God commands us to do good works, even as he clearly differentiates them from salvation. In his profound love for us, God created in our nature the capacity to be so awed and appreciative of his mercy and forgiveness, his grace and bounty, that the desire to do good works emerges from the profound gratitude for what God has done for us!

The biblical writer, James, links good works (deeds) with faith as practical and spiritual counterparts:

> *What good is it, my brothers and sisters, if someone claims to have faith but has no deeds? Can such faith save them? Suppose a brother or sister is without clothes and daily food. If one of you says to them, "Go in peace; keep warm and well-fed." But does nothing about their physical needs, what good is it? In the same way, faith by itself, if it is not accompanied by action, is dead. But someone will say, "You have faith; I have deeds." Show me your faith without deeds and I will show you my faith by my deeds. You believe that there is one God. Good! Even the demons believe that—and shudder. You foolish person, do you want evidence that faith without deed is useless? Was not our father Abraham considered righteous for what he did when he offered his son Isaac on the altar? You see that his faith and actions were working together, and his faith was made complete by what he did. And the scripture was fulfilled that says, "Abraham believed God, and it was credited to him as righteousness." And he was called God's friend. You see that a person is considered righteous by what they do and not by faith alone.* (James 2:14–24)

There are both practical and spiritual imperatives for engaging in good works. There is a lasting value of good works that transcends temporary benefits and the reflection of gratitude. *Good works accrue treasure in God's eyes and in human character.*

What are good works? They are many and varied, just as circumstances, needs, and personal talents and motivation vary. Look around and see what needs to be done for the good of others. Answer a request; fill a need. Consider others more important than yourself, and put their needs ahead of yours. Show compassion and mercy.

He has shown you, O mortal, what is good. And what does the Lord require of you? To act justly and to love mercy and to walk humbly with your God. (Micah 6:8)

Search your heart for what is right and for the strength and will to carry it out. Follow the rules and play fair. Ask God to show you the high road and to give you the strength to travel on it.

GODLY CHARACTER

As we travel through life, we are preoccupied with the daily tasks of survival in a material world. We have to take care of our physical and less tangible needs; often, we must also take care of others. We learn that security and money are important, and we find that material things provide comfort, pleasure, and security. We respect the power and necessity of money, and we become impressed by those who can command it. We are highly motivated to get money, feel good when we succeed in its acquisition, and often measure ourselves and others by the yardstick of material possessions. When overextended, the necessity to live practically and the desire to live comfortably and powerfully become idolatry. The downside of taking pride in one's own abilities, in achievement and self-sufficiency, is that it can become a form of worshiping something other than God—and this leads away from God.

Efforts, desires, thoughts, feelings, beliefs, aspirations, values, tendencies, likes, dislikes, and reactions all constitute your character. In essence, *your character is the continuing act of being you.* You have a basic nature, and this nature becomes chiseled and modified over time by how you live and the choices you make. Whether you realize it or not, your choices and character have tremendous impact and importance in the present world and hereafter as well. Who you are and what you do now affects you and those in the future, even after you are not around to experience or care about these effects. To get a glimpse of this truth, just think for a moment about what you don't have that you would like or that you would like more of—money, looks, a certain body type, health, wellness, freedom, power, and influence. Think about the many times you blamed your family and ancestors (and others who came before you and your time) for setting you up for the hardship and limitations you endure. Upon such reflection, do you still doubt that what and who came before you directly matters and influences you?

Don't take this perspective as fatalistic or deterministic. I am pointing out that your nature (genetics and human nature to be selfish, survive, and prevail) and your choices push you in directions that have consequences in the present life and in the life beyond for you and for others. There *is* a future. Indeed, we are living in the future of those who preceded us.

In storing up treasure for the present and the future, it is wise to work toward that which has lasting impact. Character has lasting impact and value. We all have a character. It is at the core of who we are, yet it is quite modifiable. If character does not seem tangible to you, consider that it manifests in what we get and become and, more profoundly, in how we respond to what we get and become. None of us has the control we'd like over what transpires. We know that circumstances change and that things get taken away. It is our individual character that predicts our responses and ultimately results in our adaptation, contentment, contributions, and how pleasing we are to God.

LOVE

Love is the overarching dynamic that binds everything together. Love connects us with each other and with the tangibles and intangibles in life and beyond. We experience love materially and spiritually. We choose among the different kinds of love and sometimes settle for and into a shadow love that is less than what God wants and models for us.

Decades ago, I had a respected mentor who quite succinctly summarized that "Love is need." I thought this was a catchy and practical mantra, but this was before I became saved. In addition to aspiring to fill my love/need entitlement, I assessed (and devalued) others by whether they realized that their actions and *love* motives were basically attempts to meet their own needs. I know now that this attitude was and is a rationalized selfishness.

Over the years, I have loved and needed and come to a profound awe of what love may be.

Consider 1 Corinthians 13:4–8:

Love is patient, love is kind. It does not envy, it does not boast, it is not proud. It is not rude, it is not self-seeking, it is not easily angered, it keeps no record of wrongs. Love does not delight in evil, but rejoices with the truth. It always protects, always trusts, always perseveres. Love never fails…

What a marvelous and inspiring description of love by the apostle Paul! How humbling and challenging to innate selfish pride, greed, and desire!

God loves us and has loved us from the beginning of creation, including the conception and creation of each of us. God's love is so fundamentally profound and encompassing that it is difficult to understand from the limited human perspective. We are left to bask in his love, to accept it, rejoice in it, and share it with others. We can love only because God first loved us! (1 John 4:19)

I consider loving others the highest goal and greatest achievement. I constantly look for love—by this I mean not only to experience love, attraction, and acceptance for myself but to recognize, observe, and savor the love that others experience. I am a voyeur of true and selfless love!

Promoting and proclaiming love is a lasting treasure. It is a practice of experiencing God in his essence. It is the future for those who are saved, and it is knowable in this present life on a regular basis. It can and should be a way of life.

I love to observe acts of consideration, sacrifice, humility, and reconciliation. I love when human weakness gives way to God's strength. I know that as I fade away, the record of my acts of love will remain. They live and strengthen in the light and appreciation of others. They live in the memory and pleasure of God.

SACRIFICE AND MAKING A DIFFERENCE

At various times in my life, I've found (much to my surprise) that people value and want from me things and qualities I think are not important or worth much. It's the little things that count, as the saying goes, but remembering the little things involves paying attention to the needs and requests of others and letting those needs and values replace my priorities.

One way to practice this sacrifice is to accept what people find attractive and value about me above what I see as worthy in myself. Putting myself in the shoes of others as they see me requires deference to their needs and views. It is not self-doubt or people–pleasing. Deferring my own pride and ego to the opinions of others regarding me necessitates empathy and the sacrifice of my own views as paramount.

Sacrificing often necessitates more than merely changing an opinion; it requires action. I have discovered intermittently that I can offend people without meaning to or even knowing about it until their resentment boils over into an attack. Feeling and believing that such wrath is unmerited and undeserved, I instinctively defend myself and query the logical basis for the perception of offense or wrongdoing. As you might imagine, this seldom settles matters. What it takes, I've found, is the vulnerable willingness to apologize for transgressing on a person's sense of boundaries and integrity, even when I'm sure that the other person is mistaken and has behaved badly. Often, this type of sacrifice is needed for the sake of the other person's feelings even when I don't know what I may have done wrong or when the allegations are contrived or imagined.

Sacrificing and making a difference happens in a multitude of small ways. The people around me seek repeated explanations about matters I think are obvious and clear. I must take time to do so and exert care to protect them from feeling stupid or inadequate. I don't feel as though I'm better than others, but I do bear the responsibility of teaching and sharing my know-how. For me, this requires the constant vigilance of maintaining sensitivity to the feelings and esteem of others and fighting off the nemesis of my instinctive attitude that they should get over it. It requires persistent effort and sacrifice for me to remember and live out the awareness that "people don't care how much you know until they know how much you care."

Here are some examples. At times, my wife insists that I apologize for perpetrations she "imagined" I committed against her. She won't bury the hatchet but pursues me with it, seeking justice for the government of which she is queen. To reconcile seems like a concession of righteousness and truth. It requires a sacrifice of selfhood for the repair and edification of a loved one's wounds and integrity, even when (in my view) they are self-inflicted.

My son, Jeremy, pits his great intellect against the emotional immaturity that struggles to keep pace with his young adult certainty of the way things should be. I am asked, in effect, to stitch and soothe the dissonance. His routine sarcasm and questions about the rampant hypocrisies of people and inequities in life challenge me to supply explanations and justifications for the way things just *are*. This requires patience, effort, and time that compete for the precious and diminishing quantity of those resources from my depleted reservoir. I take the time and make the effort, repeatedly. The real sacrifice is giving up my need to be appreciated. This equity appraisal—effort repaid by appreciation—is an embarrassing reminder of my worldview of justice and ego commerce.

Make no mistake: I love these people intensely and with great compassion. I can extol their many virtues, and I am regularly thankful for them in prayer. As much as I love and appreciate them, ministering to their needs and allowing their idiosyncrasies to make an impact on what is convenient for me requires sacrifice. It is the small efforts that matter, as well as the hugely painful forfeitures that comprise sacrifice.

Kind and sensitive gestures for unknown beneficiaries make a difference too. It may seem like a small or insignificant deed to donate clothes or food, to host a meeting, or to recycle for the good of the environment. Yet, such acts require effort and sacrifice and are often performed in the absence of direct appreciation or knowledge of any specific beneficial effects. Sacrifice is given without regard for return on investment.

Sometimes, sacrifice shows significant and palpable connection with an expressed need. In the wake of Neal's death, his mother showed a voracious appetite for his memorabilia. Though I had no qualms about giving her Neal's personal effects that she wanted, I encountered great pain and difficulty in attempting to mourn with her and provide solace for her grief and agony. We had not communicated for many years after our acrimonious divorce. When I called to tell her about Neal's passing, we began a tenuous rapprochement. How do you deal with estrangement from the mother of your child when that child has died?

Barbara and Neal had been estranged for much of his adult life. Try as I did, I could not close that gap. It seemed like I made no progress in healing their wounds. There were brittle resentments on both their parts, and I felt caught in the middle. Neal and I were close; I supported him financially. I long suspected that Barbara assumed that I had bought Neal's affection away from her because I supplied his financial needs and sustained that dependency. This had been another wedge in the marriage and its denouement. Barbara had missed out on much of Neal's life after he left for college (the time of our incipient divorce), and he rarely initiated contact with her or responded to her calls.

Thus, when Barbara confided in me what a terrible time she was having dealing with his death, I tried to console her and meet her needs—a crushing effort I had failed at during the twenty-eight years of our relationship. I responded to her requests for information about Neal's adult years, which she had missed. I gathered pictures and names of friends. I made arrangements, met with her, offered help, withheld many opinions, watched her suffer, and let it *just be* without trying to fix her pain or dismiss it. For me, this was excruciating. It was a sacrifice I was willing to give. I couldn't be the husband she wanted, but I hope these acts made a difference.

MERCY

It is said that grace is receiving something good that we don't deserve, and mercy is not receiving something bad that we do deserve. God gives abundantly both his grace and mercy. He sets an example for us, showering us with love and blessings. He wants us to also to be merciful.

God favors good works and sacrifice. But he places a higher value on mercy.

It's so tempting and habitual for me to be judgmental—to assess people and circumstances through the lens of my values, pride, and self-righteousness. It is through prayer and the sense of God's presence that I'm reminded to become more humble and accepting, less judgmental and rigid in my outlook. Turning the other cheek, not seeking revenge, one-upmanship, or even to prevail in an argument or opinion is a humility and attitude of deference toward which I aspire and work.

I'm fortified by values and strong opinions. They have accumulated through experience, and they help me survive, function, and be productive. But I cannot value them above compassion for and acceptance of others whom I am bound to love—even when they do destructive things and may disappoint or hurt me.

My mother often said, "There but for the grace of God go I." How true! And were it not for God's repeated mercy, I could suffer the grave misfortune of others.

I was humbled and profoundly moved by Pope Francis's book, *The Name of God is Mercy*. The Pope exalts mercy above other virtues and attributes in our walk with God. Pope Francis says:

Etymologically, "mercy" derives from *misericordis*, which means opening one's heart to wretchedness.

—Pope Francis, *The Name of God is Mercy*, NY: Random House, 2016

I know that I am wretched because of my sin. I am eternally grateful that God forgives me. Thus, I'm moved to show mercy and compassion upon the wretchedness of others.

Who then am I to judge? At the end of my life, what will my judgments and opinions amount to? Yet compassion, mercy, and acceptance will bring me closer to God and to the people he created.

Mercy is among the greatest treasures I want to store up.

TRUST AND SURRENDER

It is a difficult challenge to trust. This act requires vulnerability, faith, and the willingness to take risks. Perhaps the biggest risk is the acknowledgment that someone else is in control, someone more powerful or knowledgeable than we are. We depend on our senses, reason, and beliefs to carry us through the world. To defer these habits to the competence and will of another requires a transformation of personal orientation and identity. Yet, what can life be without depending upon others and giving up at least some control?

Trusting comes from innocence or desperation. We lose our innocence quickly, so most trust grows from a desperate need to connect with someone who can do or give what fulfills our need. Trust we must, for none of us can go it alone. Surrender goes against the grain of determination and independence. But surrender brings peace and humility; it is also compatible with perseverance. Trust is necessary to surrender with dignity and hope. The foundation for this confidence is found in God's character and promises. This is the basis for handling and bearing with all that is overwhelming and unmanageable.

Physical life is temporary. So are pleasures and achievement, no matter how intense or grand. In a world of shifting shadows, dubious reliability, changing allegiances, and the passing of all things created, our creator gives us glimpses of the truly valuable.

IV

LOSS

CHAPTER 14
LOSS AND TRAUMA

The aftermath of losing Neal brings great waves of sadness and unexpected periods of emotional distance from life. One might think that this is normal and to be expected after losing a loved one. But I am not used to being sad for extended periods, nor is it normal for me to feel persistently detached, regardless of the hardship or circumstances. Even writing—which is natural, habitual, and fulfilling for me—takes more motivation and effort than I am used to.

While I am in this funk, the well-intended and authentic platitudes offered by others (and which I also know are true) fall on me like incidental rain. They bring me back to reality, focus me on sensation, remind me that I should be refreshed, but mostly heighten my sense of vulnerability. "Time will heal," "Be kind to yourself," "You did everything you could," "I am so sorry," are all true and offered in compassion and comfort. Yet my comfort is limited. I am in the throes of a life injury to my soul. I toss and turn, yet cannot find a sustainable position of rest and comfort.

The thoughts come and go, and I am not much surprised by their visitation. Nor do I obsess. The perseverative restimulations occasionally cascade, but I am steady and experienced at weathering them until they fade. I am proficient at dispatching negative thoughts and emotions, and I practice this on myself with routine success. I am rarely bothered by flashbacks, even in these early stages of traumatic loss. My tools for eliminating negative emotions and my generally healthy stability serve me well. I am humbly grateful for all the condolences and for the efforts of people in my life to take time out, step forward, and express themselves (not easy for many in this regard), solicit how I'm faring, and offer help.

Still, I struggle. Bouts of crying descend upon me like rapid and unpredicted storms. Though I am physically healthy and my self-regulation, rest, and digestion are normal, well-tuned, and satisfying, it seems to take more energy than I have to get through most days. Fatigue I can bear, but creeping disinterest worries me. It is so important that I exert my best efforts and succeed at caring for and meeting the needs of others. Despite my intent and efforts, I find myself drifting away. I fight this drift, bring myself back, and function well. I'm confident that I serve people and perform my duties competently. But there is a tear in my heart, a hole in my soul, and I wonder if these will ever mend. I get hungry and eat, but I do not enjoy the food as much as I remember. I engage intimately with my wife and bask in the affection and closeness we share. But I feel so alone. I do not *feel* depressed, yet I know that I *am* depressed. I exist within a cloud.

After losing Neal, I question the importance of what I do. I don't seek reassurance from people; indeed, I rarely mention these ruminations and do so only out of compunction to share with my very small inner circle so that I do not succumb to withdrawal. Yet I wonder and worry—an unfamiliar habit for me—whether what I do really makes any meaningful and lasting difference in the lives of others. When I reassure myself with *facts* about my contributions, I still allow that I may be rationalizing and self-justifying. Do I deceive myself with aggrandizement of professional contribution and community citizenship? Do I review my good deeds only to justify my need to make a living and bolster my self-esteem?

As I ricochet between my emotional despair and my ability to positively spin and cognitively reframe, I realize I am lost. My faith—hope and belief in what is not yet seen—sustains me, as do my memories of managing and prevailing through hard times on the wings of God's help. I know that God has rescued me before, and I hope that he will find me again soon.

It is so valuable that people seek to console and comfort me. I trust that I am socially skilled and present enough to accept their offerings graciously and to make them feel ease and reward for extending the efforts. I know it must be quite uncomfortable for them too. Death is so inconvenient.

Surprisingly, I find it so painful to read the sympathy cards when they arrive. I suffer through them with bittersweet thanks and put them in a file. I find it too hard to review photos and videos of Neal, though I do not turn away from them when others share them. Neal frequently comes up in conversation, a natural and seamless bridge between the past and present, as he rightly fits into the flow of family, friends, business, and natural memories. It is when thinking of the future, a future without him, this harsh interruption of the flow, that I choke.

I am not one to wallow. I treat self-pity as excrement. I know that when life kicks me, I collect myself and rise with determination. Since I learned to defer to God's way of doing things, this gift has served me well. But now, I drag along with sadness, fear, and loneliness, this heavy ball and chain, this devastation of loss and apartness.

Should I be different? Where are the lines between pretense that everything is or will be OK and relinquishing myself to the throes of mourning and despair?

People confide that I am living everybody's worst nightmare: losing a child. But I certainly do not identify with any selection, privilege, or righteousness in suffering. In the context of what I see, my pain and damage is far less than that of others. I tend not to complain much—an achievement born of many laborious years, akin in pride to the accomplishment of losing weight—but I struggle to discern when feeling pain and licking my wounds is really being in touch with myself and when it glides into self-absorption and the seeds of resentment. I am lost. My compass is God and his promises. But I am cold and lonely, aching and vulnerable, exposed in a predatory world that moves forward inexorably. I am stuck and waiting, waiting for and on God.

The loss of my son is a catastrophic injury. He is a part of me, not attached like a limb but a genetic distribution. Though I am whole, I've lost a part of myself nonetheless. It is a trauma that has shaken me. Though I look the same and this disappearance is not physically or perceptibly observable, I've lost an important and valued part of myself. I fear that I will never be the same and that the healing will be incomplete, that the scars will bear ugly reminiscence and nondissipating hurt.

During more composed moments, I reflect on the self who remains after this tragedy. Who am I, who was I, and who will I be? Of what fabric, relationships, experiences, and identity am I composed? When God takes something away that I took for granted, how am I to relate to all the other things I assume are mine? I know they are temporary, but I am still attached to them.

Though not of this magnitude, I have lost many things, people, belongings from different dimensions—parents, friends, clothing items, jobs,
opportunities, and even physical capacities. Some of these losses were more
shocking than others. The misplaced or stolen possession can usually be
replaced. Like so many people, I have become accustomed to relief and
comfort provided by material replacement or acquisition. A car is totaled,
and a new one takes its place. A blossoming relationship or appealing opportunity often lessens the hurt or lament over something that is gone.
One learns to move on, and the healthier one is, the smoother the path is
for moving on. Overcoming past hardships, in turn, makes one healthier,
sturdier, and more resilient in the face of the inevitable new challenges that
wait around the bend in life's twisting road.

Not all loss is traumatic, and much that we lose can be taken in stride.
Many losses, however, are traumatic, and trauma has unique characteristics.
It tends to paralyze our coping mechanisms and keep us stuck emotionally.
We relive the traumatic event in emotional memory, and thoughts about
the event become fused with the startling and debilitating emotions surrounding the trauma. As with many setbacks, the ancillary effects of trauma usually diminish over time. But the core of trauma often lives within
unless deliberate and effective steps are taken to offset and even eliminate
its devastating impact.

We can lose things without necessarily being traumatized. Conversely,
however, trauma itself always involves loss. Whether or not the loss is material, there is inevitably a shocking loss of control. To be traumatized is
to lose the sense of being in charge and the associated assurance of order,
predictability, and justice. Trauma brings a fearful loss of protection, an
exposure and vulnerability previously and conveniently forgotten.

In the traumatized state of vulnerability, when the taken-for-granted
state of OK-ness is shattered, a person questions the validity of his or her
own coping resources and independence. Which is more real—the me who
can handle things, or the me I feel now, the me who thought I could handle
things, but now sees that this was an illusion?

Is there any light far down this tunnel? Any silver lining or redeeming
growth from this traumatic catastrophe?

During the recent aftermath of my great loss, I pondered these questions through raw pain and blurry overwhelm. I am ejected from known
comfort zones, shattered with grief and humility, and left with little in

the way of sensible explanation and emotional organization. How does one recover from loss and adjust to the new normal? What will that be like?

In the wake of Neal's passing, my overriding concerns have been comfort, safety, and security. My vulnerability reprises these needs. Comfort, safety, and security are the filters through which I now peer at the world, a threatening place capable of wresting from me that which I hold most dear and necessary. In this state of oversensitized vulnerability, where I must gradually trust my own feelings and control again, I gravitate magnetically toward that which palliates and comforts.

CHAPTER 15
COMFORT, SAFETY, AND SECURITY

We are creatures of habit. We thrive on structure and predictability, interspersed with adventure and novelty and punctuated by periods of surprise and suddenness. It can be hard to adjust, to alter one's habits, to acclimate to change. The saying goes, "It's hard to teach an old dog new tricks." Regardless of this insight, we do depend upon what we know, and we use knowledge and experience as base camps from which to venture into bolder and less secure territory.

Some of us are more wedded to sameness, preferring to take comfort, confidence, and sustenance from the tried and true, the known and predictable. Some people have greater needs for diversity and thrive on change, spontaneity, and the freshness that novelty brings to seeking and restlessness.

Whether you like structure, predictability, and sameness or thrive on variety and the stimulation of novelty, you have faced and will face losses. Therein lies a common challenge: accommodating these losses and adjusting to being without the items needed, wanted, felt deserved, or taken for granted.

A BREACH OF SECURITY

Loss is a breach in comfort, safety, and security. When we lose something valued, a primal sense of threat is aroused. Consciously or not, we mobilize nervous system physiological response to loss, along with emotions and thoughts compatible with the heightened alert that threat induces.

Significant loss is a *home invasion* that violates boundaries we assumed were safe, protective, and reliable. Loss can bring an onslaught of negative feelings, encumbrances, and excessive sensitivity to normal emotions. Among these are:

- grief
- sadness
- depression
- helplessness
- threat
- violation
- loneliness
- incompleteness
- abandonment
- longing, missing
- breaches of attachment
- dependence
- confusion
- anger
- resentment
- guilt
- self-recrimination
- wounds and scars
- wrenching compassion
- posttraumatic flashbacks
- obsession
- interference with competence, use of resources, or opportunities

BREACHING MY WORLD

I have experienced many of these since Neal died. The persisting detractors for me are sadness, grief, loneliness, confusion, helplessness, wrenching compassion for my son and the pain that fueled his need to escape and seek temporary comfort in a drug-induced stupor, and a deep and inconsolable craving for his companionship and love. We had a special bond that so expanded my experience of life. Being Neal's father, watching him grow, noticing his talents, ruing his mistakes, worrying about his flaws, taking pride in his accomplishments, encouraging and cheering him on, and taking on the obligations and making the sacrifices one does for a child—all of these but a pittance that in no way diminishes the joys and fulfillment of parenthood. They are the price of parenthood, one that in raising some children can be more costly, frustrating, challenging, and demanding than with others. Yet suddenly, the costs, frustrations, challenges, demands, sacrifices, joys, and fulfillments come to a screeching halt as Neal is wrested away from this life. To my limited mind and heart, it seems so cruel and wrong.

Neal was not innocent. Yet he paid the ultimate price while others who make similar mistakes and sins escape. Why? My heart wails in anguish and confusion. He was a sheep led to slaughter by his own folly, circumstance, hubris, and the unforgiving reality of natural laws.

Because of who I have grown to become, I can only experience all of this in the context of a loving and forgiving God, an all-powerful and discerning God, who chose to take from me (and others) a child so precious and dear that I would trade anything back to reengage with him, even with his difficult personality and selfish, frustrating behaviors. It is all so confusing and way beyond my intellect and emotional power to comprehend.

I am an old dog who thrives on routine. I have won my awards, and I am house-trained even into my later years. Despite the aching, aging body, I still romp and exercise, caught up in the movement, work, variety, demands, hedonism, and persistence of the daily world going 'round. My conservative nose draws me to sameness and predictability, the tried-and-true that soothes and satisfies me.

Though I am mostly a loner, I enjoy people (in limited doses as I get older), and I delight in the dispatch of social skills I have long practiced, along with the sacrifice and service that increasingly occupy my time and heart as I mature. According to the world's terms, I am well-adapted and reasonably self-sufficient, regulated, productive, and content.

Now, there's emptiness—sudden, comprehensive, and new. It's not that I've never been depressed, desperate, or bereft. I've lived decades filled with overcoming deficiencies and mistakes. What's new and different is facing disintegration when I am accustomed to being whole. Now, I am whole, but with a hole in me. And I seek comfort and people to salve the hurt and fill the hole. I feel recurring waves of need. At times, I feel like a bottomless pit into which caring people could jump and still not fill me up.

DESPERATELY SEEKING

I want security, a promise that this will stop hurting and will heal and that this monstrous experience of separation will disappear and never happen again. I struggle in doubt and despair, fearing that whatever reparations may come will be insufficient. My reason—the same reasoning powers that fail so miserably to explain and cope with my son's death—tells me that I am asking for the unobtainable. So I sail in search of a safe harbor, alone and lost, seeking comfort, safety, and security, somehow knowing that they exist beyond the storms that frighten and threaten me.

Where then lie comfort, safety, and security? Reason and logic fail to suffice; emotions are ephemeral and consuming, repositories of transience, carrying moments of succor interspersed with prolonged illusions of continuity. What can palliate this grief and loss? Can anything make me whole?

My restitution lies in the spiritual domain. The same mighty power who has limited my logical understanding and given me emotions like waves of the sea has arranged everything from beginning to end. Nothing comes to pass without God's jurisdiction and supervision, his allowance and provision. What he does *to* me or *for* me I interpret with self-centered interest; the limiting solipsism of my thoughts, feelings, senses, and prideful entitlement; and the illusory satiety of self-pity.

The comfort, safety, and security God provides come from the realization of his promises when I am in relationship with him. This includes the peace that passes understanding (Philippians 4:7), his many invitations to cast anxiety and burdens on him (1 Peter 5:7), and his everlasting presence and sameness (Hebrews 13:8). God reaches out to me and responds to me in many ways. Some of these ways are supernatural, and some are ordinary. He carries me through mystical realms by his surrounding presence. When I cry out to him, he draws close to me and soothes me with reassurance. His promises provide security (Matthew 4:20, Hebrews 13:5). He allays my fears and extinguishes their flare-ups. His comforts are many and penetrating.

The conundrum that God is always there even though I cannot access him with my senses is both frustrating and reassuring. The belief that he knows everything and can fix everything conflicts with my present pain and wanting to have my way now. What it boils down to is that I'm in a loving and dependent relationship with someone who has different ideas and intentions. The challenge is to trust and accept and to become and remain whole and loving when I cannot change the will of my beloved. Beyond this trial is the notion that the will of this other being to whom I relate is wiser and better for me than my own.

When I direct my energies to following reliable leadership, when I believe in trustworthy promises, I find comfort and relief. On the material plane, it helps that I know my mind and body and am accustomed to providing supervision in attending to their needs. I have learned that my mind and body can behave like siblings, sometimes uniting in cooperation, adventure, and enjoyment, and otherwise squabbling to the point of contention requiring stern intervention, lest there be destructive results. Toward the goal of equanimity, I revel in routine and deliberately practice habits that are healthy and make me feel good.

I subscribe to the ancient wisdom of physiological influence, experiencing habitually that my body's self-regulation and stability dictate my mind's self-control and adaptability. I worship daily the God who designed this marvel. I respect the sanctity of my body as a housing for my soul and spiritual being; thus, I strive to care for it and keep it as free from contamination as I can.

I find comfort and satisfaction in my work. Though work fatigues and often drains me, I feel needed and blessed to have some refined skills and clients who want to benefit from them. I am busy with purpose, knowing that God is watching. He could take my activities, relationships, and resources away at any moment. Rather than feel threatened by this, I find it refreshingly reassuring that God must approve in order to let me keep what I have.

How strange that painful loss can produce appreciation for and security in what remains! It is a blessed revelation, learning to possess and enjoy without being possessive.

Since my son's passing, I experience an increased need and yearning to be around people. It is not that company allays anxiety, because I am not anxious. Instead, it is that I now find human connection warm and comforting. Even the multitude of annoying habits of others is outweighed by the comfort derived from proximity and connection. This old dog feels better with familiar routine and in the presence of people he knows.

And who is more central than my wife? I bury my head in her chest, and she absorbs my tears, stroking and soothing me and staunching sporadic wailing. We have lost a child! Somehow, we must carry on, strengthen each other, and tend to this penetrating wound.

God and my wife are my bastions of support. I need them now as ever, praying and waiting to be lifted up. I am hanging on; like a weakened animal searching for food, I seek comfort, safety, and security for my survival. My beloved son is gone. I hang on but must learn to give up and let go.

CHAPTER 16
VULNERABILITY, HURT, AND GRIEF

LIFE BRINGS PAIN AND ANGUISH

Each of us has felt pain. To be human is to know hurt, anguish, and the tempering wisdom that we are indeed vulnerable. Even the hardiest and most resilient people know that they are not invincible but instead are susceptible to a spectrum of potential impingements and losses.

When we grieve, we palpably experience the vulnerability that intertwines with attachment and loss.

It is said that pain is a powerful teacher. Pain teaches us to be wary and careful and, to some extent, mistrustful. Pain provides sensory and emotional stimuli that remind us what to avoid and how to move in the world in order to stay safe and experience satiety, relief, and comfort.

Pain and distress come in different forms and intensities. From the gnawing of hunger, fear, or loneliness to the intense agony of injury or trauma, feeling hurt is an unwanted but inevitable signal that we are, indeed, vulnerable.

Life involves biological, social, and psychological development that tunes the precarious balance between an individual's competence, power, and control and his or her flaws and vulnerabilities. Though much has been written about the tragedies of history and human character, little is described about the role of *vulnerability* in managing survival. We know much about what can make us sick and hurt but less about how this knowledge can strengthen us and be used to advantage.

By vulnerability, I am not speaking merely of what makes us fallible and mortal. Vulnerability is what makes us physically and psychologically susceptible to attack and to breakdown from life's events and forces.

THE REALITY OF VULNERABILITY

Each of us is born with genetic codes that make us who we are—male, female, white, Asian, short, tall, slender, stocky, and so on. As part of these genetic codes that comprise us, we also inherit *vulnerabilities*. These are the weak links that allow us to become ill or dysfunctional in a myriad of ways. They are the genetic underpinnings for the conditions and struggles that become our individual destinies.

To validate this for yourself, examine your own struggles in the context of your family history and heritage. Ask these questions:

- What physical and psychological maladies do I or have I struggled with?
- What afflictions have my family members (extended back through generations) struggled with?
- What has caused my family members to die?
- What substances (foods, medicines, intoxicants, environmental conditions, allergens, and so on) cause me intense discomfort or adverse reactions?
- What types of weather do I like and dislike?
- What types of skills and activities do I enjoy, and what am I good at? What activities and skills are difficult or unpleasant for me?

Even a cursory review of your preferences, health status, and family history will provide stark and perhaps startling clues about your genetic vulnerabilities.

It is readily observed that conditions and predispositions tend to run in families. Illnesses such as heart disease, diabetes, schizophrenia, and so forth are noticeably more common in some family lineages than others. So are predispositions to depression, anxiety, allergies, ADHD, and a long laundry list of maladies.

Conversely, positive traits also run in families. This is evident in the proud generational recapitulation of skills and talents. Perhaps you are from a musical family, or perhaps, like your parents, you have a mechanical aptitude. Maybe you have the gift of gab, and you come from a line of talkers and those with capacious verbal ability and glibness.

The tenets of heritable characteristics are not news. However, from these reliable observations, we may draw inferences and conclusions that are strengthening and life-changing, specifically the following.

1. Though you are born with precise genetically coded information influencing your predisposition to and probability of developing certain afflictions, *these vulnerabilities are not deterministic—that is, they are, to some degree, likely but not inevitable.*
2. By becoming aware of your own vulnerabilities, you can develop a lifestyle and habits that guard against an increased likelihood that you will develop and succumb to your vulnerabilities.

In other words, even if diabetes or depression runs in your family, you don't have to fall victim to these maladies. Vulnerabilities make you commonly human, but they do not make you, per se, a victim. You play a significant role in your destiny, and you make a myriad of choices that shape small outcomes and large futures.

The particular hurts we experience and the patterns of infliction upon our vulnerabilities have a profound impact on who we become and how we weather the impending and cumulative hurts, losses, and grief that living invariably unfolds.

VULNERABILITY AND LOSS

Becoming and staying healthy requires that we are aware of our own vulnerabilities, the weak links in genetic predispositions, habits, temptations, and potentials. By gaining knowledge and exercising vigilance, we can minimize the probability of and impact from our susceptibilities. No guarantees, of course—but why not increase the odds of health and resistance?

The relationships and interconnections among loss, trauma, attachment, vulnerabilities, and health are evident. The take-home message is summed in the following two points:

1. Well-developed, practiced, and healthy attachments make accommodation of and adjustment to losses much easier and the recovery from their traumas much shorter and more complete.
2. The more accumulated and the more severe the traumas in one's life, the greater the likelihood of significant impact from loss.

It is with these insights that we seek to recognize and heal trauma and to consider what we have to lose and how to expect, cope, and deal with inevitable losses.

V

WHAT DO YOU HAVE TO LOSE?

CHAPTER 17
MORTALITY

It is obvious that we are all going to die. At various points in the unfolding and contracting of our mortal coil, we think about dying, the brevity of life, and losing someone; we think about these in different ways and with different degrees of concern and emotion.

Thoughts and feelings about the finiteness of human life occur in keeping with our life-stage maturity and with the advent of loss or potential loss of someone near and dear to us.

In accordance with mental development and the advance of conceptual and abstract thinking, children begin to appreciate the notion of *object permanence* in toddlerhood—that is, the assumption that an object doesn't cease to exist when it is not visible or tangible. It is quite a revelation that things have an existence and durability independent of our presence or act of appreciating them. This milestone precedes the ability to think of *permanence* shifting into *impermanence*—the realization that things and people can *go away*. Transformation may happen, but it is beyond the purview of young minds to make sense of it. Food disappears into the body, plants wither, garbage gets picked up and carted off, and family members, neighbors, and friends move away. And, yes, living creatures die.

When a young child tragically loses a parent or other loved one to illness or accident, a reassuring explanation is provided to help the child come to grips with the loss. "Mommy is in heaven, and she's watching over us." "God is taking good care of Fluffy, and he misses you too." These palliatives are necessary to reassure the child that he or she will be cared for, to protect against the angst of abandonment (and the reality of being, at least partially, left behind), and to help the child build cognitive and emotional resources to process and adjust to the loss. It is a reality of life that the child will need to deal with sooner or later, along with other inevitabilities and uncertainties that require adaptation. Growing throughout life requires that we modulate the practice of control with the recognition and acceptance of what we cannot control.

Helping people cope with loss—walking alongside them with sensitivity and availability—is an exquisitely intimate endeavor, a sharing that combines support, compassion, empathy, and companionship in the face of powerlessness. It is also a means by which we confront our own vulnerability, neediness, and eventual mortality.

By the time we reach adolescence, we develop the ability to think abstractly, to know that death is irreversible, and to appreciate intellectually that people live within a certain range of years. We study general science in middle school, usually become attached to pets, and typically marvel at the reproductive cycles and life spans of different species. By and large, we become knowledgeable about why organisms die—but to what extent do we really *understand* death and the brevity of life?

The explanations we espouse are highly personal and individual and are influenced by such factors as our cultural background, religious beliefs, level of education, and environment. For many, mortality is unpleasant to think about. Youth is often more easily able to dismiss it, but not always. Some folks (occasionally including children) are preoccupied with the morbid, and we generally find it difficult to interrelate for extended periods with those whom we consider to be morose. They often seem to be struggling and suffering with anxiety, depression, or obsessiveness. Interacting with people who are preoccupied with their own death (when it is not imminent) can be depleting. On the one hand, the factual certainty of death cannot be denied; on the other, in order to function, fulfill, and enjoy, we must focus on life's continuing demands and pleasures and its duties and rewards.

The struggle with mortality is universal, and some have turned it into an art form. Woody Allen, for example, has become notorious for his fixation on death. He lends comedic genius to his angst and neurotic preoccupation with attempting to reconcile the issues of meaning, hedonism, and futility in his own life. Allen bares his conflicted soul, which perceives that "Life is divided into the horrible and the miserable." In a noteworthy monologue, Allen lists reasons *not* to commit suicide—among them the delicious crab served in a New York Chinese restaurant. It's emotionally wrenching (and at the same time comedic) to see how this introspective battle repeatedly and thematically plays out in all of his films and, more often than not, brilliantly encapsulates his own doubts and his yearning to experience meaning, connection, and pleasure.

With his brilliance and unabashed angst, Woody Allen touches that nerve in those of us who ruminate about, fear, or repress coming to grips with the limits of life and our own brief place in its continuity.

It may be the need to reassure someone grieving the sudden or unexpected loss of a loved one, the onset of a threatening illness, an accident or near-death experience, the mourning of a highly respected public figure, or simply somber private reflections and ruminations that lead us to consider that, in the material world, we are temporary. It is an immutable truth that all of us must one day relinquish this mortal coil.

How does one prepare for or even think about this ultimate loss?

A good start is to think about *life*. There is an old saying that, "In order to ask a relevant question about something, you have to start by knowing something about it in the first place." Similarly, the notion of death presupposes the actuality of life. This is not distraction or positive thinking, but rather the epiphany that one's own life is a marvelous burst of creation in what seems like an unfathomable and extensive void.

Endemic to living are the instincts and striving for survival. Also, we have by nature a conscious thought process that fears and avoids *not* surviving. So when we experience or anticipate threats to survival, we think or fantasize about dying (and being absent, forgotten, nonexistent). To the survival-oriented, biologic, sensate system, such thoughts are frightening and confusing.

LIFE'S MEANING

It is no wonder, then, that the reality of terminal physical life propels us to find some meaning, order, or purpose for our time on earth.

People do this in different ways. Some immerse themselves in hedonism (*Eat, drink, and be merry, for tomorrow we shall die.* (1 Corinthians 15:32). Some strive for achievements or the amassing of wealth or power. Others find purpose in relationships, sacrifice, the building of a community, or the establishment of a legacy. And some dedicate their lives to serving others. At a very basic level, each of us *needs and wants to belong and to matter—to make a difference.*

No matter what we do or achieve, no matter how good or competent we are, we cannot escape the blatant and palpable reality that nothing is physically permanent. In tandem with that incontrovertible fact is the allied reminder that doing or being "good enough" is relative and only partially validated by some contemporary and supposedly objective societal standard or by one's own subjective assessments, rationalizations, or egotism. There's always the next event, the next leader, or the next new invention. But make no mistake. The current pinnacles will ultimately be surpassed. Some athletic superstars will, in due course, exceed all of the standing scoring records. And someone will eventually become wealthier than today's richest billionaire. All bodies and records are inevitably surpassed. The possibilities are seemingly infinite. And thus arises the need to come to terms with our *finiteness.*

Atheists and agnostics tend to believe that humans invent God and religion as a way of coming to terms with the randomness and inherent meaninglessness of life—a sort of false and insufficient psychological defense mechanism. I differ from that point of view on two counts; first, I am both sufficiently smart and psychologically sophisticated to understand that I am not capable of inventing, constructing, and connecting a schematic that is adequately elaborate, encompassing, and orderly to explain and justify my existence and the mysteries of the world. My brain does possess, however, the analytical capacity to recognize the inevitable fallacies that would be evident if I actually had the temerity and inclination to attempt to devise such a delusion and self-deception. Second, I have *information* and *evidence* (God's word and his manifestation in my life) that there is indeed a supreme and divine order and explanation for what I know and what I do not understand. This leads me to burgeoning peace and faith that someone is in charge of what happens in the past, present, and future.

This spirituality is both comforting and sufficient for me to feel taken care of and secure. It is also a basis upon which to accept the past and present and to be less worried about the future. The reliance on a power that overshadows my will and reasoning to account for mortality and loss leads me to the humility of surrendering to something unassailable, supreme, and greater than I am.

A SIMPLE METAPHOR

There is a riddle: *What moves on all fours in the morning, on two legs in the afternoon, and on three at night?*

The answer is a *person*, who crawls as an infant, walks upright in adulthood, and walks with a cane in old age and infirmity.

I am somewhere between the two- and three-legged stages. As I get older, I think more about certain topics (such as mortality, including my own) and differently about many others than I did when I was younger. I cannot perform (or carry out as well) many of the activities I did earlier in my life; others I can do much better. Aging, of course, brings physical limitations. Collaterally, in my case, getting older has favored increasing mental acuity and healthier relationships. For these things, I am so very grateful.

Aging also brings more of four cumulative existence-shaping elements: life experiences, perspective, wisdom, and losses. As we accumulate these, we become more aware of death—its impact upon us through loss, its hovering eventuality, and its pressure that drives each of us to come to grips with life, mortality, and what follows physical demise.

We also face coming to terms with our own importance as well as our finiteness.

Consider the following:

Take a bucket, fill it with water,
Put your hand in—clear up to the wrist.
Now pull it out; the hole that remains
Is a measure of how much you'll be missed…

The moral of this quaint example;
To do just the best that you can,
Be proud of yourself, but remember,
There is no Indispensable Man!

                                —Anonymous

WHAT GOD SAYS ABOUT DEATH

God is the master of life and death—the giver and the redeemer. His word, the Bible, speaks fully about life and death. An investigative biblical search reveals 1925 references to life and 1492 mentions of death. The creation and passage of life is endemic to God's plan. And life and death transcend the beating of hearts and the drawing of breaths. Human time is limited, but God's time is infinite and eternal. Our frail physical mortality is a fleeting mist in God's grand scheme. Yet each of us is precious and important. Behold what God says:

"Listen, I tell you a mystery: We will not all sleep, but we will all be changed—in a flash, in the twinkling of an eye, at the last trumpet. For the trumpet will sound, the dead will be raised imperishable, and we will be changed. For the perishable must clothe itself with the imperishable, and the mortal with immortality. When the perishable has been clothed with the imperishable, and the mortal with immortality, then the saying that is written will come true: "'Death has been swallowed up in victory.' 'Where, O Death, is your victory? Where, O Death, is your sting?'" The sting of death is sin, and the power of sin is the law. But thanks be to God! He gives us victory through our Lord Jesus Christ." (1 Corinthians 15:51–56).

"Then I saw a new heaven and a new earth, for the first heaven and the first earth had passed away, and there was no longer any sea. I saw the Holy City, the new Jerusalem, coming down out of heaven from God, prepared as a bride beautifully dressed for her husband. And I heard a loud voice from the throne saying, "'Look! God's dwelling place is now among the people, and God himself will be with them and be their God. He will wipe away every tear from their eyes. There will be no more death or mourning or crying or pain, for the old order of things has passed away.'" (Revelation 21:1–4)

As for this present life and beyond, God says:

…*"Never will I leave you; never will I forsake you."* (Hebrews 13:5)

and

…*"And surely I am with you always, to the very end of the age."* (Matthew 28:20)

CHAPTER 18
RELATIONSHIP LOSS

We are connected to the world through our abilities to bond with others, be in relationship, and maintain relationships with those around us. When important relationships falter, fail, or go asunder, we suffer great loss.

A relationship may be casual and short-lived, or it may be profound, intimate, and enduring. It may be platonic, romantic, familial, or strategic or simply reflect shared common interests, religious or political beliefs, aesthetics, or pleasures. In every case, it reveals a synergy and a mutually desired and valued connection. When it is profound and enduring, it is typically invested with emotions, expectations, dependency, reliability, trust, empathy, intimacy, effort, and regular interaction. A relationship is, thus, a living, dynamic, and synergistic entity that is characterized by a sense of belonging, kindheartedness, thoughtfulness, affection, concern, and responsibility.

Throughout life, we have many different types of relationships, some sequential or evolving (as in marriages), some overlapping (as in families), and many simultaneous (as in social friendships or job-related liaisons). We attach differing amounts of importance to various relationships, investing a great deal of dynamism in some and taking others more or less for granted.

We can also form relationships with things other than people, and we often value and bestow on these attachments significant care and attention. Some people *love* their cars, smartphones, favorite restaurants, treasured cities and countries, and cherished music, but these attachments are different from (and are not adequate substitutes for) forming quintessential relationships with people.

RELATIONSHIPS WITH OTHERS BESIDES PEOPLE

Though relationships with people should be foremost, attachments to nonpeople are also important; they add value and meaning to life, providing variety and enrichment. Pets, for example, are a great source of emotional attachment and self-regulation. They also help develop and reinforce a sense of responsibility and fidelity. They are wonderful friends, even with the obvious biological cross-species limitations. Animals can be great exchangers of emotion, and they often teach us about attachment and loss.

I remember that when I was in college, I had a sidekick German shepherd-husky dog with me constantly. In many ways, I practiced affection and responsibility by taking care of this dog at a time when my people skills and maturity were inadequately developed. One semester, I moved into a house with a graduate student who owned a collie. As we introduced ourselves and our dogs, I said, "My dog *thinks* he's human." My new roommate flashed a broad smile and retorted, "I understand. *My* dog thinks he's a psychiatrist!"

Projections and fantasies notwithstanding, we take our pets very seriously. For many people, the bonds that we develop with pets are vital relationships, enhancing emotional connection and providing companionship and fun. They furnish devotion and acceptance to lives that may be otherwise fraught with stress, insufficiency, confusion, and the overbearing or the ambiguous and taxing demands of other people. We suffer greatly when we lose these precious companions. When my first dog died a decade after I got him when I was in college, I was devastated and fell into a very deep depression.

We also form intense and consuming relationships with hobbies, possessions, and other inanimate objects. We may take pride in work done to enhance, restore, or enjoy a coveted acquisition. We may also become overly absorbed with a hobby or gadget that responds to us or provides feelings that counter anxiety or boredom.

These attachments can serve useful purposes, but there is also the potential for them to become idolatrous, consuming, and even addictive. And they should not substitute for necessary and sustaining relationships with people.

BELONGING TO PEOPLE

Many attachments can supplement and augment human relationships and the need to be *involved*. But relations between people are paramount to the needs and fulfillment of our human nature. It is how we are designed, and most of us spend our entire lives looking for worthy relationships and honing the ones we have and desire to improve.

Naturally, many relationships end, as this is also woven into the fabric of life. Though we may grieve the dissolution of a relationship, we eventually adjust, learn how to handle the parting, move on, and look for the many other fish in the sea. Sort of. Maybe. Perhaps at some points in life, we fare better than at other periods. Rarely is the end of an important relationship smooth or painless. And there are often scars and traumas. Having a relationship taken away from you can be devastating. Even when you are the one initiating the split, the emptiness and sense of loss can persist.

When a valued relationship deteriorates or dissipates, it's often difficult not to cling, imagine reunification, and review the what-ifs that might have saved the relationship. Maturity helps us console ourselves that there will be new relationships, ideally better ones and not just desperate substitutes. We rely on the reassurance from friends and from our own memories of surviving, recovering, and pressing on.

Alas, the surrogate comforts we indulge ourselves in, rationalizations we conjure up, well-meaning support and encouragement we actively or passively solicit from friends, and our own efforts to think positively often prove insufficient. We deeply *miss* the person and the relationship. There is an undeniable loss of both the beloved person and the concomitant, once joyful fulfillment that the attachment provided. The serrated blade of this loss can cut us to the core.

SURRENDERING RELATIONSHIPS

When it is clear that the relationship cannot be sustained, *surrender* is a redeeming path to peace and acceptance. Remember that surrender represents weakness and vulnerability leaving the soul and spirit. It is the renunciation of control and the capitulation to a force or will greater than one's own. *Surrender enacts the yielding of the object of attachment, not the ability to attach and to value and love.* When you surrender, you relinquish claim. Therein lies the peace that brings wholeness, regardless of possession or presence.

By surrendering to the loss of a relationship, you open yourself to adapting to new circumstances and not depending on what is no longer available. Surrender allows the process of carrying on to resume and to strengthen. Another gain is the comfort and peace that eventually accrues through acceptance. To live with what has occurred, to find new joys in the exercise of sacrifice, and to discover other attachments is to resume a life of connectedness and renewed resilience and hope.

Surrender creates a focus on the present and the future. It is a catalyst for healing. Surrender is the exercise of flexibility and deference, the acknowledgment of vulnerability, and the yielding to forces greater than one's own. Surrender helps replace the guilt, anger, frustration, and self-recrimination that often accompany relationship loss. Surrender usurps the role of blame.

When you surrender, you give up ownership and entitlement. You need not fight for what is no longer yours. You relinquish encumbrance and heaviness, and you trade continued responsibility for freedom and lightness.

Letting go of a relationship and surrendering to its loss does not mean that you give up your feelings. Instead, you become better able to feel your feelings purely. You experience them as triggered by and related to events but not mandated or continued by circumstances. You practice the graceful art of *detachment*. You exert this ability by harnessing the joint powers of your own self-control and that of the owner of all life who invites you by difficult circumstances to become humbler. Paradoxically, you learn to become less dependent on particular things and people and more dependent on the enduring promises of the one who gives all things.

Throughout our lives, relationships come and go, strengthen and weaken. Most of them ultimately dissolve with the passage of time and the development of new circumstances, opportunities, and needs in our lives. Some relationships never disappear (such as between parent and child or between siblings or best friends), although in some cases they may be torn asunder or so fraught with encrusted conflict and agony that one or both parties may try to avoid or disown the relationship. Death also happens, of course. But, in the words of writer Mitch Albom, "Death ends a life, not a relationship."

BEING IN RELATIONSHIP

There is a viable argument that living humanly is really about being in relationship with others. Some people are loners, and some become tenaciously attached to ideas, hobbies, causes, and material things. Yet all of us need other people. We cannot exist as islands, either materially or psychologically. Physical, economic, and social interdependence embody the natural order of things. Being *in relationship* means that you participate in these interdependencies. We all partake, though some of us do so more willingly, more consciously, and less selfishly than others.

Being in relationship and developing relational skills does not necessitate that you are a people person or that you become preoccupied with relationships, social neediness, or possessiveness. Having healthy relationships and relational skills presumes that you recognize the basic interdependence, vulnerability, and sacrifices that are endemic to establishing connections with others.

Relationships require models for what is involved and for how to give and receive from others. This includes acceptance of another person's faults and limitations and relinquishment of one's own possessiveness or entitlement to more than the relationship permits or the other person wants. Sustainable relationships reflect a commonality of shared values, such as the importance of love, dignity, honesty, and respect.

Relationships may end as a result of circumstances beyond our control. They may also dissolve because one or both individuals have boundaries or standards that are traumatically or repeatedly violated. The sweet joy of connection and love may lead to disappointment or heartbreak. Such are the risks inherent in loving and being vulnerable.

As discussed earlier, the capacity to create a foundation for *attachment* is critical to having and sustaining mutual and supportive relationships. When we are secure and when we can attach properly, we can give and receive in beneficial and fulfilling ways. This foundation also enables us to *let go* when relationships go awry or adrift and are clearly not sustainable.

The experiences of being in relationships and losing relationships saturate us with habits and expectations. For self-preservation and protection, we often attempt to insulate ourselves from openness, vulnerability, exposure, and trust as a defense against becoming hurt. As a result of this need to self-protect, we are at risk of sacrificing the intimacy we crave and forfeiting the resiliency to recover from the loss of the relationship. The compelling demand for safety, self-defense, and control can rob us of the freedom to love fully and retain an adequate measure of self-esteem should the relationship prove untenable.

Consider the words of Christian psychologist Larry Crabb:

The illusion that life in a fallen world is really not too bad must be shattered. When even the best parts of life are exposed as pathetic counterfeits of how things should be, the reality drives us to a new level of distress that threatens to utterly undo us. But it's when we're on the brink of personal collapse that we're best able to shift the direction of our soul from self-protection to trusting love. The more deeply we enter into the reality that life without God is sheer desolation, the more fully we can turn toward Him.

The richest love grows in the soil of an unbearable disappointment with life. When we realize that life can't give us what we want, we can better give up our foolish demand that it do so and get on with the noble task of loving as we should. We will no longer need to demand protection from further disappointment. The deepest change will occur in the life of a bold realist who clings to God with a passion only his realistic appraisal of life can generate.

Until we recognize with tears how determined we are to move away from pain and how that determination reflects our blasphemous decision to preserve our own life, we will not be able to identify the subtle ways in which our relational style violates love for others by keeping us safe. We repent by radically shifting our motivation and direction from self-preservation to trust on the basis of the belief that Christ has given and is preserving our life. The fruit of repentance is a changed style of relating that replaces self-protective maneuvering with loving involvement.

—Larry Crabb, *Inside Out*, 2007, NavPress,
Colorado Springs, CO

THE SUPREME RELATIONSHIP

Ultimately, there is an enduring relationship that never goes away. It is the eternal relationship between you and God. It is the foundational relationship that should establish and underpin your worthiness and belonging and serve as the model for all relationships. And it is the one relationship you can always depend upon, even to salve the inscrutable and sometimes devastating demise of other important relationships. Your relationship with God—which is dependent upon your choice to have and exercise that relationship—is the one that can enhance and grow all your other relationships, and it remains to sustain and comfort you when loss and disappointment strike.

...*"Never will I leave you; never will I forsake you."* (Hebrews 13:5)

...*"And surely I am with you always, to the very end of the age."* (Matthew 28:20)

CHAPTER 19
DIVORCE

About half of marriages end in divorce. It's a stunning fact. Though the stigma of divorce in American society is not what it once was, it is still a traumatic upheaval that tears apart families, decimates finances, and leaves scars and traumas that can affect people for a very long time.

Divorce brings loss that often multiplies and becomes increasingly devastating as the process of separating and untangling formerly joined lives relentlessly accelerates. There can also be relief in the separation or dissolution, especially as the tension that precedes the impending divorce siphons off the escalating pressure, frustration, and resentment. As the disillusioned partners individuate and assert themselves and their needs and wants, they may experience a range of intense feelings that include catharsis, sadness, liberation, self-righteousness, anger, and selfishness; they may have a sense that the split is for the best, that it's a smart decision, and that the union was doomed from the onset and the divorce was inevitable.

Make no mistake, however, about the fact that divorce represents a failure, regardless of the reasons. (Yes, there may be some people who strategically manipulate a marriage to gain money or some other advantage—such as citizenship—with the planned intent to dissolve the marriage once these goals are achieved. But such individuals who exploit the sanctity of their marriage vows represent only a small percentage of those who marry.)

Remember the vows of the marriage ceremony.

"Do you take this man/woman to be your lawfully wedded husband/wife, in good times and in bad, in sickness and in health, until death do you part?"

"I do."

Marriage is a solemn and sacred pledge of meaningful and enduring constancy and commitment in a world replete with inconstancy and ephemerality.

Reneging on this vow comprises a major breakdown in the family fabric. It is akin to abandoning one of life's major core elements, which is woven into the quintessential union that God intended to bind families together.

Divorce signifies the profound loss of hope and faith in what was once deemed to be a stable partnership for life. Divorce also has profound implications for collateral costs—finances; access to children, family members, and mutual friends; security; trust in love; identity; status; companionship; and unfettered participation in cherished child-rearing activities.

No one relishes these consequences, and yet they happen in conjunction with the very common pattern of adversarial relationship dissolution where lawyers and accountants often become involved.

Sometimes, people will say, "We just couldn't communicate." However, a wise and experienced marriage counselor has noted, "Divorce is an attempt to stop communicating." In other words, sadly and ironically, alienated partners do understand what each other has to say—they simply don't like it and are tired of listening to the messages. Thus, they split. For better or worse, the former partners go their separate ways. Perhaps they leave a trail of attempted reconciliations, sacrifices, efforts, and glimmers of hope that the embers of passion will reignite; perhaps there was once hope, dashed again. Often, the decision to divorce is unilateral, and the momentum toward its conclusion is all but unstoppable.

SEPARATION FROM HOPE

Divorce brings more than the loss of a partner and a lifestyle. It carries with it a loss of hope. Where there was formerly the anticipation of a developing and enriching future with a spouse, there appears instead emptiness and failure in its wake. Divorce decimates hope for that marriage relationship. There is no next season for the team.

Surely, people move on and adjust to their circumstances, and many find new love. Indeed, most people in second marriages report satisfaction with the marriage as better than their first. We can assume that people learn from their mistakes, that they mature and become more giving, understanding, and responsible. A failed marriage is devastating, but it is not necessarily a showstopper in life.

Even the most resilient and adaptive victims of divorce must weather the loss of hope. That is a monumental task. What does one do when faced with dashed dreams and hopes—when all the eggs in that basket of security, care, and attention have been broken?

Foremost in recovering from the trauma of divorce are the spiritual and psychological aspects of dealing with the battering of hope. The outside world may sympathize with your breakup and with your disrupted family, financial woes, and spousal and legal battles, but the struggle with lost optimism is a personal and private affair. It is between you and God, and it is at the crux of your relationship with him.

When your marriage crumbles, hope is taken away. It is a profound loss that challenges faith and may impede constructive motivation. The intense and ambiguous feelings that accrue from marital atrophy may spill over into one's attitude and relationship with God. This tragic life circumstance thrusts upon center stage the underlying feelings of entitlement, expectations, confidence, and the human plan for how life should work out. Suddenly, there is defeat! *How can this happen to me? And why?*

Marriage is a unique relationship; it is created and given by God with its incumbent blessings, structures, obligations, and responsibilities. In context, however, the uniqueness of marriage assimilates into the pattern of attitudes and expectations that constitute our character and reactions when life doesn't treat us the way we want or foresee. The manifestation of how we react when things don't go our way is the big issue of our identity, happiness, and relationship with the creator. Marriage and divorce (when it occurs) are crucibles for shaping our character.

In my book *Living Intact: Challenge and Choice in Tough Times*, I attempt to address many components of these broad life challenges. Specifically, the notion of expectations (as they manifest in our desires and sense of entitlement) becomes paramount in our capacity to understand and adjust when things don't work out as we might have wished. In dealing with the disappointments, demoralization, disillusionment, despair, loss of hope, and search for potential recovery, an understanding of the role that expectations play may be helpful.

LESSONS IN EXPECTATIONS

We all have expectations. They are a product of the conscious mind, the conglomeration of previous learning, the images of things to come, the desires for what we want, and the beliefs about what should happen. Without expectations, we could hardly plan or build models and concepts of the way the world operates. Expectations help us predict, categorize, and simplify. They form a cornerstone of what we know as reality. At a biological level, expectations propel our survival by guiding behavior toward fulfilling our physical needs and functions. Animals in the wild go where they expect to find food and water. People act in ways that they think will bring rewards. At a physiological level, expectations gear our nervous systems to states of arousal necessary or appropriate for anticipated physically or emotionally sustaining events. At a psychological level, expectations drive the mind's narrative to support evaluations of experience and predictions of what will happen next.

Certainly, marriage partners have expectations of each other and expectations of the course of and fulfillment provided by the union.

There is, however, a downside to expectations; desire, need, or faulty evaluation can drive expectations to the point where hopes are dashed, beliefs are unrealistic, and disappointments prevail over sensible satisfaction and fulfillment. Examples abound. A student is rejected by his or her first-choice university. A loyal employee is passed over for a promotion. A house doesn't sell for the asking price during a real estate market downturn. A spouse exhibits selfish or inconsiderate behavior and fails to meet the other's needs. Hopes and expectations are unmet and left wanting.

Expectations are mediators between reality and desire; they help us navigate through the world as it is toward the world we wish to create.

Your expectations are your assessments, your plans and schematics, aspirations, and maps of the world and yourself within the world.

GREATER AND LESSER EXPECTATIONS

Expectation connotes a general meaning with subtle nuances and variations. An expectation is a confident belief or strong hope that a particular event will happen. It can serve as a standard of conduct or performance demanded or anticipated by or of somebody. An expectation may also be a mental image of something awaited that can often be incongruent with how one's desires play out.

The term *greater expectations* indicates results hoped for or desired. Whereas *greater expectations* involve aspirations, ambitions, imagination, wishes, and dreams, *lesser expectations* refer to the results realistically anticipated based upon previous experiences and conditioning. *Lesser expectations* involve predictive validity, accuracy, boundaries, practicality, and directions.

> *Expectations reflect your conscious and unconscious assessments, plans and schematics, and maps of the world and of yourself within the world. Expectations unfold at different levels, and these levels mediate the ways that you want things to be (great expectations) with the ways you have learned through experience that they are likely to play out (lesser expectations).*
>
> *The difference between your greater expectations and your lesser expectations approximates your satisfaction and disappointment in life. It is an indicator of the extent to which you reconcile the outcomes you get with the way you would like life to work. It is also a reflection of the way you balance reality testing with desire.*

We may extrapolate that when a marriage dissolves, there has been a steady deterioration in the fulfillment of expectations, particularly *greater* expectations. It is in this morass of discouragement and hopelessness that turning to God and relinquishing futility can lead back to hope and restoration.

God gives the best living examples of his extraordinary capacity to express and model all-embracing compassion through his word (the Bible), the person of Jesus Christ, and his Holy Spirit. These mark the way for you to experience hope in your everyday circumstances. God wants to relieve your discomfort, and he gives you spiritual and secular tools to do so. He wants to strengthen you through trials and tests so that you may attain endurance and tolerance. He wants you to proactively rewrite your life story and to allow you to be filled with compassion and hope in carrying on and flourishing despite hardships. This is called transformation.

Consider 2 Corinthians 4:7–9, which says,

"But we have this treasure in jars of clay to show that this all-surpassing power is from God and not from us. We are hard pressed on every side, but not crushed; perplexed, but not in despair; persecuted but not abandoned; struck down, but not destroyed."

And Romans 5:2–5:

And we rejoice in the hope of the glory of God. Not only so, but we also rejoice in our sufferings, because we know that suffering produces perseverance; perseverance, character; and character, hope. And hope does not disappoint us, because God has poured out his love into our hearts by the Holy Spirit, whom he has given us.

Your mind's narrative gives voice to your expectations, and your narrative takes for granted your desires and your sense of entitlement. These feed into the formation of greater expectations that portray what you want and hope to get.

However, you must temper greater expectations with the reality imposed by your experiences. Divorce brings a wake-up call that your previous expectations will not be realized.

Greater expectations are inherently prone to inflated impressions. They generally make you envision the upside and place a positive spin on what you anticipate. The antidote is to possess a positive attitude coupled with discernment that can help you temper pie-in-the-sky optimism and blindsiding disappointments. You need lesser expectations—inherently more conservative—to modulate the inflated expectations that often (subconsciously) accompany a sense of entitlement, eagerness, and intensely focused desire to attain an objective that might be overlaid with wishful thinking.

We need greater expectations to energize our outlook, give us incentive, and buttress our self-image and sense of worth and potency. We require lesser expectations to dethrone us from pedestals of self-importance and privilege.

If divorce does puncture your greater expectations and deflate your hope, then you are in a submissive position before God to ask him for help in adjusting and rebuilding your life.

When life appears unfair, when disappointment, rejection, loneliness, and frustration abound, seeking to understand reality through God's eyes invariably assuages the pain and tempers the disillusionment. Greater expectations represent what you want, and lesser expectations summarize an often imperfect and unsatisfying world. Focusing on God's expectations will help you resolve the inherent differences, breakdowns, dissatisfactions, and discrepancies that result from our desires for what life should be and our actual experiences living life.

Divorce is a devastating loss. You may wonder what you did wrong or why God did not grant you a peaceful and fulfilling marriage. You may vacillate between anger and resentment about your doomed relationship and guilt that you couldn't stick it out and succeed.

God understands. He has pain when we have pain. He wants us to share it with him. He wants us to look to him for guidance and to surrender to what he rescinds and what he offers. If your marriage is in distress or deep conflict or has ended in failure, turn your sorrows, recriminations, and guilt over to the Lord. Be ready to surrender when failure overtakes you. Know that there is a heavenly perspective that salves your grief and accommodates your loss.

In the morning, O Lord, you hear my voice; in the morning I lay my requests before you and wait in expectation. (Psalm 5:3)

Set your mind on things above, not on earthly things. (Colossians 3:2)

Do not conform any longer to the pattern of this world, but be transformed by the renewing of your mind. Then you will be able to test and approve what God's will is—his good, pleasing, and perfect will. (Romans 12:2)

Marriage is a holy investment of hope and expectations. When our expectations are not realized or made manifest, we can rely for peace and hope on the care, protection, and promises of God—even when the world and the course of our lives pulls in unsatisfying directions. In Romans 5, Paul is explicit about how to deal with discrepancies in our experiences and yearnings.

> *Therefore, since we have been justified through faith, we have peace with God through our Lord Jesus Christ, through whom we have gained access through faith into this grace in which we now stand. And we rejoice in the hope of the glory of God. Not only so, but we rejoice in our sufferings, because we know that suffering produces perseverance, perseverance character, and character, hope. And hope does not disappoint us, because God has poured out his love into our hearts by the Holy Spirit, whom he has given us. (Romans 5:1–5)*

Does this mean that through our hope and faith, God will fulfill all expectations, compensate for each disappointment, and grant every desire? Surely not! If you want support and validation for the insufficiencies, lack of closure, unfulfilled promises, and unmet expectations you have suffered, then look to Hebrews 11 and you will find yourself in good company. This scripture spells out the meaning and examples of faith, listing its historic role in so many well-known anticipated promises.

> *Now faith is being sure of what we hope for and certain of what we do not see. This is what the ancients were commended for. By faith we understand that the universe was formed at God's command, so that what is seen was not made out of what was visible. (Hebrews 11:1–2)*

MY OWN DIVORCE

I am among the many who have been divorced. For decades into my marriage to Barbara, I believed that divorce was not an option. I took my vows seriously and, in my Christian walk, was determined to make the marriage work. I know that divorce breaks God's heart.

After years of trying everything I knew to save the marriage, I came to the realization that God would allow me release from my marriage. Although I'd known for years that the relationship was extremely unhealthy and dysfunctional, I was committed to sticking it out. The following factors changed my mind and my decision:

1. My children were grown.
2. For a number of years, Barbara had increasingly withdrawn from me and from the marriage—physically, emotionally, and financially. She showed no participation or commitment to engage in our marriage relationship.
3. Over the course of years of advice and counsel from my pastor, I came to understand that when there is rebellion, Scripture allows the unbeliever (Barbara) to leave, and in that circumstance, the believer (me) is not bound (1 Corinthians 7). I had done everything I could, yet Barbara had persistently and progressively chosen to leave our union.

My divorce was painful, adversarial, and costly. It took a long time. It left scars.

I was fortunate in that I remained psychologically healthy (though often stressed). I was able to provide for my children and to be there for them (although they were away at college most of the time).

After my divorce, I was blessed to find new love and a new wife. Though I had intended to remain married to my first wife, I survived divorce to become more mature, more flexible, more appreciative, and a better husband. Though I was a good and faithful spouse to Barbara, I rue the mistakes I made, and I wish I could have avoided them.

Countless times I have revisited thoughts about what role my divorce and our family breakup might have played in Neal's difficulties and demise. I review the what-ifs and realize that I may never apprehend their impact. I know that Neal had great difficulties with his mother during our marriage and after our divorce. Without reservation, I encouraged him to communicate regularly and to be in good relationship with Barbara. He had much resentment and anger toward her, and he chose to secede. Though Barbara made efforts at conciliation, it just didn't work between them. I cannot blame her.

Neal's relationship troubles were internal as well as between him and others. He also rejected Giulia (his stepmother), despite her persistent attempts to nurture him and the abounding maternal love she felt for and showed him. Somehow, he couldn't develop the trust and affiliation to let people in and to forge healthy bonds of closeness. This was tragically the case in his relationship with females—in particular with mother figures.

For me, a significant loss from divorce was the loss of hope that my children would have a continuous, intact family. The realization that my paternal leadership and all my efforts to reconcile and to compensate were not enough to help them sustain a maternal bond has been devastating and humbling.

I have surrendered all this to God and allowed him to lead me to continuing acceptance and new glimmers of understanding about what a well-meaning parent can and cannot do. My limitations are human, but God's powers and will are unlimited, even though I cannot fully understand them.

I relinquish my hurts, and I seek God's forgiveness and grace. He has given me two marriages and has blessed me with children. He's allowed me to experience love and the vulnerability that love entails. He's given me a wonderful life partner in Giulia.

I am so thankful, even though the losses hurt.

SURRENDER AND ACCEPTANCE IN FAILURE

If you have experienced divorce or are in the throes of an antagonistic or uncertain marriage, my heart goes out to you. I empathize with the agony, the mixed and volatile feelings, and the sense of diminution and belittlement that result from an inconsiderate or hostile former love.

Alas, many propitious and sacred unions go asunder. Divorce is tragic, but it is the end neither of hope nor of God's care and the extreme value he places on you.

Even when people abandon you, when you are rejected and lonely, God knows what you need and how to rebuild you. Reach out to him; you will find him waiting and welcoming!

CHAPTER 20
LOSS OF BODY FUNCTION

As we get older, things happen to our bodies. During the earlier stages of life, this is usually exciting and gratifying—we gain capabilities, strength, and autonomy as we develop and mature. The genetic codes that lie within us gradually actualize and manifest who we were meant to be.

Motor skills develop, the nervous system matures and differentiates, hormones kick in, and the brain becomes more connected and capable of higher-level and more integrated functions. We grow through the wonders of childhood and the pressures and strains of adolescence and gradually emerge as adults, ultimately able to survive and thrive independently.

This is an outline of the ideal, of course. It happens generally for most but not everyone. There are accidents, injuries, birth defects, developmental anomalies, and a myriad of traumas that can beset and derail normal development and functioning. Even in the prime of life, any person can be afflicted with a disease or accident that could derail the normal or previous operation of his or her body.

We are flesh and blood and bones—vulnerable and mortal by nature and design. In the vigor of good health, energy, and vitality, we take for granted what is obviously only temporary.

That our physical body is mortal and temporary does not (and should not) deter us from trying to preserve it. Survival instincts propel us, of course, to protect ourselves. Added to those instincts are the innate biological mechanisms of healing, the wonders of modern medicine and technology, the psychological ego's desire to look and feel good and strong, and the social impetus and reinforcement for remaining youthful, competitive, and vigorous. All of these combine to spur us to take care of ourselves and to nurture and strengthen what we have.

Each of us lives *within* a body and *with* a body. By that, I mean that we are bound to physicality and natural laws, even though most people realize that life is *something more* than the body. Some people wholeheartedly identify with their bodies in terms of looks and performance. Their identity and most of their efforts are geared toward keeping up appearances. This is a large part of our world—the culture of beauty, youth, winning, recognition, and material glory. It rubs off on us and appeals to our innate sense of wanting to be recognized and loved.

Alas, the quest for physical supremacy and endurance is a losing battle. We all wear out. In his pithy quotes about values and life observations, my father liked to say, "People wear out; money doesn't."

I'd like to focus on the people-wearing-out truth; we all eventually diminish in physical capacity. The loss of body function and prowess may be attributable to three main causes: aging, injury or trauma, and disease.

AGING

There is a natural and genetic core to the manner in which each person develops, ages, and eventually wears out. There are both common and individual patterns with many exceptions and anomalies sprinkled throughout humanity. Nowadays, people generally live longer than in previous times over the last few thousand years. There are the unusual folks who live into their nineties and some beyond a hundred years. Most people deteriorate within a shorter span; to live into old age is a mixed blessing—the survival instincts and cherishing of life along with the perspectives and wisdom are offset by the inevitable deterioration in health, comfort, functioning, and independence.

If your life is not cut short by accident, illness, or traumatic misfortune, eventually your body will wear out. It is the unavoidable destiny of human mortality.

Many worship at the altar of the fountain of youth's lifestyles and remedies. Most of us are certainly interested in living longer. Yet no matter how healthy you are, the process of getting older will diminish your body, in some ways dramatically more than others. My eye doctor cutely and diplomatically ascribes changes in vision to "having more birthdays."

It is interesting for me to observe as a neuropsychologist how many people expect and resign themselves to diminished memory and mental functioning in their fifties and sixties. Although many people do suffer cognitive loss at early ages, diminished mental capacity is by no means expected in late middle age! In fact, if you live right and are fortunate to avoid trauma and serious illness, you can be quite sharp mentally into your nineties and beyond! There is a normal slowing of motor speed and neuroprocessing as we age, and these slowdowns accelerate as one approaches the age of about seventy. At the age of eighty and older, most people do need to slow down and not encumber themselves with the responsibilities, pressures, and diversity that they once were better able to handle. But the onset of dementia or cognitive impairment is not the norm and should not be anticipated in the absence of trauma or disease (including, as we may determine, specific genetic predisposition).

However, mental diminution and even incapacitation can happen, as can declining health and associated physical limitations. To some degree, they happen eventually, so we should not be surprised by an ensuing loss of body function.

INJURY

The process of living subjects us to impingements by the environment. The world is full of things that can hurt us; it's only a matter of time until we sustain injuries. These may involve collisions of sorts with what's around us, or we may strain, pull, or overuse parts of our bodies. Though we are built with vulnerabilities, we also—fortunately—come prepared with the innate capabilities for healing. The combination of our biological recovery mechanisms, proper self-care, and the blessings of modern medicine allow us to rebound from many injuries that would otherwise leave (and historically have left) irreparable impairment and limitations.

Nonetheless, we all accumulate scars and hurts. The traumas may be cumulative or the damage so significant that we are left with permanent disabilities or limitations. The constraints imposed by injury may be uncertain, may change over time, or (as in the case of paralysis, for example) may be sudden and devastating.

Sometimes, it's hard to know or predict the healing and recovery from injuries. Many times we have setbacks or perhaps reinjure part of ourselves, not realizing the fragility that prevails. Injuries may beget injuries, especially for those who are vulnerable because of age or infirmity or even those with supposedly robust bodies because of the physical challenges and risks undertaken in sports.

We are all vulnerable, and we all get dinged by interactions with the environment. For many people, injury initiates the onset of debilitating pain and loss of the previous use and flexibility of body functioning. The degree and extent of limitation varies widely. One person may have to refrain from participating in a favorite sport or activity. Another may not be able to sit or stand without substantial pain. Many pains and limitations resulting from injury are temporary; others are ongoing or permanent.

Regardless of the manner of onset, the common experience for many is the frustration of not being able to do what was once natural, easy, and enjoyable. Injury is one way that God rescinds capabilities and freedoms we once took for granted.

DISEASE

Health is the desire and goal of almost everyone. Whether by worship, ardent lifestyle, or just prudent self-care, everyone wants to avoid illness. Yet illness and disease are the pariahs that stalk humanity.

We are the beneficiaries of better medical care, better nutrition (or at least more of it), and consequently longer average life spans and reduced early mortality rates than our ancestors. In other words, the conditions that killed most people at younger ages throughout history are no longer the scourges and threats they posed for millennia.

Sure, there are HIV, rampant heart disease, diabetes, cancer, and so on. Some folks take the fatalistic view that one thing or another is going to claim you sooner or later, so you shouldn't fret but live life fully without compulsive worry or restriction. Ideally, this is not a rationalization for careless self-indulgence. The premise is correct. However long you live, however carefully and healthfully you live, something will get you eventually. That something is likely to be disease, along with aging and possible injury to boot.

Our bodies wear out, and we succumb to disease processes that prey upon and overtake us. When an octogenarian gets cancer or has a stroke, we may say, "Well, that's tragic—but at least he had a long and full life."

It is arguably more difficult (if not similarly excruciating) to confront the reality of childhood cancer, a sports injury resulting in paralysis, or a rare disease that robs someone of body control in the prime of life.

Why does God take these things away? What possible motive, rationale, or justification could he have?

I don't have the answers. I, too, am afflicted. I've lost a son and many people I've loved as family. Though I am relatively healthy, I suffer the pains and limitations of aging, and I wonder (and *sometimes* worry) about the future decline of my body. I have heart disease, and I suffer the racking pain of arthritis and musculoskeletal degeneration on a daily basis. Though I exercise, things are not what they used to be—and I *miss, oh how I miss*, the strength, agility, and endurance I took for granted over many decades!

So, what is to be done? How are these losses to be encountered and handled?

I see that the primary and foremost adaptive response is to refrain from blaming God for taking away what he once endowed me with. It is a formidable and continuing challenge. A capable and pain-free body seems my entitlement—until I realize that I am *on loan*, all of me. My capabilities and fortitude comprise a debt that must be repaid with the forfeiture of function and ownership of my body.

With what resources and resolve can I face such monumental surrender? I can with the confidence that God gives me more than he takes away! He gives me eternal life, a certainty not yet realized in this mortal body. He gives me promises of a new body and a life where there will be *no death or mourning or crying or pain* (Revelation 21:4).

ADAPTIVE RESPONSES TO LOSS OF BODY FUNCTION

With the assumption that reduced or lost body function exacts great corporal and psychological tolls, there are ways to cope with such deterioration and loss. Along with the spiritual dimension that may partially explain and comfort us, the following can be helpful in addressing the body's functional losses.

RECOGNITION

The first step in dealing with declining or lost body function is to acknowledge what is happening. If you become suddenly injured, it won't be hard to recognize the pain and impairment. Such occurrence often overtakes and overwhelms you. In many cases, though, you may not recognize or understand the signs and symptoms for a while. Sometimes, a medical test or procedure can reveal a problem unknown to or unacknowledged by the patient.

I never knew I had cardiovascular problems until I took a stress test and failed it. I never had any symptoms (and still don't!). However, I underwent an angiogram and found out that I had three blocked arteries. Thus, I had angioplasty vascular surgery to implant stents for this condition.

On another occasion, I had a recalcitrant bladder infection that led me to several urological exams, including an imaging study. From that study, I found out that I had calcification (stones) in my kidney. This was unrelated to my bladder infection but was revealed as part of my medical exams. Again, I've been fortunate to have never experienced any symptoms of or problems with kidney stones. The bladder infection eventually cleared up, and I am left with the prudent knowledge that things are happening in my body of which I should be cognizant.

In contrast, I am *painfully* (physically and psychologically) aware of my musculoskeletal problems—arthritis and the progressive deterioration of my joints. Old injuries, genetic predisposition, and aging all contribute to my pain and physical limitations. At my height (5'6") and the height of my athleticism, I could never dunk a basketball! In my late fifties, however, it became apparent that I could not dribble or shoot a basketball without searing pain in my wrists. Numerous doctor visits and procedures have left me with an understanding and conclusions about what I can and cannot do about my conditions. Two knee surgeries have compromised many of my athletic endeavors and have compelled me to make some lifestyle changes. These events have helped me choose my activities more judiciously and anticipate what my future likely has in store in this regard.

Oftentimes, people have trouble recognizing or admitting that their bodies are not working quite the way they used to work. This may be due to the gradual onset of various conditions and to the denial of the reality of these conditions. Unfortunately, this can lead to injury and accelerated deterioration. The aging or injured athlete doesn't want to recognize or admit to lesser performance, so he or she powers through and perhaps suffers serious consequences. Or someone may get a headache or a shooting pain and only after repeated occurrences seek an examination. Subtle signs may precede more onerous symptoms or even a traumatic onset, such as a tumor or stroke.

As part of the aging process, many people notice that they are not as quick or agile as they were previously. More fatigue, a stumble here or there, a wound or cold that requires longer healing and recovery—these are some indicators that the body is losing flexibility and resiliency. Both subtle and blatant signs of body function loss often cause people great anxiety. Fearing the unknown, imagining the worst, and being inadequately prepared to adjust to changes can hamper clear awareness and adaptive adjustment.

We all wear out; don't be surprised. And don't overreact.

ADJUSTMENT, ACCOMMODATION, AND INTEGRATION

You've heard the exhortation about "rolling with the punches." This somatic metaphor is apt for making adjustments and accommodations for the lessening of body functions. These may be temporary, as in the case of a recoverable injury. Or, they may be enduring or even permanent. Whatever the case, you will have to adjust to your newer limitations and functional levels as time elapses.

There are several factors that facilitate healthier and happier adjustment. Experience, maturity, and familiarity with change are most helpful, as are family and community support, adequate medical care, psychological self-regulation and flexibility, and, especially, a sustaining spiritual faith.

Part of rolling with the punches involves making changes in lifestyles and activities that are conducive to dealing with particular physical limitations. You may have to find new ways of doing things, seek help and support for tasks you used to do independently, or give up certain activities that are no longer feasible. (I can no longer play basketball or run long distances, but that does not stop or excuse me from participating in other suitable forms of exercise.)

Yes, there may be sacrifices and perhaps transient regret over lost prowess. But God has a plan for you, even though that plan may include rescinding your former capabilities or parts of your independence. Positive adaptation can hold the excitement and promise of discovering new ways of doing things, new hobbies or healthy practices, and even new and sustaining attitudes and relationships.

When I was in graduate school, I played basketball for hours at a time, and I used to run about six miles a day. Besides being in great shape, I was highly dependent on these activities, both physically and psychologically. Then I was badly burned in a fire. I couldn't walk for weeks. I could barely sit up. I am thankful that I healed and was spared permanent disability and disfigurement. During this period, however, I was "crawling out of my skin" physically and psychologically. The excruciating pain was compounded by my severe restrictions in mobility and exercise. I had to find some release. So I took up yoga and stretching. From this challenging and unfortunate accident emerged a lifelong healthy habit of body discipline and restoration that has improved my body and enhanced my well-being. Long after healing from the burns, I retained a resource that expands and sustains me, even through progressive body deterioration.

There's an old riddle: *What moves on four legs in the morning, two in the afternoon, and three at night?* The answer: *a person—who crawls as an infant, walks upright as an adult, and uses a cane with age and infirmity.*

I have an inside joke with my wife. She likes to watch the popular TV shows *So You Think You Can Dance?* and *Dancing with the Stars.* Besides her being accomplished in art, music, and theater, my wife is considerably younger than I am. So I tease her by saying that I want to watch the shows "for very mature audiences only": *So You Think You Can Stand?* and *Dancing and Seeing Stars.*

If you are fortunate to be able to dance, remember that eventually it will get harder. At some point, you may need a cane to get around. Enjoy what you can while you are able. Be prepared to make adjustments, as that is a necessary and inevitable part of life.

A FAMILY EPISODE

My mother suffered a series of disabling strokes when she was seventy-five. Though she was previously a distinguished educator and one of the most verbal people I've known, the strokes left her with brain damage that included language impairment and persistent word-finding difficulty. I'm sure this perplexed and greatly frustrated her, but she managed to remain positive, overcome discouragement, and find ways to compensate (often by relying on others—something she was not accustomed to doing before her brain injury). Her impairment even produced some twists that she was able to appreciate and take in stride. I remember an episode when she called the local Walgreen's and asked if they had vacuums on sale. She had forgotten the word *thermos*. The following exchange ensued:

"Vacuums?" intoned the clerk. "I don't think we sell vacuums. You lookin' for a big vacuum or a small one?"

"A small one," said my mom, "for coffee."

"Coffee?"

"Yeah, you know, to keep coffee warm."

"Ma'am, I don't know whatchu want, but we don't have anything like that."

Undaunted, my mother called the Target store.

"Hello, I'm looking for a vacuum, a small one."

"How small, ma'am?"

"One I can sit with in my lap."

"In your *lap*?"

"Yes," my mother continued, "to hold in my lap."

"Why you want to hold a vacuum in your lap?"

Frustration lapped at her patience, as my mother answered this doltish inquiry, "So I can drink from it."

"You want to drink from a vacuum?"

"Yes, haven't you ever used a vacuum to keep coffee warm?"

"I-I-I don't think I can help you. Maybe you should call Sears." Click. Next...

"Hello, I'm interested in a vacuum."

Silence. "Appliances, may I help you?"

"Yes, I need a vacuum, please."

"An upright or one with attachments?"

"Well, I'm not sure," Mom faltered. "What kind of attachments?"

"Suction hoses, wide hard bristles," came the reply.

"I don't think so. That might hurt my dentures."

"Excuse me?"

Confusion engulfed Mom, as the salesman questioned impetuously. She was not used to such obstacles in purchasing an ordinary item. Mom was always an excellent communicator, a savvy consumer, and competent at getting things done.

"What do you want to use this vacuum for?"

"For liquids."

"Ah, so you want a wet vac?"

"Look, mister, I don't know what's so complicated. I just want a vacuum for hot or cold liquids, like coffee or iced tea," declared Mom.

"How much liquid?"

"A cup, maybe two."

"Ma'am, couldn't you just use a sponge?"

This episode became a family joke, and my mother was able to laugh at herself good-naturedly despite the embarrassment.

My mother's elderly decline produced unexpected blessings. Always a hard-driven, domineering person who had to accomplish and be "on-the-go," her strokes caused her to become even *sweeter* as a person. Though I wouldn't wish such trauma on anyone, I reveal in candor that my mother's loss of function somehow made her stop and smell the roses. She became more of a listener, and she was easier to be around, even with having to watch her carefully and take care of her. Years after her strokes, my mother's diabetes resulted in debilitating pain and a double leg amputation. Toward the end of her life, she couldn't eat, and her last few months were sustained on a feeding tube. Yet she remained outwardly in positive spirits and exuded interest and gentleness toward those around her. She was able to accept help and care gracefully, and she was a joy to be around. She seemed to appreciate life more, even as it slowly ebbed away from her. In her painful and limiting decline, my mother was somehow able to roll with the punches. To me, she is a model of graceful adaptation to what God takes away.

ACCEPTANCE

Consider the following homilies: "God grant me the serenity to accept the things I cannot change, the courage to change the things I can, and the wisdom to know the difference" (Reinhold Niebuhr) and "Take kindly the counsel of the years, gracefully surrendering the things of youth" (Max Ehrmann in "Desiderata").

These verses remind us of the wisdom and value of acceptance and of keeping things in perspective. Loss of capacity to function is an expected part of going through life. It is part of the surrendering we all must endure. Learn to expect it, endure gracefully what you must, and focus on what God has given you and let you keep for a time.

Accepting limitations is far different from tossing in the towel. Acceptance reflects grace, wisdom, sensitivity, and maturity. There is beauty in ripening; yet all fruit must fall from the trees and vines and must grow toward ripening and decay.

Perhaps you or a loved one has suffered a traumatic and disabling injury. Maybe there is a diagnosis with a poor prognosis or terminal implications. You wait and endure uncertainty and the pestering worry that hovers and saturates like thick fog or humidity. You vacillate between tenacious clinging and fighting and the repose of acceptance and surrender.

There are no easy answers. God has made us fallible and yet has allowed us to nurture the folly of hubris and the fantasy of invincibility. Physical life has pleasures and struggles; in the scheme of things, they are common and fleeting. God gives us this struggle. He gives us life and gifts but also the realization that our possession of them is temporary.

> *Remember your Creator in the days of your youth, before the days of trouble come and the years approach when you will say, "I find no pleasure in them"—before the sun and the light and the moon and the stars grow dark, and the clouds return after the rain; when the keepers of the house tremble, and the strong men stoop, when the grinders cease because they are few, and those looking through windows grow dim; when the doors to the street are closed and the sound of grinding fades; when people rise up at the sound of birds, but all their songs grow faint; when people are afraid of heights and of dangers in the streets; when the almond tree blossoms and the grasshopper drags itself along and desire is no longer stirred. Then people go to their eternal home and mourners go about the streets. Remember him—before the silver cord is severed and the golden bowl is broken; before the pitcher is shattered at the spring, and the wheel is broken at the well, and the dust returns to the ground it came from, and the spirit returns to God who gave it.* (Ecclesiastes 12:1-7)

God wants us to wrestle with impermanence and fallibility. He designed loss into the human condition and existence. He wants us to practice surrender. The greatest surrender is the capitulation to his gift of eternal life, there for the taking by those who will believe and accept it. By virtue of this gift and this acceptance, the surrender of tangible things—even literal parts of oneself—becomes much more endurable and integral.

For many people, loss of body function is gradual and may be depleting rather than traumatic; rather, it results from typical development and progression through life. After having children, many women find it difficult to recapture their tone and sleekness. Menopause adds an additional dimension of aging and adjustment. Sometimes this can be a relief, but this passage can also be turbulent and confusing.

Men can become impotent or experience declines in libido or erectile functioning. There are treatments and compensations, but the adjustment can be very disconcerting. The writer Stephen King has remarked, "A man goes through seventy plus years of his life being led by his penis..." The implication King makes is that sexual preoccupation—even natural, biological sexual interest—has its narrowing dimensions; somehow the release from that drive opens up other areas of life to supplant a former preoccupation.

I am not yet at that stage, and I do not look forward to it. Yet I realize that decline is inevitable but may bring unforeseen blessings.

ATTITUDES TOWARD THE BODY

Throughout history, humans have tried to come to terms with the hardships that pervade life and precede eventual mortality. In general, religions and spiritual faiths develop beliefs and regard for the physical body that support and integrate their convictions about humanity's place in the universe and in time. Some creeds espouse beliefs about reincarnation; some regard the corporal body as an ephemeral and utilitarian "housing" for the soul and spirit.

Christian attitudes toward the body incorporate a broad view of embodiment that includes the physical individual body and the body of Jesus Christ as *incarnate* (actual, made flesh) and *spiritual* (the embodiment of God). The Bible speaks of the *body* in each of these aspects.

Biblical texts and references interweave mention of the body as carnal, spiritual, and communal. The common thread is Jesus as the embodiment of God, as represented to humanity. Jesus assumes a physical body (with human vulnerabilities and limitations) as well as a spiritual body in which he transfigures into an entity much broader and more encompassing than an individual body.

The Bible speaks of the body in multiple ways. It acknowledges possession, degradation, suffering, sacrifice, transformation, belonging, unity, and redemption.

We read in the Bible that God considers the different parts of the body as integral and designed to work together with no part entitled to predominance or greater importance. In 1 Corinthians, the apostle Paul makes comparisons between parts of the human body being dependent and indispensable with individuals and communities being parts and members of the body of Christ—the idea being that we all need each other and must depend upon each other and work together, just as the parts of our bodies do (1 Corinthians 12:12–21).

In Romans 12, Paul urges us to offer our bodies "as a living sacrifice, holy and pleasing to God" (Romans 12:1). Thus we glimpse a perspective on our bodies that puts pain, function, and belongingness in a different perspective; our bodies belong to each other and to God, and we are to view ourselves as sacrificial in service—we are important, but also flexible and expendable.

The theme of belonging and possession are echoed by Malachi 2:15:

Has not the one God made you? You belong to him in body and spirit.

In 1 Corinthians 6:19-20, Paul reminds us:

Do you not know that your bodies are temples of the Holy Spirit, who is in you, whom you have received from God? You are not your own: you were bought with a price. Therefore, honor God with your bodies.

Although the context of these verses is a warning to flee from sexual immorality, the exhortation also applies to the allegiance and belonging of our bodies wholly. We may infer that our bodies do belong to God and therefore he has ownership with the right to take back our bodies in whole or in part.

When our bodies decline or hurt, we suffer. It's instructive and strengthening to refer again to what the Bible tells us about suffering in the body.

Remember that Christ took on human physicality to bear our sins and he suffered in his body. Consider 1 Peter 2:24:

He himself bore our sins in his body on the cross, so that we might die to sins and live for righteousness; "by his wounds, you have been healed."

We see that Christ's physical suffering (as well as emotional and spiritual) and death heal us spiritually, but what about human suffering in the body? What about the pain and strife we experience in the here and now?

Consider 1 Peter 4:1:

Therefore, since Christ suffered in his body, arm yourselves also with the same attitude, because whoever suffers in the body is done with sin.

What could Christ's bodily suffering mean for our pain and the loss of our bodies? Christ suffered in his body to atone for our sins. By accepting his sacrifice, we acknowledge that the body in which we live on earth is temporary and subject to sin, a fleshly nature. To be done with sin is to accept Christ's substitutionary atonement and to yield our bodies, physically and spiritually, to him. In Romans 12:1, Paul urges us to "...offer your bodies a living sacrifice, holy and pleasing to God."

Thus, we are reminded that, even while living in our bodies, we are to offer ourselves to God. He is supreme and can do with our bodies as he will. This is a surrender for which we should be prepared.

It is painful and frustrating to lose the function and control of our bodies, even though we know that we are physically temporary. However, God gives other promises and enlightenment regarding the body. Paul tells us:

But our citizenship is in heaven. And we eagerly await a Savior from there, the Lord Jesus Christ, who, by the power than enables him to bring everything under his control, will transform our lowly bodies so that they will be like his glorious body (Philippians 3:20—21).

And,

We know that the whole creation has been groaning as in the pains of childbirth right up to the present time. Not only so, but we ourselves, who have the firstfruits of the Spirit, groan inwardly as we wait eagerly for our adoption to sonship, the redemption of our bodies (Romans 8:20—21).

Experiencing the decline of one's body can be worrisome or agonizing. But for the believer in God's promises, there is hope and future glory beyond the surrender.

So it will be with the resurrection of the dead. The body that is sown is perishable, it is raised imperishable; it is sown in dishonor, it is raised in glory; it is sown in weakness, it is raised in power; it is sown a natural body, it is raised a spiritual body (1 Corinthians 15:42—44).

While in this body that wears away and is eventually taken from us, we should remember the following verses:

But we have this treasure in jars of clay to show that this all-surpassing power is from God and not from us. We are hard-pressed on every side, but not crushed; perplexed, but not in despair; persecuted, but not abandoned; struck down, but not destroyed. We always carry around in our body the death of Jesus, so that the life of Jesus may also be revealed in our body (2 Corinthians 4:10—11).

And,

Therefore we do not lose heart. Though outwardly we are wasting away, yet inwardly we are being renewed day by day. For our light and momentary troubles are achieving for us an eternal glory that far outweighs them all. So we fix our eyes not on what is seen, since what is seen is temporary, but what is unseen is eternal (2 Corinthians 4:16—18).

CHAPTER 21
LOSS OF POSSESSIONS

We are all trying to *get* things. Deriving from the basic biological survival instinct to procure food and shelter, our drive to acquire things extends into obtaining material possessions that we deem (or rationalize) as useful and necessary. But it's obvious that most of us living in the developed world of material affluence have and covet far more than is needed for basic sustenance.

When you are hungry, poor, or in dire need, the platitudes about material wealth not being satisfying can burn deeply, adding fuel to the fiery angst of needing and being without the means to meet these legitimate cravings. Much of the world endures abject poverty and hunger. Many go without shoes, adequate shelter, or sanitation and certainly without access to the medical care and technology that we take for granted.

In America, there are multitudes that cannot pay their bills or provide for basic needs, despite working or seeking work. There is much to say and reflect about inequity and injustice, but my purpose in this chapter diverges from life's unfairness and deprivation to addressing the universal problem of *loss*. We seek possessions. We acquire things throughout life. We try to hold on to them, but eventually, our things go away.

We form attachments to possessions, and some of us become overly invested in them. We can become idolatrous of material things or use them as the basis for our identities and motivation. We can even build hope around the acquisition of material goods. Let's face it: we need *stuff*, and for most of us, the money that allows us to obtain this stuff is very important in the scheme of our lives. It may sound like an overused cliché, but money does indeed "make the world go 'round." It can appear that everyone is chasing the almighty dollar.

Money—and what it can buy—signifies the ability to satisfy our survival needs; attain security, pleasure, and entertainment; supply the tools and vehicles for creativity, service, and edification; ensure the maintenance of our standard of living; and enhance the fabric of our daily lives. For many (as this is an embedded element of human nature), money may also be used as a tool for control and power.

Some pithy comedic sayings underscore the transcending cultural attitudes that are typically associated with having money in the American consumption-oriented society.

"Money isn't everything—but it's way ahead of whatever is second best!"

"Rich or poor, it's good to have money."

Though most of us exercise the innate desire to acquire things we need and like, some take this impulse to extreme lengths. You may be familiar with the biblical recounting of King Solomon's monumental explorations into the acquisition of material possessions and hedonistic pursuits. Alas, he concluded that no amount of things, pleasures, or achievements yielded any lasting satisfaction. He called it all "meaningless" and "futile." His surpassing riches and his efforts to manifest and employ those riches left him unsatisfied.

A different aspect of possessiveness is the phenomenon of hoarding. There are some whose incessant collection of things (often to the point of chaotic and filthy surroundings) shows a psychological disorder of obsessive compulsiveness. We may pity and regard such individuals with shock; however, many of us lead lives that abound with possessions that we don't use, can't find, or don't have room to store. Few among us have "just enough," and those who are wise discover that they can find contentment and joy in certain core possessions that are particularly precious or meaningful to them. A simple truth emerges: stockpiling possessions is no guarantee of increased pleasure. It simply guarantees the need for a bigger garage, a more crowded attic, and more stuffed closets and cabinets.

Then, there are those who renounce most material possessions in favor of a more ascetic existence and who strive for the satisfactions of service, self-improvement, or spiritual growth and enlightenment. There are people in contemporary society who have discovered that the rat race is not for them and who have constricted their lifestyles to lesser ambition, fewer material rewards, and, ostensibly, less stress and greater peace. For some, the unwelcome and anxiety-fraught events of job loss or lifestyle downsizing may result in a surprising adjustment to and contentment with less. Others take vows of poverty and devote themselves to helping the poor and downtrodden. They find satisfaction in humility and service.

Regardless of lifestyle or values, all people experience the loss of possessions. Setting aside ambition, greed, and drive, we must face the fact that things wear out, may become lost or stolen, or may no longer be appropriate for current circumstances, despite our emotional attachment to them. (Have you ever struggled with letting go of old clothing, trinkets, memorabilia, or other stuff that you simply no longer need?)

ACTUAL NEED AND SYMBOLIC NEED

The need for material things is quite real, and we should not belittle or diminish the efforts of people to acquire them. New clothing, a phone, or a car may serve legitimate needs. In tandem, the acquisition of such items easily coincides with the pleasure of possession and the enjoyment of owning and using them. For many, the opportunity to show off may provide satisfaction and confirmation of achievement. A large house in a more elite community, a new and luxurious car, expensive jewelry, and designer clothes may serve as testimonials to one's acumen and professional accomplishments or may be employed to elicit the envy of others who have less wealth and, thus, fewer costly possessions.

Material possessions meet actual needs and psychological needs, both rooted in our previously stated basic innate drives and requirements for survival and security. They may also meet our intrinsic needs to compete with our peers and achieve dominance and recognition.

Inevitably, though, we divest ourselves of things. But giving something up voluntarily is different from having it taken away. When things are taken from us, we experience a loss of control and trauma. At a visceral level, we feel threatened and exposed. We miss the things we've become attached to, and we wonder how we will fare without them. Few of us are affluent to the point where missing one's car doesn't really matter that much. There is actual need, and the experience of inconvenience and deprivation is amplified by the tangible absence of a critically important and highly functional possession.

But there is also *symbolic* or *psychological* need—an investment and projection of one's *self* upon objects. When my car is in the shop for repair, I don't feel completely like myself. Silly, perhaps, but for me, it's true. I may have to depend upon others, or (perish the thought) I may temporarily drive a substitute car without my accustomed music or conveniences.

For another example, I have several sets of cuff links and many neckties. I enjoy wearing them and derive pleasure from mixing and matching colors and styles. Recently, I could not find a particular and favorite pair of cuff links. I have others to suffice, but I've been obsessing about the missing pair. *Where could they be? What if I never find them? Can I afford to replace them? Should I?* When I can't locate a desired necktie among my collection, I can become irritated or obsessive. And if a favored shirt becomes torn or worn to the point of discard, I pine and rue its departure from my wardrobe.

There is absurdity to this, I admit, for I am discussing luxury. It is self-indulgent and arguably pathetic. However, for me it is emotionally very real, and it compels me to think about the nature of loss and the ways in which I react to it. I have lost other possessions, many of them far more significant than clothing items. I've never had a car stolen or had my home lost in a fire. On a scale of grand misfortune, I suppose I've been lucky. But on the continuum of trauma, I've had my share. And so have you.

Loss of possessions is not a competition involving comparative drama, scale, or relative value. It is a universal and ongoing experience that entails objective reality and subjective emotional attachment, symbolism, practical adjustment, reconciliation, and often spiritual surrender. The assigned worldly value of an item does not fairly correlate with its merit and symbolic importance to those who lose it. Whether we lose little things or big things, the manner in which we resolve our attachments is critical to our well-being and to our adjustment to life's imposing realities. It matters little if it's a diamond necklace or a pendant of sentimental value given as a Mother's Day gift—the loss may be equally painful and heartfelt and the acceptance of and adjustment to the loss may be equally challenging.

REPLACEMENT

Unlike living organisms, material losses can be replaced. Indeed, there are industries devoted to risk management, protection of assets, and the restoration of wholeness. Insurance is the business dealing with reconciliation of loss or harm.

The matters of reconciliation, replacement, and compensation do not fully address the issues of acceptance, emotional adjustment, and surrender.

Sometimes, the replacement is better than the thing replaced. Several years ago, a driver ran a red light and totaled my car. My insurance company paid what the old car was worth, and I ended up with a newer and better car than the one that was totaled. I certainly didn't plan or want the accident, and it was quite traumatic. In this case, the material loss was compensated by a replacement. It doesn't always work out that way.

Personal items of unique value may not always be replaceable. Even when things are or can be replaced, the trauma of loss may linger. When something valued is taken away, what remains is a lingering sense of our loss of control. This can be threatening, anxiety producing, and humbling.

Our lost possessions are not always replaced. Sometimes, though, God gives us something better, despite our not asking for it and despite our attachment to the prized possession lost.

OWNERSHIP

We are accustomed to owning things. The most obvious example is that of property. We are wired to want, seek, obtain, possess, and protect. Since antiquity, societies have maintained elaborate laws pertaining to the ownership of and rights to property. This has even extended to the ownership of *people* (unfortunately).

But the reality is that *none of us really owns anything—not even our "own" bodies*. Instead, each of us and all our possessions are gifts from God—bequeathed and temporary, despite what we may individually think or collectively legislate. Essentially, everything is *on loan* from God.

This doesn't mean that laws pertaining to rights and ownership may be ignored. For God hands down methods for rule and order and he appoints leaders to plan and enforce them; we are obligated to abide and obey. Although there are exceptions, the practice of following man-made laws is generally compatible with following God's laws.

Consider, though, that *ownership* is typically conceived as a legal term, rather than a spiritual one. In the spiritual domain, *ownership* and *belonging* have different meanings. Because we want and need things in our natural world and bodies, we assume that we are entitled to a variety of possessions, at least under certain conditions. But it's obvious that each of us will die and be unable to take possessions with us. Even legacies and inheritances can crumble.

From this perspective, the ownership of possessions is rightly seen as temporary. One's entitlement to things is limited. Thus, when things are rescinded, this can be accommodated as part of a continuing and natural process in which God gives and he takes away.

It is what we cherish and how we deal with attachment that can make this process a difficult problem.

WHEN STUFF GOES AWAY

Regardless of how materialistic you are or how invested you become in possessions, you will have things taken away. It is just a part of life. You may be careful with your belongings and fastidious in preserving them. Perhaps you are disorganized and tend to lose things that are important to you. Maybe you have been victimized by devastating trauma and have lost even your most basic possessions.

Whatever your situation, history, and reactions to having valued possessions gone, it's understandable that you experience loss and that you wrestle with memories, attachment, and the swirl of emotions that can accompany the loss of possessions. As mentioned above, the value of the item in terms of monetary or social importance does not equitably correlate with the sense of damage you may experience with such loss. On top of that, most of us tend to feel sheepish or guilty when we rue minor losses in comparison with the catastrophic losses suffered by victims of natural catastrophes or violence.

But the devastation of trauma (no matter how insignificant by comparison), the powerlessness caused by violation, the threat to our security, and the underlying peril to our sense of entitlement can make us prey to vulnerability and may elicit feelings of anger, resentment, insecurity, anxiety, anguish, and fear.

What, then, are constructive and viable responses in the face of losing material possessions? Here are some suggestions:

1. **Allow yourself to grieve the loss.**

    Grief is a natural emotion. Let yourself experience it, at least for a while. Grief can be a good way of saying good-bye and bringing closure to the loss and separation from the object of attachment. Grieving can help you get over the loss, and it should not be confused with complaining, resenting, or self-pity.

2. **Reflect upon the truth that God gives things and he takes things away.**

    Thank him for allowing you stewardship over the lost possession for the period of time you had it. Acknowledge that God has the right to take things away. Profess your recognition of and respect for this aspect of his power and sovereignty.

3. **Realize that you are a whole and complete person, even without the possessions you miss and desire.**

    You are not defined by what you have (or don't have). Not only will you survive the loss, but you can attain new freedom from unnecessary (or even idolatrous) attachment as you learn to live without the lost possession. Things come and go—you acquire and relinquish; yet commodities are not required for your true identity.

4. **Communicate with God about your negative emotions and confusion.**

    He accepts and understands our difficult feelings; he desires that we roll our burdens upon him.

5. **Take steps to eliminate or minimize trauma, discomfort, pain, and anguish.**

    Administration of Thought Field Therapy (TFT), either by a professional or by yourself, helps greatly in the elimination of trauma and negative feelings and in the reduction of unwanted attachment due to loss. (See my book, *Living Intact: Challenge and Choice in Tough Times*.) At times, it may be suitable and appropriate to replace the loss. But get rid of your trauma and negative feelings first.

6. **Forgive yourself and anyone else you blame or hold culpable for your loss.**

    You may have been victimized in the loss of something materially valuable. But you need not brood, blame, or nurture bitterness or resentment. Know that God is just and that he is looking out for you, even when you're hurting. As you miss the revered possession taken from you, ask God to forgive you for obsessing, resenting, moping, or clinging to it. If someone has taken from you illegitimately, ask God to forgive that person and to forgive you for your angry feelings.

7. **Reflect upon the future things you will receive (many unknown and unanticipated), and thank God in advance, asking him to supply your needs and wants.**

    It's true that God closes some doors and opens others. It's hard to envision future gifts and blessings when you're feeling the sting of present and past loss. Put your faith in what God will do for you, though it is not yet revealed. Speak to him and thank him for what he will do, even though you can't specifically name these gifts.

8. **Review all the many things God has given you and blessed you with; spend time in prayer and gratitude.**

    Count your blessings; name them repeatedly. Give praise and ratify God's faithfulness. Spend time with the almighty giver and creator, especially when you feel vulnerable, poor, inadequate, or needy.

9. **Realize that possessions come and go and—despite your attachments—they need not define you.**

    You are a precious entity—one of a kind—dear to God. Your "stuff" is like yesterday's news and weather. Greet the new day!

> *But godliness with contentment is great gain. For we brought nothing into the world and can take nothing out of it. But if we have food and clothing, we will be content with that.* (1 Timothy 6:6–7)

THE PARABLE OF THE MEXICAN FISHERMAN

An American investment banker was at the pier of a small coastal Mexican village when a small boat with just one fisherman docked. Inside the small boat were several large yellow fin tuna. The American complimented the Mexican on the quality of his fish and asked how long it took to catch them.

The Mexican replied, "Only a little while."

The American then asked why he didn't stay out longer and catch more fish.

The Mexican said he had enough to support his family's immediate needs.

The American then asked, "But what do you do with the rest of your time?"

The Mexican fisherman said, "I sleep late; fish a little; play with my children; take siestas with my wife, Maria; and stroll into the village each evening where I sip wine and play guitar with my amigos. I have a full and busy life."

The American scoffed. "I have an MBA from Harvard and can help you," he said. "You should spend more time fishing and with the proceeds buy a bigger boat. With the proceeds from the bigger boat, you could buy several boats, and eventually you would have a fleet of fishing boats. Instead of selling your catch to a middleman, you could sell directly to the processor, eventually opening up your own cannery. You could control the product, processing, and distribution," he said. "Of course, you would need to leave this small coastal fishing village and move to Mexico City, then Los Angeles, and eventually to New York City, where you will run your expanding enterprise."

The Mexican fisherman asked, "But how long will this all take?"

To which the American replied, "Oh, fifteen to twenty years or so."

"But what then?" asked the Mexican.

The American laughed and said, "That's the best part. When the time is right, you would announce an IPO and sell your company stock to the public and become very rich. You would make millions!"

"Millions—then what?"

The American said, "Then you could retire. Move to a small coastal fishing village where you could sleep late, fish a little, play with your kids, take siestas with your wife, and stroll to the village in the evenings where you could sip wine and play guitar with your amigos."

LOSING THINGS WITHOUT LOSING YOURSELF

In this life, you will gain and you will lose. It's natural to seek things that make you feel happy, interested, secure, safe, and entertained. To a great extent, the desire for things is wired into us, and it is also repeatedly reinforced. It's nice to enjoy possessions while you have them. We need things to survive. God knows this and supplies them.

But don't worship material things. You may not understand why cherished possessions are taken from you, and it may seem unfair, as your logical and self-justifying mind comes to the defense of your wounded emotions. However, *fairness* is relevant only in relation to the observance of some rule. (Without rules, there is no fair or unfair.) God is the ultimate ruler, and sometimes his decisions seem arbitrary. We may question the basis for his decisions as we plead and complain—but we may not challenge his authority and sovereignty. God has the final say.

Possessions are blessings, among the many gifts from God. You may covet them or miss them. Don't measure your security or identity by the things you have or don't have. Instead, see yourself as a precious creation, put here by God to revere him, enjoy what he gives you and how he loves you, and do good unto others.

And God is able to bless you abundantly, so that in all things at all times, having all that you need, you will abound in every good work. (2 Corinthians 9:8)

Do not store up for yourself treasures on earth, where moths and vermin destroy, and where thieves break in and steal. But store up for yourselves treasures in heaven, where moths and vermin do not destroy, and where thieves do not break in and steal. For where your treasure is, there your heart will be also. (Matthew 6:19—21)

"Therefore I tell you, do not worry about your life, what you will eat or drink; or about your body, what you will wear. Is not life more than food, and the body more than clothes? Look at the birds of the air; they do not sow or reap or store away in barns, and yet your heavenly Father feeds them. Are you not much more valuable than they? Can any one of you by worrying add a single hour to your life? And why do you worry about clothes? See how the flowers of the field grow. They do not labor or spin. Yet I tell you that not even Solomon in all his splendor was dressed like one of these. If that is how God clothes the grass of the field, which is here today and tomorrow is thrown into the fire, will he not much more clothe

*you—you of little faith? So do not worry, saying, 'What shall we eat?'
Or 'What shall we wear?' For the pagans run after these things, and your
heavenly Father knows that you need them. But seek first his kingdom and
his righteousness, and all these things will be given to you as well. Therefore do not worry about tomorrow, for tomorrow will worry about itself.
Each day has enough trouble of its own."* (Matthew 6:25—34)

*I am not saying this because I am in need, for I have learned to be content
whatever the circumstances. I know what it is to be in need, and I know
what it is to have plenty. I have learned the secret of being content in
any and every situation, whether well fed or hungry, whether living in
plenty or in want. I can do all this through him who gives me strength.*
(Philippians 4:11—13)

CHAPTER 22
LOSS OF OPPORTUNITY

When we think of *loss*, what springs to mind is the forfeiture of what was possessed. What's lost is what has been taken away, harmed, or somehow reduced. We don't typically think of loss in terms of what we never had.

Yet when it comes to *opportunity*, we may think of loss in terms of *potential* not realized or fulfilled. We have all sensed lost opportunities—chances for successful outcomes or acquisitions that never materialized; for example, missing out on a sale item or winning ticket, not getting a customer's order or business, rejection from a college or job application, a date that didn't happen or didn't go well, and so on. The list goes on and on.

I remember vividly a traumatic lost opportunity from my childhood. I was a very good speller and had won many spelling bees. I qualified to compete in the state championship, but, alas, at the time of the event, I came down with the measles, and couldn't go! At that time, I was devastated.

Lost opportunities may have been keenly desired and anticipated, such as expecting a favorable response to a request for a date when single or acceptance of a bid to buy a wanted house. The resulting disappointment of these unrequited opportunities may be very painful to assimilate at first, but, as they say, life goes on. Yet, many unreciprocated opportunities may represent very tangible losses, such as a defeat in a sports contest that results in elimination from the playoffs. The sting from these types of setbacks is sometimes more enduring, depending upon the degree of emotional and psychological investment in the particular lost opportunity.

We have all experienced disappointment in confronting and dealing with what might have been, what we were looking forward to, and what we conjectured should be rightfully ours. Some people, by nature, expressly seek opportunities, trying to make things happen and engineering personal gains by astute strategic and tactical planning and actions. Such individuals may envision potential because of their previous successful experiences and their need to continually achieve and establish new and more challenging goals for themselves. For example, many land developers have seen business and profit opportunities in geography that others have overlooked. And yet, it doesn't always work out the way one may plan and hope. Marriages fail, people get sick, accidents happen, putative friends disappoint, loved ones die, and the anticipated future opportunities vanish.

People who are more cautious may maneuver around opportunities until the prospects are carefully checked out or vetted, preferring to pour their energies and hopes into more predictable and secure endeavors. They may try to minimize disappointment, choosing to tolerate more limited gains as a viable trade-off to risky ventures and higher probability of disappointment.

Nonetheless, we all construct internal models of the world, including levels of expectation, that help us navigate the channels of opportunity through mediating hopes and ambitions with reality while concurrently assessing outcomes and probability. (I call these *greater expectations* and *lesser expectations*. See the "Loss of Innocence" chapter later in this book. For a deeper explanation, read the chapter on expectations in my book *Living Intact: Challenge and Choice in Tough Times*, where I expound upon the role that expectations play in our mental construct of reality and in our behavior and happiness.)

Using these internal models by which we construct our views of the world and how we fit in, and derive sense of what comes our way, we make continual choices about perceptions, opportunities, and consequences. As I've said in *Living Intact: Challenge and Choice in Tough Times*:

Choice is the continuing opportunity to individuate and form an identity, to exercise being you, to make a difference, and to make your mark on historical events.

Facing the challenge of choice will enable you to operate more competently in turning obstacles into opportunities and transforming brokenness into wholeness and living intact. Indeed, the fifth "secret" of living intact is *to be willing to embrace challenge as the way to turn obstacles and frustrations into opportunities and successes.*

So, you may view opportunities in the context of reconfiguring obstacles and frustrations. If you get into the habit of taking on the challenge of manufacturing opportunities out of your experiences, you will become much more focused on and enthused about present and future possibilities and will be less concerned about the disappointments of the past.

Lost opportunities can be challenges to refocus, understand ourselves, and prepare to move ahead. Just as challenges offer the opportunity to develop ourselves, so do mistakes, errors, and setbacks offer *new opportunities* to fine-tune our reality check and gauge our modus operandi. This process is typically called *learning from one's experiences* or *learning from one's mistakes*.

WHAT HAPPENS WHEN THINGS DON'T HAPPEN

Losing an opportunity represents the taking away of something you never had. Yet it can feel viscerally like it belonged to you (that is, should have belonged to you). It is a tricky and false temptation to count your eggs before they hatch. We all do this, as we all have expectations, ambitions, and desires. Without anticipating and acting upon opportunities, we would not be very motivated to organize and plan our behaviors to survive and accomplish.

The problem, however, is that opportunities can also become *entitlements*—situations, things, and people's actions that seem to be our due. Out of need and expectation, the mind automatically "justifies" why the opportunities should materialize to our satisfaction. And sometimes they do. But when God would have it another way, it is easy to feel cheated.

When you become envious or possessive of something that was never really yours, you are beset by confusion and resentment. It can seem *unfair*, a point of view that, in reality, is oriented to rules that you established, often supported by your own emotions and needs.

Sometimes life is unfair, at least by our own perception. People do get cheated when others make mistakes or don't play by the rules. Chance or human error and mischief can and do cause lost opportunities. Still, the world is not out to get you. God is always in control, even when there seems no reason for your misfortune.

It is natural and tempting to think about the past and imagine what might have been. Because you are human, you've made mistakes. Perhaps you revisit and regret them, as you rue the opportunities they may have obstructed or despoiled. Don't fall into the trap of bemoaning the what-ifs. You can't reshape the past. You can only learn from your mistakes and develop a more longitudinal view of the directions God has for you.

Beware of the path of resentment, as it has many forms and disguises. Resentment is a burden you don't need. Aside from brooding about opportunities that didn't bear fruit for you, the comparison with or envy of the fortunes of others can become bondage. Yes, it takes maturity, effort, and fortitude to feel good for others in their successes (when perhaps you think it should have been you). But the alternative is bitterness and covetousness; these attitudes and practices will surely steer you away from wholesome and happy living.

WHAT YOU WANT AND WHAT YOU NEED

Oftentimes, it just seems hard to catch a break. It may feel like life is passing you by. Others are getting ahead, enjoying the fruits of their labors and the prosperity and gifts that come their way. You may ask, "When will it be my turn?"

Perhaps you are in desperate need of a job. Maybe your efforts to have children have failed, or possibly you feel too old or ill-equipped to have or raise children. You may have missed a good chance to patch up a broken relationship or even had a dear one pass away before you could communicate or make amends. These are but a few examples of wrenching lost opportunities that are not the result of greed, entitlement, or self-pity.

There are many events and circumstances that cause us to question whether God is around and paying attention to our needs and desires. We may also wonder and doubt our worthiness in the face of life's episodic periods of harshness and turbulence. Between neediness and sensitivity and the human tendency to complain about being left out or underserved, we vacillate from crying out or lashing out to gradual acceptance that we didn't get what we wanted.

Surely, God understands, and he hasn't forgotten or deserted you. Sometimes, a person will lament that "I pray to God regularly, but he doesn't answer." An apt human reply is that God *does* answer prayer—in the following ways: "Yes, no, or not now."

In the larger scheme of things, God has a unique plan for you. Living a godly life involves not only following his rules and worshiping him but also waiting on him and living to discover his will for you. It's not easy to be patient. It's even harder to combine faith with attentiveness to God's ways and communications, which are not always tangible or logical in the manner to which we are accustomed. He is supreme, omniscient, and omnipresent, and he *cares for everybody*.

Because each of us is self-centered, it seems unnatural to think of our own lost opportunities as necessary for someone else's gain. So very many times in my life, I was certain that I would get the position, score the win, make the most of the opportunity—only to have my hopes and plans crushed amid my own resentment and self-pity. *How could God overlook my interests? Surely, there must have been an oversight, a mistake that must be made up to me!*

In disappointment and want, one tills the soil of discovery, often germinating other opportunities. It may take time, but often something comes along that's better than what we agonized to obtain. Yet lost opportunities are not always serendipitous. The silver lining we hope for often does not appear.

Could it be that God's plan is to gift and benefit someone else with what we thought he should give to us? It's so uncomfortable—particularly when tugged by desire or need—to entertain the idea that a lost opportunity is *not about us* after all! Your loss was someone else's gain, and you were not even consulted!

YOU ARE AMAZINGLY SPECIAL

Do not consider my words insensitive or mocking. I feel for you in your need and disappointment. I share your swirl of difficult emotions over being deprived. Having walked the tiring walk of self-importance, I've grown progressively more responsive to God's powerful love and the messages that he has my best interests under his watch and control, that he will never leave me or forsake me, and that his grace is sufficient for all my needs. I reflect upon the following words of the apostle Paul:

But he said to me, "My grace is sufficient for you, for my power is made perfect in weakness." Therefore, I will boast all the more gladly about my weaknesses, so that Christ's power may rest on me. (2 Corinthians 12:9)

I am not saying this because I am in need, for I have learned to be content whatever the circumstances. I know what it is to be in need, and I know what it is to have plenty. I have learned the secret of being content in any and every situation, whether living in plenty or in want. I can do all this through him who gives me strength. (Philippians 4:11—13.)

God knows your yearnings and your disappointments and heartaches. He wants you to compete and to put forth your best efforts but not to ruminate or brood over lost opportunities. He knows what's in store for you, and he really loves you. He has loved you from the very beginning.

This may be a peculiar thought, but it is true: the fact that you exist is the result of lost opportunity for millions of sperm!

CHAPTER 23
LOSS OF INNOCENCE

Aside from death, perhaps the greatest loss we can experience is the loss of innocence. Upon knowing something, we can never revert to the existence of not knowing. Like the passage of time, it can never go backward. We must live with the history and move forward, doing the best we can with the scars and knowledge of mistakes and transgressions. The reality of sin and the awareness and conviction of our transgressions mean that we can never again be totally pure and blameless.

We lose innocence gradually and relentlessly. It almost seems as though the loss of innocence is a cost directly related to the incremental acquisition of wisdom, sophistication, and practical survival skills. Life impinges upon us, tampers with our sense of wholeness, plays upon our gullibility, and progressively replaces our naïveté with a combination of skepticism, caution, suspicion, and pessimism.

We all become damaged goods. The loss of innocence accrues not only in regard to our individual wrongdoings but in a collective socialization process that teaches us to highlight and express disillusionment with the foibles and inconsistencies of others and the imperfections in the world. Losing one's innocence often leads to crises of hope, faith, and belief in goodness. Reality and disillusionment can also taint our confidence that our needs and desires will be met and accommodated. The erosion of innocence makes the world seem less reliable.

CHILDHOOD INNOCENCE

We tend to regard childhood as the age of innocence. Children are naïve, gullible, vulnerable, uninformed, and ill-equipped with the basic skills, knowledge, and experience needed to survive and function independently in the world. It takes humans many years to develop and master even the rudiments of self-sufficiency and self-help abilities, acquire control over their bodies and minds, assimilate a full range of cause-and-effect principles and associated controls, and integrate a pragmatic understanding of and capacity to apply consistently the requisite social skills and behavioral exchanges that will permit them to interact meaningfully, safely, and productively with others.

As we gain experience and hone our abilities and thinking skills, we ideally become less impulsive, better at decision-making, more organized, more adept at referencing what has worked in the past, and more likely to exercise good judgment.

Children are naturally prone to be more easily manipulated and taken advantage of for obvious reasons. Thus, we take great care and exert caution in nurturing children in order to protect them from harm and exposure to situations, conditions, and influences that might *rob them of their innocence.*

What exactly is meant by that phrase? Like all people, children are not innocent of sin, selfishness, and hurtful thoughts, feelings, and acts. They have had less time to practice transgressions, yet they are indeed culpable. It is said that a child develops distinct and guiding notions of what is right and what is wrong by about the age of six or seven. Many societies rely on this developmental demarcation in the attitudes and expectations that hold a child morally and spiritually responsible for the consequences of his or her behavior.

Children may have an adequate basic understanding of right and wrong in early childhood, but they have many years to further experience the varieties of danger, trauma, brokenness, and loss that will affect their views of the world, themselves, their security, and their expectations.

As a child grows, innocence is chipped away, not only by what each person does, but also *by what happens to and around him or her.* It is ironic that even as we become better prepared to withstand and defend against life's threats and impingements, we become more aware of life's complexity and unpredictability and come to the sagacious realization that what you see is not always what you get.

Learning that life doesn't give us all that we want in the manner and times we would have it confronts each of us with fundamental challenges. These challenges force us to construct and revise models of belief, expectations, and feelings about the way the world and life really are, about who we are, about what we are worth and are here for, and about the role and importance of other people.

This process—while natural and necessary to survival and maturity—results in the loss of innocence, a gradual erosion of our naïveté, trust, and high expectations about life's potential and its likelihood of favoring us.

The accumulation of traumas and losses reshapes our perspective on the world and infiltrates a previously simplistic view of what can truly hurt us.

TAINTED BY LOSS

As children, most of us have experienced many examples of God taking things away before we began to consciously grapple with who God is or struggle to develop a relationship with him.

A pet dies, a friend moves away, a preferred toy breaks, a bicycle is stolen—the youngster cries out in angst, resentment, disbelief, and even bitterness. *How could this happen? And why did it happen to* me?

Losses are inevitable; but some people are afflicted by traumatic losses that seem horrific and unfair, especially when they occur with such devastation to those so vulnerable—a child loses his or her health to illness, a parent dies or abandons the family, or a body is robbed of function by a genetic anomaly, disease, injury, or accident. Such traumas burst the bubble of a vision of life unfolding the way it might have been imagined and portrayed in a children's storybook.

As reality encroaches, often with unforeseen and painful consequences, the blemishes of misfortune crumple the innocence of guileless expectation that life will proceed happily.

When what we depend on or take for granted is suddenly gone, what never gets fully replaced is the innocence that was lost with it.

GUILTY AS CHARGED

Innocence is the opposite of guilt. So, as we lose innocence, do we become guiltier?

Delving into this polarity, we see that innocence has more than one connotation. The innocence previously discussed describes a state of unawareness of guile, malice, or danger. Such innocence refers to naïveté or lack of discernment. This is not the same as culpability or acts of commission. You can be a victim of something that happens to you or around you—blameless of the perpetration, yet sullied by its effects. In this sense, you can lose innocence without being guilty.

However, just having a human nature ensures that each of us will also become guiltier and guiltier as we progress through life, even if we never commit a statutory crime. We are all sinful, and it behooves us to become ever more mindful of that reality. Neither the best intentions nor the most magnificent works excuse or exonerate us from a nature and habits that predispose us to violate God's laws and his holiness.

Some people live for themselves, heedless of consequences, responsibilities, or the damage they cause. Others become more conscientious, sensitive, and more spiritually and socially mature. Whether you commit perpetrations or faux pas, your transgressions will multiply as you grow—for none of us is perfect.

The godlier you aspire to be in your behavior and thoughts, the fewer transgressions you are likely to commit. It is ironic, however, that your *awareness* of guilt will increase because your standards for displaying godliness and your adherence to what is right will become more stringent. As the saying goes, "Damned if you do and damned if you don't." But don't throw caution to the wind just because you will never be blameless. It's clearly better to strive to be less offending than to be mindlessly and habitually locked into a pattern of miscreant behavior and repeatedly commit more offenses.

The point is that we lose innocence in either way—and in both ways. We transgress, and we are most likely aware that we transgress, although we may try to deny, rationalize, or justify our transgressions. Even as we make amends and restitution and seek forgiveness and reconciliation, we cannot delude ourselves that by so doing we have become more innocent. It's a loss that can never be recaptured. Through a genuine atonement for our sins, however, we may feel some relief, but we cannot ever wipe the slate clean.

We can nonetheless seek to counterbalance lost innocence with the gaining of wisdom, along with a commitment to penitence for our transgressions and the fervent seeking of forgiveness from God and alliance with him.

HOPE, EXPECTATIONS, AND THE LOSS OF INNOCENCE

We all have expectations. They are a product of the conscious mind, the conglomeration of previous learning, the images of things to come, the desires for what we want, and the beliefs about what should happen. Without expectations, we could hardly plan or build models and concepts of the way the world operates. Expectations help us predict, categorize, and simplify. They form a cornerstone of what we know as reality. At a biological level, expectations propel our survival by guiding behavior toward physical needs and functions. Animals in the wild go where they expect to find food and water. People act in ways that they think will bring rewards. At a physiological level, expectations gear our nervous systems to states of arousal necessary or appropriate for anticipated events. At a psychological level, expectations drive the mind's narrative to support evaluations of experience and predictions of what will happen next.

There is, however, a downside to expectations; desire, need, or faulty evaluation can drive expectations to the point where hopes are dashed, beliefs are unrealistic, and disappointments prevail over satisfaction and fulfillment.

(In my book *Living Intact: Challenge and Choice in Tough Times*, I expound upon the role that expectations play in our mental construct of reality and in our behavior and happiness.)

The following excerpt is from *Living Intact: Challenge and Choice in Tough Times*:

"Expectations are mediators between reality and desire: they help us navigate through the world as it is toward the world we wish to create."

"Your expectations are your assessments, your plans and schematics, aspirations and maps of the world and yourself within the world."

GREATER AND LESSER EXPECTATIONS

Expectation connotes a general meaning with subtle nuances and variations. An expectation is a confident belief or strong hope that a particular event will happen. It can serve as a standard of conduct or performance demanded or anticipated by or of somebody. An expectation may also be a mental image of something awaited that can often be incongruent with how one's desires play out.

The term *greater expectations* indicates results hoped for or desired. Whereas *greater expectations* involve aspirations, ambitions, imagination, wishes, and dreams, *lesser expectations* refer to the results realistically anticipated based upon previous experiences and conditioning. *Lesser expectations* involve predictive validity, accuracy, boundaries, practicality, and directions.

> *Expectations reflect your conscious and unconscious assessments, plans and schematics, and maps of the world and of yourself within the world. Expectations unfold at different levels, and these levels mediate the ways that you want things to be (great expectations) with the ways you have learned through experience that they are likely to play out (lesser expectations).*
>
> *The difference between your greater expectations and your lesser expectations approximates your satisfaction and disappointment in life. It is an indicator of the extent to which you reconcile the outcomes you get with the way you would like life to work. It is also a reflection of the way you balance reality testing with desire."*

With regard to losing innocence, the disappointments we experience in life—especially significant or traumatic losses—chip away at our expectations of what life could (and, perhaps, should) be like. In effect, losing innocence narrows the discrepancy between *great expectations* and *lesser expectations* with regard to predictions about and acceptance of the realities that beset us.

SURRENDERING INNOCENCE

The irony about losing innocence is that it can never be fully replaced or reinstated—yet many of us resist and bristle against this loss with desperate attempts to revert and recapture innocence.

Recapitulating from *Living Intact: Challenge and Choice in Tough Times*:

Once upon a time, life was better. It was easier, simpler, more rewarding. Or so we imagine. Human history clearly belies our fantasies about humankind's more idyllic past. Life, in fact, has always been challenging. From man's traumatic expulsion from the Garden of Eden to the painful daily encounters with our own traumas, we are reminded of the challenges. On some level of consciousness, we are aware of our falls from the grace of whole-ness, when life seemed workable and when we felt together and intact.

Life provides us with scars, and its conditions affect our health, well-being, and attitudes. As we proceed along the path, we become both stronger and weaker, fortified and shaken by patterns and sequences of events that often distort our notions of certainty, predictability, "OK-ness," and self. What is inevitable is that each of us will face brokenness—insult, injury, transgression, deteriora-tion, separation, insufficiency, insecurity, and loss—that detracts from the experiences of intactness and satisfaction.

What then should be our attitude about losing innocence, and how should we accept or even embrace it?

It seems that God uses many processes, events, and circumstances to bring us closer to him in knowledge and relationship. He gives us things, blesses us, and sometimes rescinds what we become attached to, take for granted, or claim as our own. He gifts us with the provenance and enjoy-ment of material things, relationships, and fleeting happiness; but he wants us to know that all things are subservient to a relationship with him and are transient, except for a relationship with him. Consider 1Corinthians 6:19—20:

Do you not know that your bodies are temples of the Holy Spirit, who is in you, whom you have received from God? You are not your own; you were bought at a price. Therefore honor God with your bodies.

That God takes away innocence during our lifetime should not be sur-prising. One terrible price of sin is the loss of innocence. Thank God that he forgives our sin through Jesus Christ!

In surrendering to Christ, we confess our sin and helplessness. We acknowledge that evil and guilt have tainted us, and we accept the sovereignty of God in saving us and in providing for the course of our lives, as well as for our eternal salvation. Surrendering innocence is a small price for what God gives in return.

Through God's mercy, we are saved. Through his sovereignty, we are bought at a price. That price includes giving up our innocence and our notions about and insistence upon what should be and, ultimately, submitting to a dependence upon his will.

VI
AFTERWARD

CHAPTER 24
MOVING ON

THE INEVITABILITY OF LOSS

To paraphrase a friend, "Living with loss is ongoing, and reminds me just how much living means losing. They are intertwined."

Experiencing loss is not only inevitable—a natural part of the life cycle—it is also a crucible for developing the skills and wisdom to cope with life and its natural limitations. During the time each of us spends in this mortal coil, we gain and acquire things, capacities, opportunities, and relationships. We lose them eventually—some by attrition or voluntarily and some suddenly, unexpectedly, or tragically.

Weathering and suffering loss may be difficult or at times devastating. However, we should expect losses to invade our lives, and we should be prepared emotionally and spiritually to face them.

For most people, the most difficult losses are those of loved ones and the close relationships that nurture, provide companionship and meaning, and allow us to exchange affection, the meeting of needs, and often the deepest yearnings and connections of our souls. Losing people (or other living beings) close to us can induce grief and aloneness, causing bereavement and leaving us to question the meaning and worthiness of our existence.

Loss is a universal experience, and it is a challenge to our sense of security and humility. How we deal with loss will considerably influence the purpose and confidence with which we handle our responsibilities and the uncertainties of the future. Losing what is important can have a devastating impact and lead to decreases in motivation and emotional health and stability. It can turn us inward and make us dwell on wounds that can fester into an attitude of mistrust and bitterness. Yet it doesn't have to be this way. Despite the hurt and impact of loss, such experiences can make us stronger and more compassionate, sensitive, and attuned to priorities that more humanely serve us and others.

Accepting and recovering from loss requires courage and honesty. Such healing begs for human connection and for mature and functional ways to share and deal with vulnerability. The experience of loss can be the seeds of new beginnings. Loss challenges us to hope, to believe and expect that something worthwhile looms on the horizon, even if it is currently out of view.

The inevitability of loss does not mean that it must be devastating.

HEALTHY ATTACHMENT

As expounded earlier in this book, it is the ability to *attach* that makes sentient the experience of loss. The precious qualities of loving, needing, connecting with, depending upon, providing for, and experiencing joy and sorrow with another living being inherently include the vulnerability and potential for grief, hurt, loneliness, anguish, and suffering. That which enables self-actualization and fulfillment by relating to others is imbued with vulnerability to trauma, hurt, and grief when what one loves is taken away.

Life is a struggle between powerful sets of emotions—attaching, yearning, acquiring, protecting, and developing and detaching, surrendering, yielding, letting go, and giving up. Loss is an instrument that God uses to separate us from the sovereign ownership that is truly and only his. God gives many gifts and is able to supply all needs. In addition to the many things and people that comprise his blessings, he gives us the priceless gift of the ability to grow fond of them. The ability to claim God's blessings and enjoy his provisions must often be tempered by the humbling sacrifice of relinquishing what is taken away. To accept such sacrifices, we must understand and even embrace the paradox of surrender.

Healthy attachment requires the ability to become involved, dependent, vulnerable, and trusting. Though it develops from early neurological growth in the presence of nurturance, intimacy, and emotional bonding, it is also strengthened through the reinforcement of needs being met, security being perceived and provided, and the practice of establishing and maintaining rewarding and sustaining relationships.

Ironically, it may be that one of the most critical values of practicing healthy attachment in relationships is that it sustains the coping capacity to lose and surrender what holds for us the most important meaning.

DEALING WITH TRAUMA

Though much that we lose can be taken in stride, significant losses can be traumatic, and trauma has unique characteristics. It tends to paralyze our coping mechanisms and keep us stuck emotionally. We relive the traumatic event in emotional memory, and thoughts about the event become fused with the startling and debilitating emotions surrounding the trauma.

We can lose things without necessarily being traumatized. Conversely, however, trauma itself always involves loss. Whether or not the loss is material, there is inevitably a shocking loss of control. To be traumatized is to lose the sense of being in charge, the sense of order, predictability, and justice. Trauma brings a fearful loss of protection and an exposure to vincible experiences previously and conveniently forgotten.

Moving on from the paralysis of trauma often involves some form of psychological treatment. My colleagues and I have found that EEG neurofeedback and Thought Field Therapy are instrumental in relieving and eliminating—*yes, eliminating*—the stranglehold of trauma. You are invited to learn how these techniques can help you and those about whom you care. Visit my website, www.marksteinberg.com, and read my book *Living Intact: Challenge and Choice in Tough Times* for more information.

An important point to remember about trauma is that it has cumulative effects. The more trauma a person has experienced (and the more trauma that has gone untreated and unresolved), the more difficult it is to cope with loss.

Remember always that God is the supreme healer. He invites us to roll our burdens upon him and to seek his shelter, comfort, protection, and healing. Go to God with your traumas. Ask him for relief and for freedom from the encumbrances of trauma and loss. He may direct you to humanly administered help, but he will also provide divine healing. Just ask him.

SURRENDER TO GOD

Let's review what it means to surrender and how it plays a vital role in moving on with your life.

The paradox of surrender is that you gain by giving up. As stated earlier, surrender is weakness and vulnerability leaving the soul and spirit. It is the renunciation of control and the capitulation to a force or will greater than one's own. *Surrender enacts the yielding of the object of attachment, not the ability to attach and to value and love.* When you surrender, you relinquish claim. Therein lies the peace that brings wholeness, regardless of possession or presence.

What do you gain by surrendering to loss? One gain is a resolve to adapt to new circumstances and not depend on what is no longer available. It is not easy to do without. Certainly, there is no replacement, nor is there adequate salve for the pain of losing a loved one. Surrender allows the process of carrying on to resume and to strengthen. Another gain is the comfort and peace that eventually accrues through acceptance. To live with what has occurred and to find new joys in the exercise of sacrifice and other attachments is to resume a life of connectedness and renewed resilience and hope.

Surrender creates a focus on the present and the future. It is a catalyst for healing. Surrender is the exercise of flexibility and deference, the acknowledgment of vulnerability, and the yielding to forces greater than one's own. It is not weakness or destitution; rather, it is the participation in a universe of natural cycles of exposure and erosion, nurture and protection, hurt and healing.

Most important, surrender is the process by which God can manifest his rightful place as creator and owner of the universe and let us experience his vast love, comfort, presence, grace, mercy, and protection.

When you surrender, you give up ownership and entitlement. There is no reason to fight for what is no longer yours. You relinquish encumbrance and you trade continued responsibility for freedom and lightness.

When God takes away, he closes doors, often unexpectedly. In his providence, new doors open and opportunities unfold to discover and live out what God has in mind. Loss can be an opportunity to turn disappointment and longing regarding the past into hopeful longing and eagerness about the present and future. With God, the future is brighter. Surrender allows us to let go and move more fluidly toward what God has in store.

LIVING IN HOPE AND SECURITY

In this world of shifting shadows, flux and change, abundance and scarcity, blessing and misfortune, one eventually questions what is reliable. Relationships come and go, and people get sick, move away, turn against us, or die. Bodies deteriorate, opportunities vanish, good fortune has limits and reversals, and happiness is fleeting.

What remains in this world of transience is God's presence, his sovereignty, his control, and his word. He has given us promises and revelation. He has told us that he gives and takes away. He has made a covenant by which we can feel secure, holding the knowledge that he is reliable and that he never lies. He leads us through comfort, direction, protection, example, spiritual presence, and hope. He wants us to worship him and to be in fellowship with him. He wants us to surrender to his love and control, submit to his will, seek to enter into his rest, and have faith.

The losses you face will challenge you in many ways—emotionally, spiritually, attitudinally, and perhaps economically. Before you had the things you lost, God knew what he would give you and when he would rescind his offerings. But he will never take away his love and his eternal life for you, if you will accept these and allow him to help you live in this light.

It is God's blessings that have allowed you to experience, possess, and enjoy. It is through his magnificent power and protection that you can have the flexibility of being able to manifest sufficient courage, accept vulnerability, and gather the requisite trust in God to let go.

IN THE END

There is a tendency in human nature to overwrite the past with interpretations and emotional memories that color one's history with tones of glory or misery. Elapsed time and life's changes elicit reflections that make past events, actions, and people seem either worse or better than they occurred to us when we lived through them.

In the face of loss and its accompanying pain, the past may seem idyllic. We may pine for what we lost, mourning a previous sense of wholeness before the loss happened. The impact of trauma, the tremors of vulnerability, and anxieties about the future can render memories of life before the loss to be healthier and more intact than in the aftermath of loss.

Alternatively, the experience of significant loss may be so wrenching that we may resolve to put it behind us. Walling off memories or constructing a story that represses the positives preceding the loss helps the emotional mind adjust. Chalking up painful history as a prelude to a better present time may also sort out and rationalize the hurtful event.

As we remember the past—nostalgically, pleasantly, painfully—our minds tend to reinterpret what happened to make it fit in with our life stories and our emotional assimilation of events. Sometimes, in recalling the pleasant enjoyment we had before a crushing loss, we may see ourselves as naïve in taking for granted what we had before the loss; in the better times, we were simpler and more innocent, not knowing the harsh reality of loss that awaited. Alternatively, we may develop a fatalistic attitude about loss, rationalizing it and interpreting loss as inevitable or somehow better in the long run.

In either transformation, the reconstructed memories and their integration with present circumstances lead us to the realization that the now is more real and more pressing than what we may miss and long for but never recapture. And therefore we must adjust and move on.

To deal with reality, live responsibly, make the most of what we have, and find purpose in our lives, we must face the fact that we exercise choice. Even when our options seem limited and we may be hurting, we always have choices about our responses, attitudes, perceptions, interpretations, and behavior.

The reality is that each of us has a limited time in our individual physical bodies on earth. Yet each of us is also eligible for eternal life, should we make the *conscious decision to choose it* when confronted at this crossroad. This awareness transforms the experience of loss. Indeed, it changes everything.

As I am fortunate to get older, I am dealing with losses and their associated hurts much better than I used to cope. This is fortuitous, since I seem to sustain more traumatic losses than I remember from earlier in my life. Surely, the loss of my son Neal weighs upon me. I miss him constantly, even as my memories are suffused with the mixture of his charming ways, our precious connection, and the alienating, hurtful behaviors that were also a part of him.

In the years since Neal passed, I have been learning to live without him, without the future I imagined and helped him work toward. To give him life and have him for twenty-seven years was and is such a blessing! As painful as losing him has been, it has awakened me anew to the constant presence of God and his care for me.

Living with Neal and losing him cannot be separated from my surrender to whatever God has revealed and has in store for me. The continuing process of yielding to God's will, growing closer to him, and anticipating what his future shall bring gives me the courage, hope, and joy to face my coming days.

It is my hope that Neal's story and my reflections about coping with loss and integrating surrender into the natural fabric of life will enable you to face hardship with greater ease and blessing.

One of Neal's birthday presents to me

ABOUT THE AUTHOR

Dr. Mark Steinberg is a licensed psychologist with expertise in clinical, educational, and neuropsychology. He appears regularly on television to offer his psychological expertise on topics pertaining to health, behavior, and living a more satisfying and productive life. He treats children, adolescents, and adults, offering a range of services dealing with attention and mood disorders, behavior problems, family and communication issues, developmental disabilities, educational and learning problems, parenting challenges, habit change, addictions, and neurological disorders (including headaches, seizures, and sleep disorders).

Over the course of his practice, Dr. Steinberg has administered over sixty thousand evaluation and treatment procedures.

By blending the latest technological advances with traditional and scientific methods, Dr. Steinberg improves functioning and eliminates problems that have persisted for years. He is well-known for his pioneering work with EEG neurofeedback and Voice Technology, the treatment that eliminates negative emotions in minutes.

Dr. Steinberg has made many appearances on local and national television. He is widely consulted as a medical expert, and has won local and statewide awards. He is the author of three acclaimed books: *Confessions of a Maverick Mind: A Psychologist Shares Stories and Adventures, Essays and Articles, and Poems and Songs; Staying Madly in Love with Your Spouse; Guide to a Happier Marriage; Living Intact: Challenge and Choice in Tough Times;* and coauthor of the popular book, *ADD: The 20-Hour Solution.*

He offers individual services, as well as seminars and trainings.

His clinics, Mark Steinberg, Ph.D. & Associates, are located in Redwood City, CA, San Francisco, CA, and Walnut Creek, CA. For information, call (408) 356-1002 or visit **www.marksteinberg.com.**